residential Report Writing & Case Studies

2nd Edition, 2nd Printing

D1208409

HONDROS LEARNING™

HONDROS LEARNING™

4140 Executive Parkway

Westerville, Ohio 43081

www.hondroslearning.com

19 18 17   3 4 5

978-1-59844-226-7

Table of Contents

Preface

Hondros Learning™ is proud to present *Residential Report Writing & Case Studies* as part of the market-leading textbook series for appraisal qualifying education. Written specifically to correspond to the most recent Appraisal Qualifications Board's course topic requirements, *Residential Report Writing & Case Studies* features **clear writing**, **real-world examples, work problems** and **case studies**, useful **illustrations**, challenging chapter quizzes, and a **glossary** of key terminology, making this text the most up-to-date tool available for achieving mastery of and applying site valuation and the cost approach in appraisal practice.

In addition to following the *AQB content guideline* for qualifying education, all texts in our appraisal series are *affordably priced* and feature a *clear writing style* and *numerous study aids* to assist students with comprehension and application of the material. Concepts range from simple to slightly complex, illustrating the application of the material in various appraisal scenarios. **Key terms** are highlighted and defined throughout and compiled along with other related terms in a useful *glossary.*

Instructor materials are available separately to make using this text in the classroom a seamless experience.

Exam Prep

Additional appraisal products available from Hondros Learning to help students prepare for the licensing exam include the *Appraisal Review Crammer™, 3rd edition*—a valuable self-study or classroom exam preparation guide; and *CompuCram™ Appraisal Exam Prep Software.*

About the Author

Timothy Detty has taught thousands of real estate and appraisal students over the course of his teaching career at Hondros College. A practicing Certified General Appraiser, he has also written numerous real estate and appraisal courses and served as both author and expert reviewer for several real estate and appraisal textbooks. He has been awarded the designation of Certified Distance Education Instructor (CDEI) from the International Distance Education Certification Center (IDECC) and is an Associate Member of the Appraisal Institute. In addition to being certified by the Appraiser Qualifications Board of The Appraisal Foundation as a USPAP instructor, Tim serves as an at-large representative to the Education Council of Appraisal Foundation Sponsors (ECAFS), is a member of the Education and Research Advisory Committee of the Ohio Real Estate Commission, and is a frequent guest lecturer and contributor to various real estate and appraisal publications.

Reviewer Acknowledgements

Hondros Learning™ would like to thank the following expert reviewer for her comments and suggestions:

Beth Sigg

Certified General Appriaser
AQB Certified USPAP Instructor

Suggested Syllabus

Residential Report Writing and Case Studies

COURSE DESCRIPTION:

Residential Report Writing and Case Studies is deeply rooted in appraisal professional standards and best practices of an appraiser when communicating the opinions and conclusions of a residential appraisal. The course commences with a detailed discussion of USPAP Rules and the reporting options permitted by STANDARD 2. Appraisal writing skills are then overviewed along with several examples of how the reasoning of an appraiser is expressed in typical appraisal reporting situations. Common reporting issues are then explored to illustrate the level of detail required in appraisal commentary so that appraisal reports are clear and not misleading (or fraudulent). Finally, the most common residential appraisal reporting form, the Uniform Residential Appraisal Report (URAR), will be fully illustrated along with the requirements of the Uniform Appraisal Dataset (UAD). The course concludes with an overview of several of the most common residential appraisal forms. Within each section of the course are numerous compelling case studies to assist reinforcement of learning. The current version of USPAP is recommended for reference during the course.

COURSE OBJECTIVES:

- Describe USPAP appraisal reporting requirements.
- Explain the level of content and detail necessary in compliance of the USPAP reporting options permitted by Standard Rule 2-2 as well as to address the needs of intended users.
- Apply reasoning skills for composing expanded explanation of certain reporting elements.
- Recall common appraisal reporting issues that appraisers must manage.
- Describe the processes for reporting appraisal information on the URAR and Market Conditions Addendum.
- Demonstrate proper data entry of required fields that conform to the Uniform Appraisal Dataset for appraisal submission.

TEXTBOOK: *Residential Report Writing and Case Studies, 2nd Edition*, Hondros Learning™, ©2013

COURSE CREDIT HOURS: *Pre-licensing:* 15 credit hours (14 hours class work plus 1-hour exam)
Continuing education: 14 credit hours (final exam not required)

INSTRUCTION METHOD: Lecture and group exercises

COURSE OUTLINE—Note: *Attendance is mandatory to receive course credit.*

DAY ONE (*Total classroom hours day one*: 7.5)
Suggested Time Increments:

3.5 hours	Introduction and Overview
	Chapter 1 Appraisal Reporting and USPAP Compliance
1.0 hour	Lunch
0.5 hours	Chapter 1 Appraisal Reporting and USPAP Compliance (continued)
2.2 hours	Chapter 2 Effective Writing and Reasoning Skills in Appraisal Reporting
1.3 hours	Chapter 3 Common Issues in Appraisal Reporting

DAY TWO (*Total classroom hours day two*: 7.5)
Suggested Time Increments:

0.5 hours	Chapter 3 Common Issues in Appraisal Reporting (continued)
3.0 hours	Chapter 4 Residential Appraisal Reporting Forms
1.0 hour	Lunch
1.6 hours	Chapter 4 Residential Appraisal Reporting Forms (continued)
0.8 hours	Appendix A: Case Studies
0.6 hours	Appendix B: Overview of Other Common Appraisal Forms
1.0 hour	Final Examination
(1 hour)	Final Examination/Student Surveys

Chapter 1

Appraisal Reporting and USPAP Compliance

Introduction

While much of this course will focus on what an appraiser "should do" to provide a **credible** appraisal report, this chapter will focus on what an appraiser "must do" in compliance with the **Uniform Standards of Professional Appraisal Practice (USPAP)**. USPAP sets the *minimum* ethical and performance obligations for appraisal practice, which includes appraisal reporting. The discussion in this chapter begins with general reporting obligations and then continues with specific requirements for each of the reporting options permitted by USPAP under STANDARD 2 – REAL PROPERTY APPRAISAL REPORTING.

Bias A preference or inclination that precludes an appraiser's impartiality, independence, or objectivity in an assignment.

Confidential information Information that is either identified by the client as confidential when providing it to an appraiser and that is not available from any other source; or classified as confidential or private by applicable law or regulation.

Credible Worthy of belief.

Intended User The client and any other party as identified, by name or type, as users of the appraisal or appraisal review report by the appraiser on the basis of communication with the client at the time of the assignment.

Report Any communication, written or oral, of an appraisal or appraisal review that is transmitted to the client upon completion of an assignment.

Signature Personalized evidence indicating authentication of the work performed by the appraiser and the acceptance of the responsibility for content, analyses, and the conclusions in the report

Uniform Standards of Professional Appraisal Practice (USPAP) Professional appraisal standards promulgated by The Appraisal Foundation, and widely recognized throughout the United States as accepted standards of appraisal practice.

Key Terms

USPAP and General Reporting Obligations

USPAP contains the minimum standards for appraisal development and reporting. In this chapter, the discussion will focus on the reporting element of the appraisal process.

Within USPAP there are numerous requirements and prohibitions related to appraisal reporting that will be discussed in this section.

Definition of a Report and the USPAP Preamble

The discussion of USPAP compliance in appraisal reporting should commence with the USPAP definition of "**report**".

> **REPORT:** *any communication, written or oral, of an appraisal or appraisal review that is transmitted to the client upon completion of an assignment*

The comment, following the USPAP definition of "report", acknowledges (in part) that most appraisal reports are written. Oral reports are not the common type of report for most common uses of appraisal reports.

The PREAMBLE of USPAP references (in part) appraisal reporting through a general caveat:

> *It is essential that appraisers develop and communicate their analyses, opinions, and conclusions to intended users of their services in a manner that is meaningful and not misleading.*

Appraisal Reporting and USPAP Rules

Throughout USPAP Rules are various obligations which, among other topics, address what an appraiser must and must not do when reporting the opinions and conclusions of an appraisal.

General Reporting Obligations of the ETHICS RULE

The <u>Conduct</u> section of the ETHICS RULE of USPAP commences with an overall obligation for an appraiser to perform assignments impartially, objectively, and independently. This portion of the rule goes on to prohibit **bias** and advocacy when in the role of an appraiser. This prohibition could certainly extend to reporting when bias on the part of the appraiser or advocacy for the interests of a party or issue, causes the appraisers report to become misleading or fraudulent due to the appraiser's inclination or position. The <u>Conduct</u> section of the ETHICS RULE contains several prohibitions regarding communication of a misleading or fraudulent report. In some cases, this action by an appraiser could be considered criminal activity, which is also prohibited by this section of the rule.

Avoiding Discrimination in Reporting

The <u>Conduct</u> section of the ETHICS RULE also cautions that an appraiser:

> *must not use or rely on **unsupported*** conclusions relating to characteristics such as race, color, religion, national origin, gender, marital status, familial status, age, receipt of public assistance income, handicap, or an **unsupported*** conclusion that homogeneity of characteristics is necessary to maximize value* (*Bold added for emphasis)

At first, this statement may seem to primarily address an appraiser's development process; however, USPAP Advisory Opinion 16 (*Fair Housing Laws and Appraisal Report Content*) illustrates the applicability of the prohibition in appraisal reporting. It is recommended that appraisers review and acquaint themselves with the contents of the Advisory Opinion. According the guidance offered there, appraisers are responsible for ensuring that their opinions and conclusions are *impartial and objective* and do not illegally discriminate through subjectivity or stereotypical assumptions.

This can create a perplexing conundrum for appraisers in some circumstances, as the Advisory Opinion acknowledges that in some cases even supported assumptions relating to the fore mentioned characteristics may be prohibited by applicable law. Thus, great care must be used so that statements used in an appraisal report do not appear discriminatory.

Even unintentionally, certain words or statements may be perceived as being discriminatory or biased. While there is no recognized succinct reference for words and phrases that appraisers should avoid, fair housing advocacy groups and others have long been vocal to discourage use of certain language in connection with real estate advertising and appraisal. While it is difficult to achieve consensus among the appraisal industry for some of these opinions, most agree that appraisers should not use terms such as *"white (or blue) collar neighborhood"* or *"high (or low) income area"*. As well, words such as "exclusive" may be misinterpreted if left unexplained. The use of a term such as this should be carefully elaborated so that it is clear to the user of the report the context for its use. For example, if a neighborhood is exclusive because property ownership is limited to members of a particular country club, the use of the term may be appropriate (in most states). However, if the term is used to describe a certain level of social or economic status, it may be perceived to be discriminatory and should not be used in this context. Good judgment and reasoning skills should prevail when considering this sensitive issue.

Appraisal Report Signatures

Appraisal report **signature** requirements are addressed in the <u>Management</u> section of the ETHICS RULE. Whether handwritten or electronically placed, an appraiser affixes his signature, or authorizes the use of his signature to **certify recognition and acceptance of his obligations to USPAP**. The signature of one appraiser must not be affixed by another without the signing appraiser's consent. Authorization to affix or use an appraiser's signature can only be granted on an **assignment-by-assignment basis**.

Specific Disclosure Requirements per USPAP Rules

When applicable, USPAP Rules contain certain disclosure requirements. Some of the disclosures must be included in specific sections of an appraisal report, such as any letter of transmittal (see sample on Page 4) in which conclusions are stated, or the report certification (discussed later in this chapter). Other disclosures must be simply contained within the report.

The <u>Conduct</u> section of the ETHICS RULE requires disclosure by an appraiser in an appraisal report of:

- Any current or prospective interest in a subject property or the parties involved in the assignment
- Any services as an appraiser, or in any other capacity, regarding the subject property performed within a three-year period prior immediately proceeding acceptance of the assignment

In addition to the disclosure made prior to accepting the assignment or one made if discovered any time during an assignment, **disclosure must be made in the certification** of the report. Disclosing this information is important to preserving public trust, and it gives the client an opportunity to evaluate the information before engaging the appraiser.

> ***Note:*** *Effective January 1, 2012 with the 2012-2013 Edition of USPAP, appraisers must disclose if they have, or have not, performed a prior service, as an appraiser or in any other capacity, regarding the property within the three-year period immediately preceding acceptance of the assignment. See discussion of Standards Rule 2-3 on page 11.*

The disclosure regarding prior services cannot be made if the appraiser has agreed with the client in a prior assignment not to disclose the prior service. In USPAP, the <u>Comment</u> to this portion of the <u>Conduct</u> section of the ETHICS RULE provides specific advice regarding how these requirements interact with the appraiser's obligation of confidentiality:

> <u>Comment</u>: *Disclosing the fact that the appraiser has previously appraised the property is permitted except in the case when an appraiser has agreed with the client to keep the mere occurrence of a prior assignment confidential. If an appraiser has agreed with a client not to disclose that he or she has appraised a property, the appraiser must decline all subsequent assignments that fall within the three year period.*

The <u>Management</u> section of the ETHICS RULE requires that fees, commissions, or things of value relating to the procurement of an assignment **must be disclosed**.

> *An appraiser must disclose that he or she paid a fee or commission, or gave a thing of value in connection with the procurement of an assignment.*

> <u>Comment</u>: *The disclosure must appear in the certification and in any transmittal letter in which conclusions are stated; however, disclosure of the amount paid is not required. In groups or organizations engaged in appraisal practice, intra-company payments to employees for business development do not require disclosure.*

File No. 123456789

Any Bank
487 Main Street
Forty, OH 43417

File Number: 123456789

To Whom It May Concern:

In accordance with your request, I have appraised the real property at:

123 Main Street
Some City, OH 43120

The purpose of this appraisal is to develop an opinion of the market value of the subject property, as improved.

In my opinion, the market value of the property as of   01/01/2011   is:

$123,000
One Hundred Twenty-Three Thousand Dollars

The attached report contains the description, analysis and supportive data for the conclusions, final opinion of value, descriptive photographs, limiting conditions and appropriate certifications.

Sarah McDreamy
Licensed Appraiser

- Is specific to a particular assignment and does not reference gifts or other things of value provided to a client as a "thank you" or other appreciation for business in general.
- Does not need to state the amount (or value) of the payment, only that a payment was made.

The COMPETENCY RULE of USPAP sets forth steps an appraiser must take during the development process to address a lack of competency in a particular assignment as well as certain disclosure mechanisms that must take place in the reporting process regarding the lack of initial competency and the steps that were taken to complete the assignment.

From a reporting perspective, whether the lack of competency was initially recognized or was discovered at some point during the assignment, an appraiser must:

> *describe, in the report, the lack of knowledge and/or experience and the steps taken to complete the assignment competently*

The SCOPE OF WORK RULE of USPAP specifies three fundamental duties that must be performed by appraisers in an assignment. The first two duties are related to the development process – identification of the problem to be solved and determining the appropriate scope of work. The third duty is to *disclose the scope of work in the report.*

The disclosure obligations of the SCOPE OF WORK RULE provides the following requirement:

> *The report must contain sufficient information to allow intended users to understand the scope of work performed.*
>
> <u>Comment</u>: *Proper disclosure is required because clients and other intended users rely on the assignment results. Sufficient information includes disclosure of research and analyses performed and might also include disclosure of research and analyses not performed.*

USPAP Advisory Opinion 28 (Scope of Work Decision, Performance, and Disclosure) offers additional guidance regarding disclosure of the scope of work through these excerpts:

- *An appraiser must disclose research and analyses not performed when such disclosure is necessary for intended users to understand the report properly and not be misled.*
- *These disclosure requirements apply to the scope of work performed, rather than the scope of work initially planned by the appraiser.*
- *The appraiser must disclose the type and extent of research and analyses that were actually completed in the development process.*
- *Additionally, the information required to allow intended users to understand the scope of work may include disclosure of research and analyses not performed.*
- *There is no requirement for the scope of work description to be in a particular or separate section of the report.*

Finally, the JURISDICTIONAL EXCEPTION RULE of USPAP specifies certain disclosure requirements when there is an exception to USPAP due to applicable law or regulation. The reporting compliance requirements of the rule consist of two distinct reporting steps in an assignment involving jurisdictional exception – *an appraiser must:*

1. *clearly and conspicuously disclose in the report the part of USPAP that is voided by that law or regulation; and*

2. *cite in the report the law or regulation requiring this exception to USPAP compliance.*

Confidential Information and Reporting

As an aside from what an appraiser must disclose in an appraisal report, the <u>Confidentiality</u> section of the ETHICS RULE addresses the prohibition of disclosure of **confidential information** and exceptions when disclosure of confidential information is acceptable. First, the USPAP definition of confidential information should be reviewed:

CONFIDENTIAL INFORMATION: information that is either:

- *identified by the **client*** as confidential when providing it to an appraiser and that is not available from any other source; or*

- *classified as confidential or private by applicable law or regulation.* (*Bold added for emphasis)

The <u>Confidentiality</u> section of the ETHICS RULE sets forth the following prohibition for disclosure of confidential information and exceptions for when disclosure is permissible.

An appraiser must not disclose (1) confidential information; or (2) assignment results to anyone other than:

- *the client;*

- *parties specifically authorized by the client;*

- *state appraiser regulatory agencies;*

- *third parties as may be authorized by due process of law; or*

- *a duly authorized professional peer review committee except when such disclosure to a committee would violate applicable law or regulation.*

An appraiser must take reasonable steps to safeguard access to confidential information and assignment results by unauthorized individuals, whether such information or results are in physical or electronic form.

An appraiser must ensure that employees, co-workers, sub-contractors, or others who may have access to confidential information or assignment results, are aware of the prohibitions on disclosure of such information or results.

A member of a duly authorized professional peer review committee must not disclose confidential information presented to the committee.

Appraisers are sometimes asked to submit sample reports to others, such as a prospective client who is considering adding the appraiser to their approved appraiser list. It should be noted that such a scenario is not the same as a duly authorized professional peer review committee. The <u>Comment</u> to the preceding rule provides explanation of how the appraiser may proceed without client consent.

<u>Comment</u>: When all confidential elements of confidential information and assignment results are removed through redaction or the process of aggregation, client authorization is not required for the disclosure of the remaining information, as modified.

Redaction can be achieved by concealing certain identifying information through use of a marker pen, or typewriter correction fluid or tape. For residential appraisals, this is usually the most common method. Aggregation, for example, may be achieved by jumbling information so that it becomes meaningless or the information could be removed completely.

USPAP STANDARD 2 and Reporting Options

STANDARD 2 of USPAP addresses the obligations of an appraiser for reporting a real property appraisal and correlates with the final step in the appraisal process. In addition to an introduction, the standard contains four Standards Rules (2-1 through 2-4):

- Standards Rule 2-1 addresses general reporting obligations

- Standards Rule 2-2 provides a checklist for each reporting option

- Standards Rule 2-3 illustrates and elaborates on the appraiser's certification

- Standards Rule 2-4 specifically addresses oral appraisal reports

The discussion in this section will focus on the introduction and Standards Rule 2-1 through 2-3.

Introduction to STANDARD 2

The Introduction to STANDARD 2 reiterates the appraiser's obligation found in the ETHICS RULE to not report a real property appraisal in a manner that is misleading or fraudulent:

In reporting the results of a real property appraisal, an appraiser must communicate each analysis, opinion, and conclusion in a manner that is not misleading.

The <u>Comment</u> accompanying the Introduction contains general clarifications regarding STANDARD 2 and real property appraisal reporting:

- The standard addresses the **content and level of information** required in a report and does not dictate the form, format, or style of the report.
- The form, format, and style of a report are **specific to the needs of intended users and appraisers**.
- The substantive content of a report determines **compliance with the reporting options** permitted by STANDARD 2.

It should be specifically noted that reporting and the report option chosen is not a function of the scope of work. Rather, the reporting option and the form, format, or style are specific to the needs of **intended users**. This often becomes confused as the intended user is identified during problem identification along with other elements that assist an appraiser in determining the type of report for communicating his conclusions. However, this determination is not part of the scope of work decision.

Standards Rule 2-1 – General Obligations

Standards Rule 2-1 contains **general obligations** for all written and oral real property appraisal reports:

Each written or oral real property appraisal report must:

(a) clearly and accurately set forth the appraisal in a manner that will not be misleading;

(b) contain sufficient information to enable the intended users of the appraisal to understand the report properly; and

(c) clearly and accurately disclose all assumptions, extraordinary assumptions, hypothetical conditions, and limiting conditions used in the assignment.

Standards Rule 2-2 – Reporting Options

Standards Rule 2-2 is somewhat lengthy as it comprises two separate checklists of reporting obligations for each of the two **reporting options permitted** by STANDARD 2:

- Appraisal Report
- Restricted Appraisal Report

A Report Comparison Chart detailing the content requirements for each reporting option is found in USPAP Advisory Opinion 11. Advisory Opinion 11 and Advisory Opinion 12 contain important illustrations regarding reporting and should be consulted for further understanding.

Throughout STANDARD 2 and other parts of USPAP and its addenda, each reporting option may be referenced by a Standards Rule number and subsection, rather than by title. Therefore, it is helpful to be familiar with these references:

- 2-2(a) –Appraisal Report
- 2-2(b) – Restricted Appraisal Report

The two reporting options permitted by STANDARD 2 are also related to distinguishing terms that set each reporting option apart from the other; these terms are **summarize** and **state**.

These distinguishing terms reflect the level of information **significant to the solution of the appraisal problem**.

- An Appraisal Report "summarizes" this information.

- A Restricted Appraisal Report "states" this information.

Throughout the discussion of STANDARD 2, these distinguishing terms will be used. USPAP Advisory Opinion 11 should be reviewed as it provides examples of summarizing and stating information.

Standards Rule 2-2 – Choosing the Appropriate Reporting Option

Standards Rule 2-2 begins by emphasizing that the appraiser must report his conclusions and opinions of a real property appraisal by using one of the two reporting options.

The Standards Rule also obligates the appraiser to **prominently state in the report** which reporting option is being used:

> *Each written real property appraisal report must be prepared under one of the following options and prominently state which option is used: Appraisal Report or Restricted Appraisal Report.*

The Comment to the introduction of Standards Rule 2-2 contains important information and clarification. Important points contained in the comment include:

- The Restricted Appraisal Report option can be used only when the client is the only intended user.

- The Appraisal Report option must be used when there are intended users other than the client.

- The essential difference among the two reporting options is the content and level of detail of the information reported.

The level of information necessary in a report and the reporting option chosen by the appraiser depends on the **intended use and the intended users** in an assignment. Great care must be taken by an appraiser when characterizing the type of report and level of information that is contained in the report. An appraiser may use any other label (i.e., narrative format, form format) **in addition to but not in place of** the label of Appraisal Report or Restricted Appraisal Report.

Standards Rule 2-2 – Minimum Report Requirements

STANDARD 2 sets forth the **minimum requirements** for the level and content for each report type. An appraiser must supplement a report form, if necessary, with other information, addenda, exhibits, etc., so that intended users are not misled and the report complies with the content requirements of Standards Rule 2-2.

Receiving a copy of a report, regardless of the reporting option, **does not make that party an intended user** unless that party has been identified by the appraiser as an intended user at the time of the assignment.

Standards Rules 2-2(a) and (b) – Reporting Checklists

The next portion of Standards Rule 2-2 commences the reporting checklist for each report type. Each Standards Rule contains a checklist item specifying obligations represented by i – xii, which corresponds to the sub-categories found in Standards Rules 2-2(a) Appraisal Report and 2-2(b) Restricted Appraisal Report.

Standards Rule 2-2 – Identity of the Client and Other Intended Users

Standards Rule 2-2(a)(i) includes the following obligation for Appraisal Reports regarding information about the client and any other intended users in the assignment.

> *(i) state the identity of the client, unless the client has specifically requested otherwise; state the identity of any intended users by name or type;*

Standards Rule 2-2(b)(i) is somewhat different in that it has been expanded to include reporting obligations specific to a Restricted Appraisal Report.

(i) state the identity of the client, unless the client has specifically requested otherwise; and state a prominent use restriction that limits use of the report to the client and warns that the rationale for how the appraiser arrived at the opinions and conclusions set forth in the report may not be understood properly without additional information in the appraiser's workfile

The <u>Comment</u> to Standards Rule 2-2(a)(i), in part, contains obligations of an appraiser and clarifications for an Appraisal Report:

> *<u>Comment</u>: An appraiser must use care when identifying the client to avoid violations of the Confidentiality section of the ETHICS RULE. If a client requests that the client's identity be withheld from the report, the appraiser may comply with this request. In these instances, the appraiser must document the identity of the client in the workfile and must state in the report that the identity of the client has been withheld at the client's request.*

The <u>Comment</u> to Standards Rule 2-2(b)(i) contains similar language to that previously discussed but continues with additional admonishments specific to a Restricted Appraisal Report.

The <u>Comment</u> reminds appraisers that:

> *The Restricted Appraisal Report is for the client's use only. Before entering into an agreement, the appraiser should establish with the client the situations where this type of report is to be used and should ensure that the client understands the restricted utility of the Restricted Appraisal Report.*

Standards Rule 2-2 – Intended Use

Standards Rule 2-2(a) and (b)(ii) refer to the appraiser's obligation to report the intended use of the appraisal and is the same with **BOTH** reporting options.

> *(ii) state the intended use of the appraisal*

A <u>Comment</u> accompanies Standards Rule 2-2(b)(ii) which reminds an appraiser that the intended use of a Restricted Appraisal Report must be consistent with its limitations—the report is for the client's use only.

Standards Rule 2-2 – Information Regarding the Subject Property

Standards Rule 2-2(a) obligates appraisers to:

> *(iii)summarize information sufficient to identify the real estate involved in the appraisal, including the physical and economic property characteristics relevant to the assignment*

Standards Rule 2-2(b)(iii) is slightly different for a Restricted Appraisal Report where the appraiser must:

> *(iii) state information sufficient to identify the real estate involved in the appraisal*

Standards Rule 2-2 – Property Interest/Type of Value/Effective Date

Standards Rule 2-2(a) and (b)(iv-vi) require the reporting of the real property interest being appraised, the type and definition of value in the assignment, and the effective date of the appraisal and date of the report.

These general obligations are the same for **BOTH** reporting options:

> *(iv) state the real property interest appraised*
>
> *(v) state the type and definition of value and cite the source of the definition*
>
> *(vi) state the effective date of the appraisal and the date of the report*

While the general obligations are the same for both reporting options to "state" these elements, <u>Comments</u> to the requirements for an **Appraisal Report** elaborate on **additional diligence that is required** on the part of an appraiser.

> *(iv) <u>Comment</u>: The statement of the real property rights being appraised must be substantiated, as needed, by copies or summaries of title descriptions or other documents that set forth any known encumbrances.*
>
> *(v) <u>Comment</u>: Stating the definition of value also requires any comments needed to clearly indicate to intended users how the definition is being applied.*

When reporting an opinion of market value, state whether the opinion of value is:

- *in terms of cash or of financing terms equivalent to cash, or*

- *based on non-market financing or financing with unusual conditions or incentives.*

When an opinion of market value is not in terms of cash or based on financing terms equivalent to cash, summarize the terms of such financing and explain their contributions to or negative influence on value.

√ **Note:** While these are NOT requirements of a Restricted Appraisal Report, the appraiser must ensure that the resulting report will not be misleading.

Standards Rule 2-2 – Scope of Work

Standards Rule 2-2(a) and (b)(vii) address an appraiser's obligation (depending on the reporting option) to summarize or state the scope of work used to develop the appraisal.

Comments to this section provide further guidance for **BOTH** reporting options:

Comment: Because intended users' reliance on an appraisal may be affected by the scope of work, the report must enable them to be properly informed and not misled. Sufficient information includes disclosure of research and analyses performed and might also include disclosure of research and analyses not performed.

Depending on the reporting option:

When any portion of the work involves significant real property appraisal assistance, the appraiser must summarize or state the extent of that assistance. The signing appraiser must also state the name(s) of those providing the significant real property appraisal assistance in the certification, in accordance with Standards Rule 2-3.

Standards Rule 2-2 – Information Analyzed and Methodology Used

Standards Rule 2-2(a)(viii) obligates appraisers to:

(viii) summarize the information analyzed, the appraisal methods and techniques employed, and the reasoning that supports the analyses, opinions, and conclusions; exclusion of the sales comparison approach, cost approach, or income approach must be explained

Standards Rule 2-2(b)(viii) is slightly different in that the information is stated with less detail and reference is made to the appraiser's workfile.

(viii) state the appraisal methods and techniques employed, state the value opinion(s) and conclusion(s) reached, and reference the workfile; exclusion of the sales comparison approach, cost approach, or income approach must be explained

There are several lines of Comments to section (a)(viii) of Standards Rule 2-2.

Some key points of the obligations include:

- Appraisal Reports must include sufficient information to indicate that the appraiser complied with the development requirements of STANDARD 1.

- Appraisal Reports must provide sufficient information to enable the client and intended users to understand the rationale for the opinions and conclusions, including reconciliation.

In a market value assignment, **BOTH** reporting options require a **summary** of the results of analyzing the subject sales, options, and listings in accordance with Standards Rule 1-5. If the information is unobtainable, a statement on the efforts undertaken by the appraiser to obtain the information is required. If the information is irrelevant, a statement acknowledging the existence of the information and citing its lack of relevance is required.

Standards Rule 2-2 – Use of the Property/Highest and Best Use

Under Standards Rule Standards Rule 2-2(a) and (b)(ix), **BOTH** reporting options require an appraiser to state the **use of the property** on the date of the value opinion and as reflected in the appraisal.

Per Standards Rule 2-2(a) and (b)(ix) in part, the appraiser must:

> *(ix) state the use of the real estate existing as of the date of value and the use of the real estate reflected in the appraisal*

Standards Rule 2-2(a)(x) places obligations on an appraiser, for an Appraisal Report, to summarize the support and rationale for an appraiser's opinion of highest and best use when such an opinion has been developed by an appraiser in the assignment.

Standards Rule 2-2(b)(x) requires that for a Restricted Appraisal Report, the appraiser's opinion of highest and best use, when it is developed in an assignment, must be stated.

Standards Rule 2-2 – Extraordinary Assumptions/Hypothetical Conditions

Standards Rule 2-2(a) and (b)(xi) address an appraiser's obligation for **BOTH** reporting options to:

> *(xi) clearly and conspicuously:*

- *state all extraordinary assumptions and hypothetical conditions; and*
- *state that their use might have affected the assignment results*

Standards Rule 2-2 – Signed Certification

The final obligation of Standards Rule 2-2 is the inclusion of a **signed certification** in compliance with Standards Rule 2-3.

To comply with Standards Rule 2-2(a) and (b)(xii), **BOTH** reporting options require an appraiser to:

> *(xii) include a signed certification in accordance with Standards Rule 2-3*

Standards Rule 2-3 – Signed Certification Language

Under Standards Rule 2-3, all written real property appraisal reports (for **BOTH** reporting options) must contain a signed certification containing language similar to the following:

> *I certify that, to the best of my knowledge and belief:*
>
> *— the statements of fact contained in this report are true and correct.*
>
> *— the reported analyses, opinions, and conclusions are limited only by the reported assumptions and limiting conditions and are my personal, impartial, and unbiased professional analyses, opinions, and conclusions.*
>
> *— I have no (or the specified) present or prospective interest in the property that is the subject of this report and no (or the specified) personal interest with respect to the parties involved.*
>
> *— I have performed no (or the specified) services, as an appraiser or in any other capacity, regarding the property that is the subject of this report within the three-year period immediately preceding acceptance of this assignment.*
>
> *— I have no bias with respect to the property that is the subject of this report or to the parties involved with this assignment.*
>
> *— my engagement in this assignment was not contingent upon developing or reporting predetermined results.*
>
> *— my compensation for completing this assignment is not contingent upon the development or reporting of a predetermined value or direction in value that favors the cause of the client, the amount of the value opinion, the attainment of a stipulated result, or the occurrence of a subsequent event directly related to the intended use of this appraisal.*
>
> *— my analyses, opinions, and conclusions were developed, and this report has been prepared, in conformity with the Uniform Standards of Professional Appraisal Practice.*

— I have (or have not) made a personal inspection of the property that is the subject of this report. (If more than one person signs this certification, the certification must clearly specify which individuals did and which individuals did not make a personal inspection of the appraised property.)

— no one provided significant real property appraisal assistance to the person signing this certification. (If there are exceptions, the name of each individual providing significant real property appraisal assistance must be stated.)

Standards Rule 2-3 – Who Must Sign the Certification

The <u>Comment</u> to Standards Rule 2-3 is fairly extensive and, in some cases, covers a variety of appraisal scenarios. It states, in part:

A signed certification is an integral part of the appraisal report. An appraiser who signs any part of the appraisal report, including a letter of transmittal must also sign the certification.

In an assignment that includes only assignment results developed by the real property appraiser(s), any appraiser(s) who signs a certification accepts full responsibility for all elements of the certification, for the assignment results, and for the contents of the appraisal report...

Standards Rule 2-3 – Non-real Property Assets

The next portion of the <u>Comment</u> applies when the assignment additionally includes opinions or conclusions related to **non-real property assets**.

Clarification is provided that when an assignment includes non-real property assets, the **real** property appraiser signing the certification is taking full responsibility only for the **real** property related elements.

...In an assignment that includes personal property, business or intangible asset assignment results not developed by the real property appraiser(s), any real property appraiser(s) who signs a certification accepts full responsibility for the real property elements of the certification, for the real property assignment results, and for the real property contents of the appraisal report.

Standards Rule 2-3 – Work Done by Others

The <u>Comment</u> to Standards Rule 2-3 continues with obligations of a real property appraiser when he has relied on **work done by others who do not sign the certification**.

An example of such case might be (but not limited to) when a real property appraiser has relied on the opinions and conclusions of non-real property appraisers when their opinions and conclusions are incorporated into the real property appraiser's opinions and conclusions.

When a signing appraiser(s) has relied on work done by appraisers and others who do not sign the certification, the signing appraiser is responsible for the decision to rely on their work. The signing appraiser(s) is required to have a reasonable basis for believing that those individuals performing the work are competent. The signing appraiser(s) also must have no reason to doubt that the work of those individuals is credible.

Standards Rule 2-3 – Other Appraisal Assistance

The remainder of the <u>Comment</u> addresses disclosure in circumstances when **other individuals provide significant appraisal assistance** to the real property appraisers who are not signing the certification.

The names of individuals providing significant real property appraisal assistance who do not sign a certification must be stated in the certification. It is not required that the description of their assistance be contained in the certification, but disclosure of their assistance is required in accordance with Standards Rule 2-2(a) or (b)(vii), as applicable.

In more simple terms, the names of those providing significant assistance in an assignment must be stated in the certification. However, a description of what those individuals actually did that was significant to the conclusions found in the report is not specifically required to be in the certification but, depending on the reporting option, **must** be summarized or stated in the report.

Chapter 1 Case Examples

Case Example #1: Assignment Conditions

SCENARIO: A real property appraiser has been asked by a local lender to perform an appraisal of a vacant land parcel for the purpose of determining a market value. The intended use of the appraisal is for mortgage finance purposes in a sales transaction. The land parcel is being sold by a parent to one of her children. The lender has been provided with a previous appraisal of the property performed by an appraiser who was engaged by the property owner. The lender tells the appraiser that the present transaction price, between parent and child, is for an amount that is about one-half of the value indication concluded by the appraiser in that assignment.

The lender informs the appraiser that although his analysis may indicate a value opinion greater than the contract sale price, the lender's policies prohibit the appraised value in this assignment being more than 5% higher than the contract sale price as this tends to signal red flags to underwriters. The appraiser accepts and completes the assignment and communicates a report honoring the client's condition.

Has the appraiser failed to comply with USPAP?

ANALYSIS: Yes. In this case, the appraiser has accepted an assignment with unacceptable assignment conditions. The limitations placed on the appraiser have compromised the appraiser's independence and may not allow for the appraiser to develop an unbiased value opinion. Staying within "5% of the contract sale price" simply to satisfy the lender's underwriting criteria when the appraiser's unbiased value opinion is actually greater than that would be a violation of the ETHICS RULE, which requires (in part) an appraiser to perform assignments ethically and competently, and to not produce a misleading or fraudulent report. In addition, the appraiser's signed certification required by Standards Rule 2-3 acknowledges that the conclusions within the report are his personal unbiased opinions and conclusions.

Case Example #2: Disclosure of Payments by the Appraiser

SCENARIO: As a condition of receiving an assignment from a client, Appraiser Helen gave the client two tickets to the opera. The client attended the opera, and the following week Helen completed her assignment for the client, but she didn't discuss the tickets in the certification.

Was this acceptable under USPAP?

ANALYSIS: No. The <u>Management</u> section of the ETHICS RULE obligates an appraiser to disclose any fees, commissions, or things of value paid in the procurement of an assignment in the certification and any letter of transmittal in which conclusions are stated. The opera tickets are a thing of value paid to the client in connection with the procurement of an assignment. The value of the tickets, however, does not require disclosure.

Case Example #3: Confidentiality About Property Condition

SCENARIO: In the course of inspecting a subject property for an appraisal being performed for a lender-client, the homeowner has asked the appraiser to keep confidential certain information about the condition of the property in the appraisal report to the lender.

Can the appraiser treat this information as confidential?

ANALYSIS: No. The homeowner in this case is not part of the appraiser-client relationship. In fact, failing to disclose certain, pertinent information to the lender-client would not be in compliance and would produce a misleading report.

Case Example #4: Who May Have Access to Confidential Information?

SCENARIO: Barry, an appraiser, has applied for a professional designation of a major appraisal organization. As part of the approval process, Barry must submit sample appraisals reports for review by the designation committee of the organization. The committee is comprised of appraisers.

Can Barry comply with USPAP and supply the sample reports?

ANALYSIS: Yes. The <u>Confidentiality</u> section of the ETHICS RULE specifies (in part) that confidential information may be disclosed to professional peer review committees, unless if it would violate law or regulation. Since the committee in this case consists of other appraisers who are functioning on behalf of a professional appraisal organization, the sample reports could be submitted. However, the committee members must not disclose confidential information that has been submitted to the committee.

Case Example #5: Report Label and Content Level

SCENARIO: Stephanie, a real property appraiser, has completed her appraisal report for a multi-million dollar property. The appraisal will be used in a federally-related finance transaction. Based on the intended use and intended user in the assignment, Stephanie has decided that an Appraisal Report in narrative format is appropriate, which she has verbally communicated to the client. However, the appraisal report is labeled only as a "narrative" appraisal report.

In completing her report, Stephanie was very detailed in summarizing the real estate involved, scope of work, information that was analyzed, etc. However, her opinion of highest and best use was briefly stated with no discussion supporting the rationale for that decision.

Has Stephanie failed to comply with Standards Rule 2-2?

ANALYSIS: Yes. Standards Rule 2-2 requires an appraiser to prominently state in the report which reporting option is being used. An appraiser may use any other label in addition to, but not in place of, the label of Appraisal Report or Restricted Appraisal Report. Stephanie failed to comply with this requirement when she used only the label of "narrative" report. If it was her intention to provide an Appraisal Report, the report could have been labeled Appraisal Report in Narrative Format, or something similar, to have complied with the Standards Rule.

However, even though the level of detail of most of the elements of reporting were consistent with the level of an Appraisal Report, the level of stating her opinion of highest and best use, with no discussion supporting the rationale for the opinion, was consistent with the level of a Restricted Appraisal Report. Thus, the level of content for the entire report is reduced to that expected in a Restricted Appraisal Report, and therefore, would have conflicted with the necessary level determined appropriate for the intended use and the intended user.

Case Example #6: Reporting Significant Appraisal Assistance in the Report

SCENARIO: Jarrod Smith is a trainee with limited experience, and therefore, is not signing the certification in any assignment for which he provides significant assistance. In the most recent assignment for which he provided assistance, his supervisory appraiser permitted him to gather data for the subject property, choose comparable properties that were used in the sales comparison analysis, and reconcile the conclusions leading to the final opinion of value; an opinion with which his supervisory appraiser agreed.

The resulting Appraisal Report included a statement where Jarrod had provided "significant professional assistance in various phases of the appraisal process." The certification only disclosed Jarrod's assistance.

Is the disclosure in the report and the certification sufficient for compliance with Standards Rule 2-2?

ANALYSIS: No. While the disclosure in the certification was sufficient to fulfill the requirements of Standards Rule 2-2 and 2-3, merely including a broad statement of "significant professional assistance in various phases of the appraisal process" did not meet the disclosure requirements for an Appraisal Report. Standards Rule 2-2(a)(vii) requires that an Appraisal Report summarize the extent of the assistance, and therefore, the disclosure did not maintain the level of detail that should have been included.

An example of a more appropriate statement might be: **Jarrod Smith provided significant professional appraisal assistance in this appraisal assignment that included gathering data for the subject property, choosing comparable properties that were used in the sales comparison analysis, and reconciliation of the conclusions.**

Chapter 1 Case Study

The case study is intended as an introduction to introduce basic writing skills in compliance with a specific USPAP reporting option. There could be broad opinions of whether certain subject conditions are "average" or something different. There could also be varying opinions on information provided such as the effective age. However, those are development issues and not the issue here. As well, with some reporting formats and forms, this discussion might not be presented as a single discussion, but rather divided into several commentaries. Therefore, do not get caught up with how the conclusions were developed or how typical it might be to report this information within a single commentary. The purpose here is to recognize the appropriate level of reporting based on the information provided and to develop USPAP compliant narrative commentary that will be meaningful and understood by the user of the report.

Using the minimum USPAP reporting requirements consistent with an Appraisal Report; compose a narrative commentary identifying the real estate involved in the assignment and the physical and economic characteristics of the subject property by summarizing the relevant information in compliance with Standards Rule 2-2(a)(iii) using the following information:

Subject property address: 15 Robin Avenue, Anywhere, USA

Property type: Single-family residential dwelling, built on a crawl space.

Year built: 1982 – The majority of the dwellings in the immediate neighborhood were built approximately the same time period by the same developer.

Construction Quality: Average - Brick construction, composition shingle roof, double-pane windows, and concrete block foundation. The construction quality of the dwelling is consistent with, and similar to, other residential properties in the neighborhood.

Improvement Condition: Below average – The property has been well maintained and demonstrates continuous updating, which is typical of other dwellings in the neighborhood. However, a severe weather event two weeks prior to the effective date of the appraisal caused a tree to fall on the roof. The damage consists of approximately a 2' x 2' hole in the roof on the west side of the dwelling, approximately 2 feet from the south end of the roof, and 3 feet down from the ridge of the roof. Exterior damage is limited to the hole in the roof, which was confirmed by a qualified contractor hired by the property owner. The estimate to repair the damage is $2,500. The hole immediately received temporary repairs to prevent any water permeation into the attic area of the house or the finished living space. No interior evidence of damage was observed.

Gross living area: 1,475 square feet.

Legal description: Phase II, Lot #47, Wild Bird Subdivision. Public property records, Book 157, Page 39

Design: One-story ranch

Purpose of appraisal: Market value in its as-is condition

Effective age: 40 years

Lot size: 75' x 90', rectangular

Property features: 2-car attached garage, concrete driveway, patio in rear, small covered front porch

Location: Average – The subject is located on the west side of the street. All neighborhood properties share similar locational attributes and are equally desirable to market participants. Single-family properties in the neighborhood are a mix of single-story ranch style and one and one-half story dwellings of similar age as the subject.

The neighborhood is predominately single-family residential dwellings, with 10% 2-4 family, 15% public service use (schools and parks), and 5% vacant land reserved for future residential construction.

The neighborhood is approximately 5 blocks from the center of Anywhere. The center area of Anywhere is the location for shopping, medical services, major employers, transportation hubs, and recreational centers. Several arteries connect the designated neighborhood to the center of Anywhere.

Functional utility: Average – 3 bedrooms and 2 full baths. The floor plan is similar to other dwellings in the neighborhood and considered market acceptable.

Site topography: Mostly level

Zoning: R-1, medium density residential, and is limited to one-story and one and one-half story single-family residential dwellings of at least 1,200 square feet for one-story dwellings, and at least 1,800 square feet for one and one-half story dwellings. The subject conforms to all set-back and side-yard area requirements.

Neighborhood boundaries: Finch Avenue to the north, Bluebird Street to the south, Blackhawk Drive to the west, and Sparrow Street to the east.

Summary

1. The Uniform Standards of Professional Appraisal Practice (USPAP) sets the *minimum* ethical and performance obligations for appraisal practice, which includes appraisal reporting. Appraisers must develop and communicate their analyses, opinions, and conclusions to intended users of their services in a manner that is meaningful and not misleading.

2. The <u>Conduct</u> section of the ETHICS RULE contains several prohibitions regarding communication of a misleading or fraudulent report. In some cases, this action by an appraiser could be considered criminal activity, which is also prohibited by this section of the rule.

3. Appraisers must not use or rely on unsupported conclusions relating to characteristics such as race, color, religion, national origin, gender, marital status, familial status, age, receipt of public assistance income, handicap, or an unsupported conclusion that homogeneity of characteristics is necessary to maximize value.

4. Whether handwritten or electronically placed, an appraiser affixes his signature, or authorizes the use of his signature to certify recognition and acceptance of his obligations to USPAP. The signature of one appraiser must not be affixed by another without the signing appraiser's consent. Authorization to affix or use an appraiser's signature can only be granted on an assignment-by-assignment basis.

5. Disclosures that must be made in an appraisal report include any current or prospective interest an appraiser may have in the subject property or with the parties involved; prior services as an appraiser or in any other capacity within the previous three years; fees, commissions, or things of value paid by the appraiser in connection with the procurement of an appraisal assignment; the scope of work performed in an assignment; the part or parts of USPAP that was of no force due to jurisdictional exception, and citation of the law or regulation causing the exception.

6. Reporting and the report option chosen is not a function of the scope of work. The reporting option and the form, format, or style are specific to the needs of intended users. There are two reporting options permitted by USPAP: Appraisal Report and Restricted Appraisal Report. Distinguishing terms reflect the level of information significant to the solution of the appraisal problem: An Appraisal Report "summarizes" this information and a Restricted Appraisal Report "states" this information.

7. All written real property appraisal reports (for BOTH reporting options) must contain a signed certification. An appraiser's present or prospective interest in the subject property or with the parties involved; prior services as an appraiser or in any other capacity within the previous three years; fees, commissions, or things of value paid by the appraiser in connection with the procurement of an appraisal assignment; and any significant appraisal assistance are among the items that must be included in the certification when applicable.

Chapter Quiz

1. *Katy is appraising a property owned by her best friend. Katy would feel badly if the appraisal did not meet the needs of her friend and feels inclined to consider the property being appraised in the most positive manner. The __Conduct__ section of the ETHICS RULE applies here, as it makes clear that an appraiser must NOT perform an assignment with _____.*

    a. bias

    b. neutrality

    c. objectivity

    d. subjectivity

2. *Zachary's client instructs him to report a specific property value as a condition of the assignment. The assignment _____.*

    a. is an acceptable assignment condition

    b. is allowed as long as the appraiser confirms the value

    c. permits the appraiser's independence

    d. is a violation of the ETHICS RULE

3. *Anthony received an appraisal assignment for a property that was previously appraised by him. He understands that he must handle confidential information appropriately. What else must Anthony do?*

    a. get a release from the client of the prior assignment

    b. make proper disclosure regarding the prior assignment

    c. refuse the assignment since re-appraisal of the same property is prohibited under USPAP

    d. update the prior assignment and use it for the new assignment

4. *A real property appraiser has paid a fee to procure an appraisal assignment. According the __Management__ section of the ETHICS RULE, where must the fee be disclosed?*

    a. in the body of the appraisal report

    b. in the certification and any transmittal letter

    c. in the letter of engagement

    d. in a separate disclosure to the client

5. *According to the __Management__ section of the ETHICS RULE, an appraiser affixes his or her signature in an assignment for what purpose?*

    a. authenticate the work of the appraiser

    b. certify recognition and acceptance of USPAP responsibilities

    c. comply with federal copyright law

    d. prove that he personally inspected the property

6. *Which is a requirement when submitting an appraisal report to a professional peer review committee?*

    a. Any confidential information must be redacted.

    b. A fee to the appraiser must be charged for the submission.

    c. Client consent is required.

    d. Members of the committee must treat the information as confidential.

7. *The scope of work disclosed in an appraisal report must include the_____.*

    a. appraiser's final conclusions and value opinion

    b. initially planned scope of work at the onset of the assignment

    c. intended use in the assignment

    d. scope of work that was actually performed

8. *Which is NOT one of the specific requirements that an appraiser must follow when an assignment involves a jurisdictional exception?*

    a. cite in the appraisal report the law or regulation requiring the exception to USPAP compliance

    b. comply with the law or regulation

    c. identify the law or regulation precluding the compliance with USPAP

    d. indicate in the report how the law or regulation adds to the requirements of USPAP

9. *Standards Rule 2-1 requires that appraisal reports contain _____ to enable intended users to understand the report properly.*

    a. definitions of appraisal terms

    b. exhibits and photographs

    c. simple and common language

    d. sufficient information

10. *Standards Rule 2-2 requires an appraiser to _____ which reporting option is being used in the assignment.*

   a. document in the workfile
   b. keep confidential
   c. prominently state in the report
   d. specify in the certification

11. *In an appraisal report, sufficient information regarding the scope of work includes disclosure of research and analyses performed and might also include disclosure of _____.*

   a. the client's objectives for the assignment's results
   b. confidential information used in development
   c. fees and things of value paid to the appraiser
   d. research and analyses not performed

12. *An appraiser who _____ must also sign the certification.*

   a. contributes significant real property appraisal assistance
   b. physically inspects the subject property
   c. proofreads a report for typographical errors
   d. signs any part of the appraisal report including a letter of transmittal

Chapter 2

Effective Writing and Reasoning Skills in Appraisal Reporting

2

Introduction

In Chapter 1, we covered the USPAP requirements of what an appraiser, at minimum, must do and must not do in appraisal reporting; in this chapter, the attention now turns to what an appraiser **should do** or **should not do** in an effort to produce a meaningful and effective appraisal report. Basic writing skills and ability on the part of an appraiser to communicate the reasoning for his conclusions are important for effective appraisal reporting.

Key Terms

Curable Item Repairable or able to be fixed; something that *can* be repaired or replaced at a reasonable cost with the value added to the property being more than the cost.

Deferred Maintenance A physical deterioration that has occurred because of a failure to perform regular maintenance and upkeep.

District An area consisting of one particular land use. There could be several districts within a neighborhood and several neighborhoods comprising a market area.

Economic Life The period of time when a structure contributes positively to a property's value; considers physical deterioration, functional obsolescence, and external obsolescence.

Effective Age Estimated by an appraiser and based on all forces of physical deterioration and functional and external obsolescence.

External Obsolescence When something outside the boundaries of a property and the control of the property owner makes it less desirable. The factors causing the obsolescence may be economic or location factors.

(continued on page 25)

Basic Report Writing Skills

In some cases, an appraiser may have the opportunity to actually sit down with the client, and possibly any other intended users, to detail the steps taken in an appraisal for the development of the appraiser's conclusions found in a written appraisal report. However, this is *typically the exception rather than the rule*. And, even in those circumstances, not spelling out the appraiser's diligence and the basis for conclusions in the written report can later haunt the appraiser, often during a subsequent review of the appraisal report by a review appraiser or a regulatory investigator. In most assignments, the appraisal report is the **only** vehicle used to fully communicate the appraisal process, the steps taken by the appraiser, and the reasoning supporting the appraiser's conclusions.

One Size Does Not Fit All

Sometimes, there is a misconception that all appraisal reports should be written the same way—using the same level of discussion and industry terminology—and that every client and user of an appraisal will comprehend the content of the report. Nothing could be further from the truth. Clients and users of appraisal reports have different needs and expectations from an appraisal report. Depending on the intended user(s) and intended use of an appraisal report, some will obviously be interested in the final opinion of value, while others, for example, may be most focused on the highest and best use of the property or the conclusions of the cost approach. This is the reason that the *level of content and detail found in a report should address the **needs of the intended users**, based on the intended use of the report*. These are certainly elements that require clarification at the time of the assignment and for which the appraiser must be mindful when writing the appraisal report.

Many users of appraisal reports, such as lenders, are quite familiar with appraisal reports, most of the industry terms, and the appraisal process. Others may be reading an appraisal for the first time and have no comprehension of industry terms, such as extraordinary assumption, hypothetical condition, effective age, or economic life. And most certainly, those individuals and others likely cannot grasp the extent of the development process undertaken by the appraiser. In those circumstances, industry terminology and the developments steps taken by the appraiser must be much more comprehensively explained.

Appraisal Reporting Forms

Most residential appraisals are communicated using standardized appraisal reporting forms. (Residential appraisal reporting forms will be discussed in Chapter 4.) A common misconception of some appraisers, as well as some clients and intended users, is that simply reporting information using the provided checkboxes, or inserting abbreviated responses in the various fields of the reporting form, is sufficient to satisfy USPAP obligations and what an appraiser "should" do for communicating the opinions and conclusions of an appraisal. Appraisers have been known to say "If it is not on the form, I do not have to report it". To be clear, the appraiser has the responsibility to ensure the particular form and its contents meet USPAP requirements and the needs of clients and intended users, *not the form*.

In almost every assignment, the appraisal report must be expanded through **narrative commentary**, often carried to report addenda, in order to clearly communicate elements of the appraisal and other significant information for the appraisal report to be understandable to the user(s). Many users of appraisals, such as Fannie Mae and Freddie Mac, require additional explanation with certain responses on the forms. Additional information and exhibits are almost *always* necessary in every appraisal report, including those communicated on a reporting form.

Exercising Pride in Reporting

An appraisal report should be thought of as a demonstration that will result in repeat and new business for the appraiser. Poor reports could prevent another assignment from a client, or might end up in the hands of someone who could reject future appraisal opportunities. This does not mean going over the top; it just means producing a quality report for which the appraiser can be proud.

Here are some tips:

- For form reports, do **not** type in ALL CAPS—it gives the appearance of laziness.

- Make sure the report is clear and understandable, without being too technical or complicated.
- The information should flow as if telling a story, whether writing a full narrative report or completing the comment fields in a report form.
- Do not assume that the client and other intended users know what is being discussed or referenced—a little reflection here goes a long way.
- The more complex the assignment or the property, the more detailed the report should be.
- Check for proper grammar, punctuation, and spelling (use spellchecker and take a remedial writing course, if necessary).
- Proofread, proofread, proofread!

It is always good to review every appraisal report one last time before submitting to the client, and consider whether the report contains the content and level of detail necessary to satisfy an appraisal licensing regulatory official at some time in the future. As well, the completed appraisal report should reflect the quality for which the appraiser can be proud.

Expression of Reasoning in Appraisal Reporting

Regardless of the level of depth and detail that an appraiser applies to develop his conclusions, those efforts pale when users of an appraisal do not understand the reasoning surrounding those conclusions. Some conclusions are based upon fact and may not require extensive discussion—although an explanation of what those facts mean may be necessary. Other conclusions are based on the results of various analyses that must be carefully explained for the user to comprehend the process and mindset leading to the conclusion. This section of our textbook, while certainly not all inclusive, we will provide an opportunity to consider, using case studies, several required reporting elements that are notoriously abbreviated in many residential appraisal reports.

Discussing Neighborhood Boundaries and Locational Characteristics

Since location is such an important aspect of property value, it is important to effectively describe the **market area** or **neighborhood** boundaries in a manner that will allow the reader of the report to clearly understand the defined boundaries and the reasoning of why those particular boundaries were chosen by the appraiser. **Locational characteristics**, whether favorable or adverse, are also critical to the appraiser's conclusions and should be elaborated. Certain elements outside the defined neighborhood boundaries may also have an influence, either positively or negatively on the subject's neighborhood, which should be included in the neighborhood discussion.

Functional Obsolescence When a building is less desirable because of something inherent in the design or nature of the structure.

Incurable Item Something that *cannot* be repaired or replaced at a reasonable cost with the cost of the repair being more than the value added to a property.

Long-lived Item A component of a structure that is *not* expected to be replaced during the life of a property.

Market Area An area where properties would be located that would be considered competition for the subject property.

Neighborhood A compilation or group of complimentary land uses.

Physical Deterioration The diminishment of condition of a structure or other improvement, or a component of the structure or improvement due to age, the elements, or other forces.

Short-lived Item A component of a structure that *is* expected to be replaced during the life of a property.

Useful Life Relates to the period of time a structure or a component of the structure can be expected to function for the purpose for which it was designed; applies only to physical deterioration.

Key Terms

Technically, a market area is usually a broader category and may encompass quite a large area. A **market area** is usually considered *an area where properties would be located, which would be considered competition for the subject property*. In some smaller communities, the entire city or village, for example, could be defined as the market area. A **neighborhood** is *a compilation or a group of complimentary land uses*. When describing a neighborhood, the appraiser should illustrate **all** of the uses, even though varied, which create the overall environment. The complementary uses could be a mix of residential, commercial, and service, as well as other amenities. In the neighborhood description, the neighborhood may be delineated further by identifying separating single-family homes, apartment complexes, retail areas, etc., into districts. A **district** is *an area consisting of one particular land use*. There could be several districts within a neighborhood and several neighborhoods comprising a market area.

In most cases, it is common to use *geographic boundaries*, natural or man-made, as one way to define and describe a neighborhood. Examples are typically streets or other thoroughfares, corporation limits, flowing bodies of water, etc. As will be seen in Chapter 4, Fannie Mae, Freddie Mac, and other lending entities require the boundaries of the defined neighborhood or market area to be initially described using directional boundaries – *North, East, South, and West.*

Once the initial neighborhood boundaries have been described, characteristics of the neighborhood should be detailed that allow the reader to create a mental image of the neighborhood and provide vital information that will assist in supporting other analysis, such as highest and best use and overall marketability. As such, this is a very important description that somewhat sets the stage for much of the discussion in other areas of the appraisal report. In many assignments, the client and other users may not be at all familiar with the area and must rely on the appraiser's description to understand the neighborhood characteristics.

Example

A poorly composed neighborhood description might be:

The subject neighborhood is located in a northern suburban area. The area consists of various styles and ages of housing, both single-family and apartment complexes. Proximity to conveniences and schools is average. Marketability is also average.

Make A List

Keeping in mind that the neighborhood discussion should focus on the general characteristics of the neighborhood and not the locational positives and negatives of the subject's specific location, consider the information that should be included in the neighborhood description and make a list of those below:

_____

_____

_____

_____

_____

Case Study— Neighborhood

Using the information provided, write a neighborhood description that assists the reader to envision the subject neighborhood. **Do not simply copy the information given.** *Rather, compose the information in a manner that has proper flow and is grammatically and structurally correct. The resulting neighborhood description should be informational and not sound like a sales pitch. The illustration below depicts the neighborhood and provides some of the information needed to write the description. Additional information follows.*

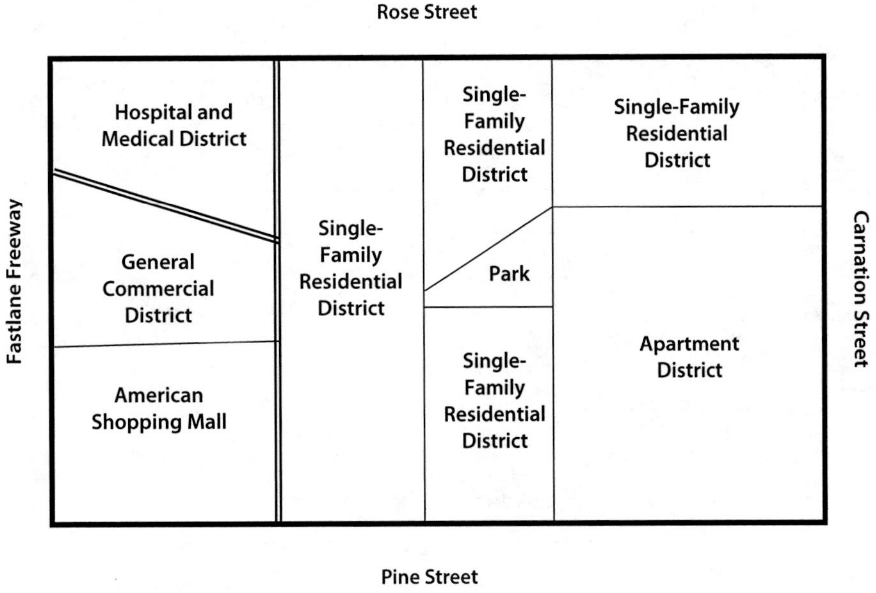

Rose Street

Hospital and Medical District		**Single-Family Residential District**	**Single-Family Residential District**
General Commercial District	**Single-Family Residential District**	**Park**	**Apartment District**
American Shopping Mall		**Single-Family Residential District**	

(Left side: Fastlane Freeway; Right side: Carnation Street)

Pine Street

Additional neighborhood information and results of the appraiser's analysis:

- Suburban area known as Ridgeway, which is located immediately Northwest of the city of Chesterville, approximately eight miles from the center of the city
- Fire and police protection are provided by Brown Township in which Ridgeway is located
- Public transit lines run along main arteries throughout the neighborhood
- The neighborhood is about 95% built-up with about 5% vacant land, which is mostly vacant building lots owned by adjoining homeowners
- Single-family housing is a mix of two-story, one and one-half story, and ranch style homes, with ranch style being predominate (about 75%)
- Most houses (about 80%) are frame construction, with the remainder being either brick or stone
- Housing age ranges from 10-15 years, with most houses being 15 years old
- Single-family housing prices range from $250,000 to $325,000, with $275,000 being the median
- Houses range from 1,800 square feet to just over 2,400 square feet, with 2,000 square foot homes predominate
- Most lots have mature trees and landscaping and are generally level in topography
- Houses in the neighborhood are generally three- or four-bedrooms and are built on crawl spaces
- Some houses have fireplaces, which is preferred by the market
- All houses have either a one-car or two-car garage and a rear patio or deck

- The area is served by the Chesterville North School District (six miles away) with busing provided
- Houses are typically on the market for 30-60 days with the exception of brick and stone houses, which have demonstrated a slightly shorter marketing time
- Three apartment complexes, which, in total, contain approximately 300 units, are located in the southeast portion of the neighborhood, have about 2% vacancy, and comprise about 25% of the land use
- The apartment complexes, as well as the non-residential uses, do not appear to detract marketability, except for houses that are directly exposed to those uses
- Housing near to and surrounding the park are market preferred

Discussing the Basis for Effective Age

The **effective age** of a structure is *based on all forces of physical deterioration and functional and external obsolescence*. In other words, the effective age considers:

* A structure's physical condition
* How acceptably functional a structure is
* Any external factors that influence a structure

Estimating the effective age of a structure, or other improvement, requires support by good judgment and reasoning skills on the part of the appraiser that comes through experience. The results of the cost approach can be skewed by not reasonably estimating effective age. Appraisers must be thoughtful and use great care, as subjectively setting the effective age without support of sound reasoning and logic, as well as not communicating the reasoning and logic sufficiently in the appraisal report, are frequent causes for disciplinary action by state-appraiser regulators.

A few concepts and terms should be reviewed to assist with the reasoning that the appraiser will discuss in the appraisal report regarding effective age:

* **Physical Deterioration** The diminishment of condition of a structure or other improvement; or a component of the structure or improvement due to age, the elements, or other forces. This type of depreciation is often observable during the appraiser's personal inspection of the subject property. Regular maintenance can slow this process; deferred maintenance results in items that need immediate attention.
* **Functional Obsolescence** When a building is less desirable because of something inherent in the design or nature of the structure. Functional obsolescence can be curable or incurable.
* **External Obsolescence** When something outside the boundaries of a property and the control of the property owner makes it less desirable. The factors causing the obsolescence may be economic or location factors.
* **Deferred Maintenance** A physical deterioration that has occurred because of a failure to perform regular maintenance and upkeep. Most deferred maintenance would be classified as curable (repairable), provided the severity of the condition is not beyond economical repair or replacement, but not all physical deterioration is curable.
* **Curable Item** Repairable or able to be fixed; something that *can* be repaired or replaced at a reasonable cost with the value added to the property being more than the cost.
* **Incurable Item** Something that *cannot* be repaired or replaced at a reasonable cost with the cost of the repair being more than the value added to a property.
* **Short-lived Item** A component of a structure that *is* expected to be replaced during the life of a property.
* **Long-lived Item** A component of a structure that is *not* expected to be replaced during the life of a property.
* **Economic Life** The period of time when a structure contributes positively to a property's value—considers physical deterioration, functional obsolescence, and external obsolescence.
* **Useful Life** Relates to the period of time a structure, or a component of the structure, can be expected to function for the purpose it was designed for and applies only to physical deterioration.

Since estimating effective age is primarily based upon the appraiser's supported judgment and opinion, there could be disagreement among appraisers as to exactly where the effective age should be estimated, or if a particular condition is curable or incurable in various scenarios. As examples of effective age are presented, do not get caught up in these issues as this is not the point of this section of the textbook. The purpose here is effectively communicating the reasoning behind the estimated effective age determined by the appraiser to the user of the report.

The discussion of effective age should include:

* *Specific* information regarding physical condition of the improvements considered in the estimated effective age, such as particular items that have been updated, replaced, repaired, renovated, or refurbished

- A statement regarding the absence or presence of any functional or external obsolescence, and if present, a specific description of the condition(s) and how the effective age has been affected

For Example

A common, yet poorly composed, explanation of the appraiser's reasoning might be:

The effective age is estimated to be five years, which is less than the actual age due to condition.

Case Study #1— Effective Age

A house is 20 years old (its actual age). The owner replaces the roof, floor coverings, repaints all of the rooms, spruces up the exterior, replaces dated lighting and plumbing fixtures, and installs a new HVAC system, thus bringing the house to current day standards and tastes. Since most short-lived curable items have been addressed, the appraiser has estimated the effective age as five years. There was no condition of functional or external obsolescence present.

Write an explanation for the reasoning of the estimated effective age of five years. The explanation may be brief but should allow the user of the report to fully understand the basis for the effective age.

_____

_____

_____

_____

Case Study #2— Effective Age

For this example, a single-family dwelling evidences poor functional utility, which is considered to be incurable. The functional obsolescence is a result of the primary front entrance of the dwelling opening into the kitchen, and the only bath in the dwelling being located off the kitchen.

Actual age of the dwelling is 60 years. The dwelling has been extensively renovated with all curable items meeting present day standards and very little deterioration of incurable items. The structure is very well maintained and is consistent with other residential properties in the neighborhood. There is no external obsolescence present. Absent the functional issues, the appraiser would have estimated the effective age at 25 years, however, considering the functional obsolescence present, the appraiser has estimated the effective age at 50 years.

Write an explanation for the reasoning of the estimated effective age of 50 years. The explanation may be brief but should allow the user of the report to fully understand the basis for the effective age.

Appropriate Discussion of Highest and Best Use

Highest and best use is *the most reasonably probable legal use of a property, as vacant land or as improved, that is physically possible, adequately supported, financially feasible, and results in the greatest value.* Determining the highest and best use for the subject property is a critical step in the appraisal process and is at the heart of the valuation process when the type of value in an assignment is market value. Its purpose is to decide whether the property is being used for its most profitable permitted use. In some cases, a change from the current use could maximize the property value.

Admittedly, in many single-family residential appraisal assignments, determining highest and best use is somewhat of a brief process as zoning and private restrictions limit use of the site to the present use. Also, it will probably not be an everyday event to encounter a property when the dwelling has reached the end of its economic life. However, this does not mean that the discussion of highest and best use should be absent or overly abbreviated in the appraisal report.

Reporting highest and best use in residential appraisal assignments is often performed on some type of appraisal form. In such forms, the highest and best use reporting consists of marking an appropriate checkbox. If the particular appraisal reporting form is considered an **Appraisal Report** (which many are), USPAP requires the appraiser to *summarize the support and rationale for that opinion.* Therefore, simply checking off the box that the present improvements or use of the property are the highest and best use does not fully comply with USPAP without the appropriate level of explanation for the reasoning.

Even when some level of explanation for the highest and best use conclusion is presented, often times the reasoning is overly abbreviated. While in many residential circumstances the explanation does not need to consist of multiple paragraphs, the rationale should at least:

- Reference that the value of the site "as-vacant" was at least considered and why this was not the conclusion of the appraiser
- Discuss any alternatives that were considered, and if no alternatives would be more profitable or productive, the reasoning (If there were multiple alternatives considered, they should be discussed)
- Provide support for the highest and best use conclusion that is credible and will be understood by the user

For Example

A highest and best use explanation that is poorly written might be:

The current improvements represent the highest and best use of the property.

Case Study #1— Highest and Best Use

This first example likely represents the type of assignment that many appraisers will encounter in everyday appraising. The subject property is a ten-year old single-family residential dwelling in a residential subdivision. The subject's R-1 (one-family residential dwelling) zoning limits use of the site to single-family residential dwellings, as do the restrictive covenants of the subdivision. There is no significant physical deterioration or functional or external obsolescence present. The appraiser concluded that the highest and best use was its present use.

Write a brief, but convincing, explanation that details the reasoning for the appraiser's highest and best use conclusion.

_____

_____

_____

_____

_____

Case Study #2— Highest and Best Use

A vacant parcel is being appraised for which (R-2) zoning only permits multiple residential apartments of up to four units. There is no evidence that the vacant parcel should remain vacant, as assemblage of the site with an adjoining parcel is not likely. The appraiser has therefore determined that the highest and best use of the parcel is for a 2-4 unit apartment building, which in conformity with maximum lot coverage requirements of zoning, contains 4,000 square feet. Upon further analysis, the appraiser has concluded that the ideal improvement for a vacant parcel is a three-unit apartment building with each unit having three bedrooms and two baths, based on the following information.

Number of Units	Unit Description	Estimated Cost	Completed Value (based on income approach)
Two	4-bedroom, 3-bath	$268,000	$170,000
Three	3-bedroom, 2-bath	$196,000	$202,360
Four	2-bedroom, 2-bath	$180,000	$177,000

Write an explanation for the appraiser's rationale that supports the appraiser's highest and best conclusion.

_____

_____

_____

_____

_____

_____

_____

_____

_____

_____

Summary

1. Clients and users of appraisal reports have different needs and expectations from an appraisal report. The level of content and detail found in a report should address the needs of the intended users, based on the intended use of the report. These elements require clarification at the time of the assignment and for which the appraiser must be mindful when writing the appraisal report.

2. Many users of appraisal reports are familiar with appraisal reports, industry terms, and the appraisal process. Others may be reading an appraisal for the first time and have no comprehension of certain industry terms or the extent of the development process in an appraisal, which may require the appraiser to be much more comprehensive in his explanations.

3. A common misconception is that simply reporting information using the provided checkboxes, or inserting abbreviated responses in the various fields of a reporting form, is sufficient to satisfy USPAP obligations and what an appraiser "should" do for communicating the opinions and conclusions of an appraisal. The appraiser has the responsibility to ensure the particular form and its contents meet USPAP requirements and the needs of clients and intended users, *not the form*.

4. In almost every assignment, the appraisal report must be expanded through narrative commentary, often carried to report addenda, in order to clearly communicate elements of the appraisal and other significant information for the appraisal report to be understandable to user(s).

5. Some conclusions in an appraisal report are based upon fact and may not require extensive discussion—although an explanation of what those facts mean may be necessary. Other conclusions are based on the results of various analyses that must be carefully explained for the user to comprehend the process and mindset of the appraiser leading to the conclusion.

Chapter Quiz

1. *The level of content and detail in an appraisal report should address the needs of intended users,*

    a. and be the same in every report.
    b. based on the intended use of the report.
    c. consistent with the fee being charged.
    d. while containing no greater information than required by USPAP.

2. *In circumstances where the client is not familiar with appraisal reports or industry terminology, an appraiser must*

    a. ensure there is an additional intended user who possesses understanding.
    b. explain, in the report, the terminology and the development steps more comprehensively.
    c. provide an oral report in addition to providing the written report.
    d. report no more than he would for a client who has familiarity.

3. *When using a residential appraisal reporting form required by Fannie Mae, an appraiser should*

    a. avoid the expansion of commentary beyond the comment fields in the forms.
    b. not append the form with exhibits or additional commentary.
    c. only complete the specific fields of the reporting form.
    d. use addenda for extra commentary to ensure that intended users understand the report.

4. *The responsibility to ensure that a particular appraisal reporting form and its contents meets USPAP requirements and is appropriate to the needs of clients and intended users rests with the*

    a. appraiser in the assignment.
    b. client requiring the form.
    c. entity which developed the form.
    d. specifications found in STANDARD 2 of USPAP.

5. *When developing commentary for neighborhood boundaries and locational characteristics, an appraiser must*

    a. also discuss influences from outside the defined area.
    b. never reference the price ranges of housing in the area.
    c. refer only to positive qualities within the defined area.
    d. reference the area as a specific district.

6. *The neighborhood description is often a basis for*

    a. defining the ethnic composition of a market area.
    b. particular interest rates to be charged in the area.
    c. rejection of an assignment by an appraiser.
    d. supporting other analysis performed in the assignment.

7. *Which is a TRUE statement regarding effective age?*

    a. Clients and intended users furnish the effective age to be used in the assignment.
    b. Estimating effective age is limited to the observation of physical deterioration.
    c. The report should contain the reasoning and logic for its estimation by an appraiser.
    d. Unless there is external obsolescence, effective age and actual age are always equal.

8. *Using the Appraisal Report option permitted by USPAP, the support and rationale for the appraiser's highest and best use conclusion must be*

    a. contained in the certification.
    b. described in the report.
    c. stated in the reconciliation.
    d. summarized in the report.

9. *A quality neighborhood description should*

    a. be informational to the client and other intended users.
    b. exclude any non-residential uses present in the neighborhood.
    c. make the client and other users want to live there.
    d. not include a reference to a particular school system

10. *In an appraisal report, if an appraiser describes a component of a structure as long-lived, the discussion within the report should allow users to understand that this term means the*

    a. cause is due to external obsolescence.
    b. component is not expected to be replaced during the life of the structure.
    c. economic life of the component is therefore greater than the actual age.
    d. item or component cannot be physically repaired or replace.

Chapter 3:
Common Issues in Appraisal Reporting

Introduction

USPAP is specific to many issues in appraisal reporting. Some of these issues, such as appraisal reporting obligations found in STANDARD 2, are mostly direct and to the point. Other issues are integrated into other prohibitions and obligations found in USPAP Rules and other communication of the Appraisal Standards Board, such as Advisory Opinions.

In this section, two specific appraisal reporting issues will be the topic of discussion in context of USPAP compliance and in observance of best practices. First is a brief discussion of client direction and instruction in the reporting process. The discussion then turns to illustrate five of the most common reporting issues and how they should be handled in appraisal reporting.

Bracketing A process in which an appraiser identifies comparable data that is inferior and superior to the subject data. The appraiser then determines where to apply the indications within that range.

Gross Rent Multiplier (GRM) A factor derived from comparable rental data, which is then used to develop an opinion of value of the subject property.

Market Rent What the subject property could rent for in the open market if currently vacant and available.

Paired Data Analysis The process of determining the value of specific property characteristics or features by comparing pairs of similar properties. Also called **Matched Pair Analysis**.

Regression Analysis A statistical measure that attempts to ascertain the source of change in variables.

Transition A complete change of land use.

Key Terms

Client Direction

It is very common, and is certainly logical, that during the course of the engagement process and during problem identification, the client may have certain requests regarding the appraisal report issued by a particular appraiser in a specific assignment. Many of the requests are reasonably typical and part of many appraisal assignments, and therefore not an issue of concern. Most often these particular specifications or requests come in the form of assignment conditions – diligence over and above what might be required by USPAP. Very often, these additional specifications present themselves as requirements to, for example, furnish additional photographs, include certain other addenda, develop an approach to value that is not otherwise required or necessary, etc. Of course, it is the appraiser's responsibility to determine if any request or assignment condition is reasonable, within professional standards, and will result in a credible appraisal report.

There may be other requests or specifications that are **not** ethical or permitted by professional standards, however. This is where an appraiser must be vigilant, remaining steadfast by **not** accepting an assignment that is accompanied by unacceptable assignment conditions. Advisory Opinion 19, bound with USPAP, addresses this topic.

Some common examples of clearly, or potentially, unacceptable assignment conditions that might be directed by the client include (but are certainly not limited to) requests for the appraiser in residential assignments to:

- Not report a specific fact about the property, such as the actual zoning designation, zoning regulations, or zoning status of the property (or to state it differently than it is)

- Not report a property defect or a highest and best use other than its current improved use

- Misrepresent the property improvements as something they are not, such as report an obvious two-family property as a single-family property

- Not include any adverse external conditions in the commentary or in photographs, such as an objectionable non-residential use

- Not mention functional issues of the subject property, such as non-market acceptable floor plans or a unique design

- Not make adjustments in the sales comparison approach, even when warranted

- Make adjustments in the sales comparison approach, even when not warranted

- Only report that the subject site contains a land area or dimensions that differ from its actual description, and not mention the remaining land area in the report

These are just a few of some of the most common examples of assignment conditions that jeopardize an appraiser's independence and would lead to a misleading and likely fraudulent appraisal report. It may be possible that if the unacceptable nature of the request is pointed out to the client, the request or condition may be withdrawn and the appraiser may proceed. However, compliance with such requests is contrary to professional ethics.

Appraisal reporting should present a true and precise picture of the property that is the subject of the assignment. The appraiser is doing a disservice to himself and to all involved when an appraisal report is misleading, and is participating in criminal activity when the report is fraudulent. Facts regarding the property should **never** be fraudulent, or for that matter, sugar-coated.

Five Critical Reporting Issues

Although there could potentially be innumerable appraisal reporting missteps and failures which could produce a poor quality appraisal report and either serve as a discredit to the appraiser abilities or be adjudged as not in compliance with USPAP, five critical report issues are among the most commonly cited issues in appraisal reviews and the disciplinary actions of state appraisal regulatory officials:

1. Failure to disclose and discuss physical deterioration and functional obsolescence

2. Failure to disclose and discuss locational issues or external obsolescence

3. Failure to adequately disclose and discuss prior sales and relevance

4. Failure to discuss the support for adjustments, or for not making adjustments in the sales comparison approach

5. Failure to adequately discuss how market rent potential and rates of capitalization were established

While some of these critical issues may be simply oversight or overly abbreviated in some cases, in other cases, issues such as disclosing or adequately discussing deterioration and obsolescence might be omitted or pasteurized in order to satisfy the client or other users of the appraisal report. Regardless, appraisers must exercise special care in these areas so that appraisal reports are clear and not misleading.

Issue #1 - Failure to Disclose and Discuss Physical Deterioration and Functional Obsolescence

Physical deterioration and functional obsolescence were discussed in Chapter 2. **Physical deterioration** is *something to do with the condition of the structure*, while **functional obsolescence** pertains *to something about the design or functional acceptability of the structure*. In the previous discussion, how these conditions influence the effective age was described. In this section, the discussion focuses on the hazards of not fully disclosing and discussing the physical and functional characteristics. Failure to provide a *true picture of these characteristics* will result in a misleading, or in some cases, a fraudulent appraisal report.

Case Study
. . . .

A residential dwelling is approximately 45 years old. The exterior had vinyl siding installed only on the front portion of the structure about three (3) years ago, while the sides and rear of the house have significant chipping and peeling paint, with much exposed wood siding and paint chip residue present on the ground. Four windows in the front of the house received insulated tilt-out replacement windows when the siding was installed. The remaining windows on the sides and rear are the original single-pane wood windows, which are deteriorating.

Inside, all rooms were repainted in the past six months. However, the bedrooms and living room are painted black, and the bath and kitchen are bright mustard yellow. The floor covering in the kitchen was removed, evidently some time ago, and only has the particle board subfloor exposed. The furnace was removed three months ago and a new furnace is in the box and sitting on the covered patio at the rear of the dwelling.

This is the appraiser's commentary regarding the physical and functional characteristics…

The dwelling is approximately 45 years of age; however, the structure has undergone extensive renovations. The exterior recently received new vinyl siding and insulated tilt-out replacement windows. The interior has recently been redecorated in a contemporary color scheme. Kitchen floor coverings were in the process of being replaced at the time of the inspection. The furnace is also new.

The issues with the appraiser's commentary should be obvious. Rewrite the commentary so the users of the report have a clear picture of the property in its "as-is" condition.

_____

_____

_____

_____

_____

_____

_____

_____

Issue #2 - Failure to Disclose and Discuss Locational Issues or External Obsolescence

External obsolescence, also discussed in Chapter 2, reflects *conditions outside a property's boundaries and can present itself due to locational conditions that are objectionable to market participants,* such as railroad tracks, industrial exposure, or noise; or from economic conditions, such as change taking place with the economics of a market. This is not as common with residential properties but might present itself with a property that is over-improved in comparison to properties surrounding it, or if the property is located in an area of **transition**, which is *a complete change of land use,* ssuch as an area of single-family homes transitioning in use to high-density multi-family apartments.

This is an area of reporting for which many appraisers demonstrate poor reporting practice by not saying anything. Often, this is accompanied in the report by including photographs that purposely avoid depicting the particular external issue. Such practice can lead to a misleading or fraudulent report.

Case Study

A single-family subject property is situated across the street from a chemical distribution plant. The side of the street on which the subject is situated consists of all residential homes. There are also residential homes on each side of the chemical distribution plant. A rail line runs behind the chemical distribution plant and the houses on each side of it. In addition to a continuous odor emitting from the facility, heavy truck traffic proceeding in and out of the facility is constant—24 hours per day. A freeway entrance ramp is at the end of the street, about 300 yards from the subject property. Properties in this particular block have consistently experienced lengthy marketing periods and a significant impact on selling prices.

This is the appraiser's commentary regarding the external characteristics…

The subject property is located on a street that predominately consists of single-family residential dwellings with a mix of non-residential uses typical for the immediate area. Access of the area is considered to be good with convenient access to various modes of transportation and highways.

Rewrite the commentary so the users of the report have a clear picture of the external characteristics of the property and how the conditions have historically affected the immediate market.

_____

_____

_____

_____

_____

_____

_____

_____

Issue #3 - Failure to Adequately Disclose and Discuss Prior Sales and Relevance

As was discussed in Chapter 1, all reporting options permitted by USPAP require a **summary** of the *results of analyzing the subject sales, options, and listings in accordance with Standards Rule 1-5.*

- If the information is **unobtainable**, a statement on the efforts undertaken by the appraiser to obtain the information is required.

- If the information is **irrelevant**, a statement acknowledging the existence of the information and citing its lack of relevance is required

The portion of Standards Rule 1-5, which is referenced in the preceding reporting obligation, applies to **all agreements of sale, options, and listings** of the subject property **current as of the effective date of the appraisal; and all sales** of the subject property that occurred **within the three (3) years prior to the effective date of the appraisal.**

This USPAP obligation applies to market value assignments. Appraisers sometimes do not report sales and transfers that are not arm's length, such as Sherriff's sales, foreclosure sales, transactions between relatives, etc.

- Per USPAP Advisory Opinion 4, reporting of *foreclosure sales and voluntary deeds in lieu of foreclosure* is **required** and are considered sales.

- The obligation for reporting *other casual transfers*, such as those between family members, which are not arms-length, is not specifically addressed, but those transfers, in most cases, would likely not be relevant. However, these transfers should still be reported as such, and the lack of relevance noted.

Prior sale and transfer information is often important information for the user of the appraisal report. It also demonstrates the appraiser complied with the analysis obligations of Standards Rule 1-5.

Case Study

A residential property is being appraised for the purpose of developing an opinion of market value for use by a lender client for mortgage financing in a purchase transaction. The purchase price in the current agreement to sell is $245,000. The property transferred to the seller in the current transaction, James Green, two (2) months ago. No sale price was declared as the transfer was part of an estate with Mr. Green inheriting the property from his late uncle, John Frank. Another transfer occurred one (1) year prior – which was a transfer via a foreclosure sale. In this transaction, the late Mr. Frank purchased the property at a Sheriff's auction for $105,000. According to Mr. Green, the late Mr. Frank spent approximately $110,000 renovating the property, which was in a distressed condition when he acquired it.

This is the appraiser's commentary regarding the prior sales history of the subject property...

No arm's-length transactions of the subject property were found in the three (3) years previous to the effective date of this appraisal.

Rewrite the commentary so the users of the report are informed of the transfer history of the subject property.

_____

_____

_____

_____

_____

_____

_____

Issue #4 - Failure to Discuss the Support for Adjustments or For Not Making Adjustments in the Sales Comparison Approach

While USPAP does not specifically call out this obligation, the necessity for discussing the adjustments, or for not making adjustments in the sales comparison approach, are integral with Standards Rule 2-2(a)(viii) for an Appraisal Report, which (in part) obligates the appraiser to **summarize** the information analyzed, the appraisal methods and techniques employed, and the reasoning that supports the analyses, opinions, and conclusions.

For a **Restricted Appraisal Report**, Standards Rule 2-2(b)(viii) requires only that the appraisal methods and techniques employed must be **stated**.

When discussing the rationale in support of why and how an adjustment was derived and applied, as well as the reasoning supporting why an adjustment was not applied, an appraiser must remain mindful of the level of understanding possessed by the user(s). Certain terms and concepts may be foreign to the user(s). At a minimum, the appraisal report should discuss, at the appropriate level, the:

- **Methodology used** for deriving adjustments and the necessity of doing so.
- **Rationale** for not making an adjustment when there is a difference.

The discussion of the necessity and methodology for adjustments is *not limited to physical differences*, but is warranted for other elements as well, especially market conditions (date of sale).

Case Study

A 4-bedroom residential dwelling is being appraised, which contains 2,300 square feet of gross living area. Three comparable properties have been chosen, one which has 3-bedrooms. All of properties have slightly differing gross living area than the subject. It is noted that the appraiser has applied an adjustment for the difference for the fourth bedroom for Comparable Sale #2 at $2,250. No adjustments have been applied for the slight differences in gross living area.

	Subject	Comparable Sale #1		Comparable Sale #2		Comparable Sale #3	
Address	4 Glenn Dr.	8 Glenn Dr.		2 Howard Ln.		6 Ridge Dr.	
Sale Price	--------------		$250,000		$248,000		$247,000
GLA	2,300 SF	2,320 SF		2,280 SF		2,290 SF	
Bedrooms	4	4		3	+2,250	4	
Adjusted Sale Price	-------------		$250,000		$250,250		$247,000

The appraiser derived the contributory value of the fourth bedroom from paired data analysis using four sets of paired data, and then used a **regression analysis**, *a statistical measure that attempts to ascertain the source of change in variables,* for observing the conclusions.

Paired Data Set	GLA	Extracted Contributory Value of 4th Bedroom
3	1,800 SF	$1,500
1	2,000 SF	$1,800
2	2,200 SF	$2,100
4	2,400 SF	$2,400

The appraiser observed that since the subject property contained 2,300 square feet of gross living area, the indicated support was at the halfway point between the conclusions of paired data set #2 and #4, which contained 2,200 square feet and 2,400 square feet, respectively. Thus, the appraiser's conclusion for application to the subject was bracketed between the $2,100 and $2,400 contributory value indication as $2,250. **Bracketing**, in this case, *is demonstrated by the value indications that are superior and inferior to the subject, with the subject's relevance positioned in between.*

For the gross living area (GLA), the appraiser's analysis indicated that small differences are not typically recognized by the market, and therefore no adjustment was required.

The appraiser offered no comments regarding the bedroom adjustment or the lack of an adjustment for differences in gross living area.

Write a commentary so that users the report, of even an elementary level of understanding, will comprehend how the bedroom adjustment was derived and why no adjustment was made for differences in the gross living area.

_____

_____

_____

_____

_____

_____

_____

_____

_____

_____

Issue #5 - Failure to Adequately Discuss How Market Rent Potential and Rates of Capitalization Were Established

The previous discussion regarding the information analyzed, the appraisal methods and techniques employed, and the reasoning that supports the analyses, opinions, and conclusions is applicable to data used to develop an income approach in a residential appraisal, as well. When an income approach is necessary for credible assignment results, most residential appraisals employ the **gross rent multiplier (GRM)** technique of monthly **market rent.** The commentary for the income approach should include:

- Information regarding the quality and quantity of data that was analyzed to determine market level rent, and the indications produced by the data, including the reasoning of the appraiser for the data chosen for analysis as well as his conclusions

- How and why the market level rent concluded by the appraiser differs (or is similar to) the contract rent of the subject property

- Methodology employed to derive a market level rate of capitalization to be used in the approach (typically a GRM or an overall capitalization rate)

It should be noted that the most common residential appraisal reporting forms (discussed in Chapter 4) require an appraiser to **summarize** the income approach, including support for market rent and the GRM applied in development of the approach.

Case Study

A 3-bedroom, single-family rental property is the subject of an appraisal. The subject property contains 1,150 square feet, is equipped with central air-conditioning, and has a 1-car detached garage. The appraiser has estimated monthly market rent of the subject at $600 and derived a GRM of 123.34 to be applied in the assignment from the data below.

Market Rent Analysis

	Rental #1	Rental #2	Rental #3
Bedrooms	3	3	2
Gross Living Area	1,150 +/-	1,150 +/-	1,150 +/-
Central Air-Conditioning	Yes	Yes	Yes
Garage	1-car	1-car	1-car
Monthly Rent	$600	$600	$550

GRM Analysis

	Sale Price	Monthly Rent	(Formula)	GRM
1	$66,200	$530	(66,200 ÷ 530)	124.91
2	$73,000	$590	(73,000 ÷ 590)	123.73
3	$75,000	$610	(75,000 ÷ 610)	122.95
4	$65,000	$525	(65,000 ÷ 525)	123.81
5	$65,500	$500	(65,500 ÷ 500)	131.00
6	$70,000	$575	(70,000 ÷ 575)	121.74
7	$72,800	$650	(72,800 ÷ 650)	112.00
8	$68,000	$520	(68,000 ÷ 520)	130.77

The appraiser's analysis concluded that $600 per month was a reasonable market rental rate for 3-bedroom dwellings, which have other similarities with the subject (note the 2-bedroom rental at $550), and 123.34 was a reasonable GRM to be applied based on the data bracketing the subject's estimated market rent.

(The value conclusion of the income approach was $74,000 [123.34 x $600], which is also bracketed within the sales analyzed.)

The appraiser's commentary regarding the summary of the income approach in support of the market rent and GRM used in the approach…

Market rent of the subject was estimated to be $600. A GRM of 123.34 was deemed applicable.

Rewrite the commentary so that users the report, of even an elementary level of understanding, are convinced of the rationale, the methodology used to estimate market rent, and how the GRM was derived.

_____

_____

_____

_____

_____

_____

_____

Summary

1. The client may have certain requests regarding the appraisal report issued by a particular appraiser in a specific assignment, which are typical and part of many appraisal assignments, and therefore not an issue of concern. However, an appraiser must be vigilant and remain steadfast by not accepting an assignment that is accompanied by unacceptable assignment conditions.

2. Appraisal reporting should present a true and precise picture of the property that is the subject of the assignment. The appraiser is doing a disservice to himself and to all involved when an appraisal report is misleading, and is participating in criminal activity when the report is fraudulent.

3. Failure to provide a true picture of the physical and functional characteristics of a property of locational issues or external obsolescence will result in a misleading, or in some cases, a fraudulent appraisal report.

4. **Both** reporting options permitted by USPAP, in a market value assignment, require a summary of the results of analyzing the subject sales, options, and listings in accordance with Standards Rule 1-5. If the information is unobtainable, a statement on the efforts undertaken by the appraiser to obtain the information is required. If the information is irrelevant, a statement acknowledging the existence of the information and citing its lack of relevance is required. This also applies to all agreements of sale, options, and listings of the subject property current as of the effective date of the appraisal; and all sales of the subject property that occurred within the three (3) years prior to the effective date of the appraisal.

5. When discussing the rationale in support of why and how an adjustment was derived and applied, as well as the reasoning supporting why an adjustment was not applied, an appraiser must discuss, at the appropriate level, the methodology used for deriving adjustments and the necessity of doing so; and discuss, at the appropriate level, the rationale for not making an adjustment when there is a difference.

6. When an income approach is necessary for credible assignment results, most residential appraisals employ the **gross rent multiplier (GRM)** technique using monthly **market rent.** The commentary for the income approach should include information regarding the data that was analyzed and the indications produced by the data, including the reasoning of the appraiser for his conclusion of market level rent; and how and why the market level rent concluded by the appraiser differs (or is similar to) the contract rent of the subject property, as well as the methodology employed to derive a market level rate of capitalization to be used in the approach.

Chapter 3 Quiz

1. *If a client requests additional exhibits, photographs, maps, and other documentation be included in an appraisal report, the request should be considered*

   a. a reasonable and typical request.

   b. an unacceptable assignment condition.

   c. as a challenge to an appraiser's objectivity and independence.

   d. contrary to the ETHICS RULE of USPAP.

2. *Advisory Opinion 19, which is bound with USPAP, addresses*

   a. deriving a gross rent multiplier.

   b. reporting options permitted by USPAP.

   c. unacceptable assignment conditions.

   d. updating an appraisal report.

3. *In a Restricted Appraisal Report, Standards Rule 2-2(b)(viii) requires that appraisal methods and techniques employed in an assignment must be*

   a. described, along with the reasoning supporting the analysis.

   b. included in the certification of the appraisal report.

   c. stated.

   d. summarized, along with the reasoning supporting the analysis.

4. *Using the following scenario, if an appraiser concludes a GRM of 126.50 is supported, his conclusion is _____ by the data.*

   GRM Analysis

Comparable Rental #	Sale Price	Monthly Rent	GRM
1	$125,000	$1,000	125.00
2	$121,600	$950	128.00

   a. bracketed

   b. contradicted

   c. pinpointed

   d. targeted

5. *Which reporting option(s) require a summary of the results of analyzing subject sales, options, and listings in a market value assignment?*

   a. both reporting options

   b. Restricted Appraisal Reports only

   c. Appraisal Reports for mortgage lending purposes only

   d. Appraisal Report for any purpose only

6. *A particular neighborhood is undergoing a complete change of use from residential to commercial. An appraiser should refer to the occurrence in the appraisal report as*

   a. diminishing returns.

   b. gentrification.

   c. progression.

   d. transition.

7. *In the sales comparison approach, if there is a difference between the subject and a comparable sale and no adjustment has been made, to address the lack of an adjustment, the appraiser should*

   a. apply a GRM instead.

   b. consider the assignment unacceptable.

   c. discuss, in the report, the rationale for not making an adjustment.

   d. place N/A next to the item in the sales comparison grid.

8. *An appraiser accepted an assignment from a client who asked her to disregard the residential property's commercial zoning and not report it. By accepting the assignment with this condition, it could cause the appraiser to*

   a. allow a hypothetical condition.

   b. lack independence.

   c. readdress the report.

   d. violate a jurisdictional exception.

9. *A residential dwelling being appraised is located across the street from a factory that the appraiser has determined is negatively affecting the value of the subject property. The appraiser applied a location adjustment in his sales comparison approach. However, the client asked that the factory not be discussed in the appraisal report. Since the appraiser addressed the condition with an adjustment, has he complied with USPAP?*

   a. no, because USPAP requires explanation for each adjustment

   b. no, omitting the discussion could produce a misleading report

   c. yes, since an adjustment was included

   d. yes, since the client requested the omission

10. *An observation using a statistical measure that attempts to ascertain the source of change in variables is being referenced in an appraisal report, which is more commonly known as a(n)*

    a. adjustment.
    b. GRM.
    c. paired data analysis.
    d. regression analysis.

Chapter 4

Residential Appraisal Reporting Forms

Introduction

This text has concentrated so far on acceptable methods that appraisers can employ in order to communicate their conclusions in a manner that is meaningful and not misleading. The discussion and exercises could be applied to narrative reporting or reports communicated on an appraisal form. In this chapter, the most common appraisal form will be fully discussed and illustrated.

There are numerous appraisal forms available from various sources and integrated with most appraisal software products. Many of these forms were developed collaboratively by Fannie Mae and Freddie Mac for use with a mortgage finance transaction. Other forms may be labeled as "general purpose" forms and may be used for intended uses other than financing.

Certain report forms for use in a financing transaction by Fannie Mae and Freddie Mac now have specific requirements. Therefore, this chapter will discuss the background of what led to newer methods of residential reporting for these entities as well as the standards of those entities that must be applied by the appraiser in communication of his opinions and conclusions. Due to the depth of the discussion here, only the Uniform Residential Appraisal Report (URAR) form will be illustrated along the Market Conditions Addendum, which is required to accompany the reporting form when used for various lending industry participants. The discussion of this specific form could certainly be applied to other types of forms, as well.

The Appendix of this text includes several other report forms that are commonly used for residential appraisal reports.

Uniform Appraisal Dataset (UAD) Defines all fields required for an appraisal submission for specific appraisal forms and standardizes definitions and responses for a key subset of fields to enhance data quality and promote consistency.

Government Sponsored Enterprises (GSEs) A financial services corporation created by the United States Congress. Their function is to enhance the flow of credit to targeted sectors of the economy and to make those segments of the capital market more efficient and transparent.

URAR (Uniform Residential Appraisal Report) Developed collaboratively by Fannie Mae and Freddie Mac for use with a mortgage finance transaction of single-family residential property. Also adopted by other entities such as FHA, VA, and some primary lenders for residential appraisal reporting.

Key Terms

Uniform Appraisal Dataset

At the direction of the Federal Housing Finance Agency, Fannie Mae and Freddie Mac developed the **Uniform Appraisal Dataset (UAD)**. According to Fannie Mae, the Uniform Appraisal Dataset *defines all fields required for an appraisal submission for specific appraisal forms and standardizes definitions and responses for a key subset of fields to enhance data quality and promote consistency.* The purpose of the UAD is to improve the quality and consistency of appraisal data on loans delivered to Fannie Mae and Freddie Mac, which are considered **Government Sponsored Enterprises (GSEs)**.

Several key issues led to the creation of the UAD:

- Terminology differs among appraisers for the same descriptions (e.g., waterfront / ocean front).
- Framework descriptions differ (e.g., good / average, brick / vinyl).
- Condition descriptions are improperly categorized (e.g., good and average appear often, whereas fair and poor appear infrequently).
- Number and date formats vary (e.g., taxes are written as dollars or percentages).

Uniform Mortgage Data Program

As a background for the Uniform Appraisal Dataset (UAD), it should be pointed out that the UAD is a component of the Uniform Mortgage Data Program (UMDP). The purpose of the UMDP is for Fannie Mae and Freddie Mac to combine their efforts to implement uniform appraisal and other loan delivery data standards, including a joint appraisal data delivery system for single-family loans they purchase. Reasons for development of the UMDP include:

- Capture consistent data
- Drive improved loan quality
- Manage risk effectively

The Uniform Collateral Data Portal (UCDP) collects and submits electronic appraisal data via a web application. The Uniform Loan Delivery Dataset (ULDD) leverages the industry-recognized MISMO® (Mortgage Industry Standards Maintenance Organization) standard which is a loan delivery dataset. MISMO is the leading technology standards development body for the residential and commercial real estate finance industries. Its mission is to benefit industry participants and consumers of mortgage and investment products. MISMO uses a format that allows business-related firms to streamline shared data in forms or reports. MISMO does not have software requirements—it dictates only how to format data for sending to another party.

The benefits of implementing the Uniform Mortgage Data Program (UMDP) include:

- Data standards will be consistent across the industry
- Data will be collected in electronic form
- Appraisal data will be machine-readable

Implementation Dates

The appraisal data must conform to the UAD and be delivered through the Uniform Collateral Data Portal. According to Freddie Mac, the **Uniform Collateral Data Portal (UCDP)** is *a single portal for the electronic submission of appraisal data files to Freddie Mac and Fannie Mae and facilitates the electronic collection of appraisal report data.*

The implementation dates for the UAD and UCDP are as follows:

- For appraisals with an effective date (date of inspection) **on or after September 1, 2011**, the appraisal report must be completed in compliance with the UAD for conventional mortgage loans sold to Fannie Mae or Freddie Mac.
- Effective **March 19, 2012**, appraisal report forms, as well as supporting documents, for all conventional mortgages must be submitted to the UCDP if an appraisal report is required, and the loan application is dated **on or after December 1, 2011**.

The implementation dates for the Uniform Loan Delivery Dataset (ULDD) are as follows:

- For application dates **on or after December 1, 2011**, lenders are required to collect additional ULDD data.

- For application dates **on or after December 1, 2011**, mortgages delivered to Fannie Mae / Freddie Mac **on or after March 19, 2012** must meet ULDD requirements and be delivered in the MISMO required file format.

However, most of this is of less concern to appraisers and more important to lenders. The primary issue facing appraisers is the UAD and the reporting compliance that accompanies the regulation.

 Note: Appraisers should obtain a copy of the latest version of *Appendix D – Field Specific Standardization Requirements*, which is available on the website of both Fannie Mae and Freddie Mac.

UAD Required Forms

Fannie Mae and Freddie Mac have developed numerous forms for reporting the appraisal of single-family, 2-4 family, condominiums, manufactured homes, etc. However, the UAD defines the required fields *only* for appraisal submission on these four specific appraisal forms:

UAD REQUIRED FORMS		
UAD Form	Fannie Mae Form	Freddie Mac Form
Uniform Residential Appraisal Report (URAR)	1004	70
Individual Condominium Unit Appraisal Report	1073	465
Exterior-Only Inspection Residential Appraisal Report	2055	2055
Exterior-Only Inspection Individual Condominium Unit Appraisal Report	1075	466

The **URAR (Uniform Residential Appraisal Report)** is an appraisal form used for a *single-family* residential property when there is an interior and exterior inspection as part of the scope of work in the assignment. The exterior-only form is most often referred to as a "drive-by" appraisal form and is also for single-family properties. The other two forms are for *condominiums,* using either an interior and exterior inspection or an exterior inspection only.

 Note: At the time of the development of this textbook, the UAD was an emerging topic and applies only to appraisals of single-family properties and condominiums. Also, only Fannie Mae and Freddie Mac require its use as presented here. However, FHA requires similar UAD reporting compliance for appraisals assigned on or after January 1, 2012, and it is not inconceivable that other lending participants might follow suit by imposing the requirement later. Appraisers should monitor industry announcements for details as they continue to emerge.

UAD Data Fields

Many of the data fields in the UAD forms are limited to certain choices. There are checkboxes, pick lists, and drop-down boxes populated with prescribed responses or input formats. Appraisal software providers have developed programs that conform to these requirements.

Here are some examples of data entry requirements:

- **Address** – Must conform to United States Postal Service standards
- **Subject Offering Dates and Price**s – Must comply with standard
- **Sale Type** – Drop-down list with specific choices

- **View from Property** – Drop-down list with specific choices
- **Condition of Property** – Specific rating from C1 to C6
- **Quality of Construction** – Specific rating from Q1 to Q6

Each form field is either a *requirement* or an *instruction*. The data entered for a required field is validated for accuracy—non-conforming data is flagged as an error. Instruction field entries are not validated, but must be transmitted, if populated.

The benefits of using UAD data fields include:

- Creating efficiency and consistency in appraisal reviews
- Improving data integrity related to home values
- Strengthening the loan underwriting process by promoting a more consistent view and understanding of appraisal data
- Supporting processes to manage and mitigate valuation risk

The Uniform Residential Appraisal Report (URAR)

The Uniform Residential Appraisal Report, commonly known in the appraisal industry as the URAR, is more formally referred to as Fannie Mae Form 1004/Freddie Mac Form 70.

Many others within the real property lending industry have also adopted use of the form, such as FHA and VA, as well as smaller primary lenders.

The URAR is the most common reporting form employed for appraising residential properties for use by a *lender client*. The form is a six-page report and provides an orderly and systematic flow of information and commentary.

 Note: The full form can be found in the Appendix.

The URAR report form is considered an *Appraisal Report,* designed to report an appraisal of a one-unit property or a one-unit property with an accessory unit, including a unit in a planned unit development (PUD), based on an *interior and exterior inspection* of the subject property. This report form is *not* designed to report an appraisal of a manufactured home or a unit in a condominium or cooperative project. In the presentation in this section, the form will be discussed using the UAD required reporting criteria.

In becoming familiar with the contents of the URAR, the first discussion should evolve around Pages 4-6 of the form. The content of these pages should be recognizable as some of the major reporting requirements of USPAP:

- Scope of Work
- Intended Use
- Intended User
- Definition of Market Value
- Statement of Assumptions and Limiting Conditions
- Appraiser's Certification

The content of Pages 4-6 commences with a discussion of the general use of the form and then continues with the reporting information necessary for USPAP compliance.

General Use Provisions of the URAR

This section generally sets forth the types of property for which the reporting form is applicable and overviews certain aspects of the assignment. Also discussed is the unacceptability of modifications, additions, or deletions to those assignment elements with the exception of the scope of work, which may be expanded. Similar limitations are also imposed regarding the appraiser's certification, with the exception of additions to the certification that are required by law or specific requirements of an appraisal organization to which the appraiser must observe membership requirements related to the certification.

> This report form is designed to report an appraisal of a one-unit property or a one-unit property with an accessory unit; including a unit in a planned unit development (PUD). This report form is not designed to report an appraisal of a manufactured home or a unit in a condominium or cooperative project.
>
> This appraisal report is subject to the following scope of work, intended use, intended user, definition of market value, statement of assumptions and limiting conditions, and certifications. Modifications, additions, or deletions to the intended use, intended user, definition of market value, or assumptions and limiting conditions are not permitted. The appraiser may expand the scope of work to include any additional research or analysis necessary based on the complexity of this appraisal assignment. Modifications or deletions to the certifications are also not permitted. However, additional certifications that do not constitute material alterations to this appraisal report, such as those required by law or those related to the appraiser's continuing education or membership in an appraisal organization, are permitted.

Scope of Work

This abbreviated description of the assignment's scope of work establishes the minimum diligence expected of the appraiser regarding inspection, research, verification, analysis, and reporting.

Certainly, the scope of work actually performed by the appraiser will be expanded in many cases from the minimum level described here. As well, the disclosure of the scope of work should include additional commentary from the appraiser to sufficiently communicate the extent of the research and analysis performed in the assignment.

The Scope of Work Rule of USPAP requires the disclosure in the appraisal report to contain sufficient information to allow intended users to understand the scope of work performed.

> **SCOPE OF WORK:** The scope of work for this appraisal is defined by the complexity of this appraisal assignment and the reporting requirements of this appraisal report form, including the following definition of market value, statement of assumptions and limiting conditions, and certifications. The appraiser must, at a minimum: (1) perform a complete visual inspection of the interior and exterior areas of the subject property, (2) inspect the neighborhood, (3) inspect each of the comparable sales from at least the street, (4) research, verify, and analyze data from reliable public and/or private sources, and (5) report his or her analysis, opinions, and conclusions in this appraisal report.

Fannie Mae guidelines acknowledge that while the appraisal process may be guided by the form, the form does *not* limit or control the appraisal process. The appraiser's analysis should go beyond any limitations of the form, and expanded with additional comments and exhibits in the report when needed to adequately describe the subject property, document the analysis and valuation process, or support the appraiser's conclusions.

Intended Use

This statement satisfies the USPAP requirement to state the intended use(s) of the report. The existence of this statement, integral with the form, makes using this form for other non-financing uses (e.g., marketing, estates, litigation) unacceptable.

> **INTENDED USE:** The intended use of this appraisal report is for the lender/client to evaluate the property that is the subject of this appraisal for a mortgage finance transaction.

Intended User

Satisfying USPAP requirements to state the intended user, the intended user in this case is predetermined to be the lender/client. Again, this specification eliminates the use of this form for other non-financing uses and users.

> **INTENDED USER:** The intended user of this appraisal report is the lender/client.

Definition of Market Value

There are innumerable ways to define market value. This definition illustrates the most commonly used and described method. The discussion continues with how adjustments for financing terms and concessions should be handled.

DEFINITION OF MARKET VALUE: The most probable price which a property should bring in a competitive and open market under all conditions requisite to a fair sale, the buyer and seller, each acting prudently, knowledgeably and assuming the price is not affected by undue stimulus. Implicit in this definition is the consummation of a sale as of a specified date and the passing of title from seller to buyer under conditions whereby: (1) buyer and seller are typically motivated; (2) both parties are well informed or well advised, and each acting in what he or she considers his or her own best interest; (3) a reasonable time is allowed for exposure in the open market; (4) payment is made in terms of cash in U. S. dollars or in terms of financial arrangements comparable thereto; and (5) the price represents the normal consideration for the property sold unaffected by special or creative financing or sales concessions* granted by anyone associated with the sale.

*Adjustments to the comparables must be made for special or creative financing or sales concessions. No adjustments are necessary for those costs which are normally paid by sellers as a result of tradition or law in a market area; these costs are readily identifiable since the seller pays these costs in virtually all sales transactions. Special or creative financing adjustments can be made to the comparable property by comparisons to financing terms offered by a third party institutional lender that is not already involved in the property or transaction. Any adjustment should not be calculated on a mechanical dollar for dollar cost of the financing or concession but the dollar amount of any adjustment should approximate the market's reaction to the financing or concessions based on the appraiser's judgment.

Statement of Assumptions and Limiting Conditions

The Statement of Assumptions and Limiting Conditions assists the appraiser in establishing the limitations of responsibility on the part of the appraiser. Some elements also further emphasize the scope of work performed in the assignment, such as providing a sketch of the improvements, research of flood information, and other notes regarding any unfavorable conditions found, or not found, within the subject property.

STATEMENT OF ASSUMPTIONS AND LIMITING CONDITIONS: The appraiser's certification in this report is subject to the following assumptions and limiting conditions:

1. The appraiser will not be responsible for matters of a legal nature that affect either the property being appraised or the title to it, except for information that he or she became aware of during the research involved in performing this appraisal. The appraiser assumes that the title is good and marketable and will not render any opinions about the title.

2. The appraiser has provided a sketch in this appraisal report to show the approximate dimensions of the improvements, including each of the units. The sketch is included only to assist the reader in visualizing the property and understanding the appraiser's determination of its size.

3. The appraiser has examined the available flood maps that are provided by the Federal Emergency Management Agency (or other data sources) and has noted in this appraisal report whether any portion of the subject site is located in an identified Special Flood Hazard Area. Because the appraiser is not a surveyor, he or she makes no guarantees, express or implied, regarding this determination.

4. The appraiser will not give testimony or appear in court because he or she made an appraisal of the property in question, unless specific arrangements to do so have been made beforehand, or as otherwise required by law.

5. The appraiser has noted in this appraisal report any adverse conditions (such as needed repairs, deterioration, the presence of hazardous wastes, toxic substances, etc.) observed during the inspection of the subject property or that he or she became aware of during the research involved in performing this appraisal. Unless otherwise stated in this appraisal report, the appraiser has no knowledge of any hidden or unapparent physical deficiencies or adverse conditions of the property (such as, but not limited to, needed repairs, deterioration, the presence of hazardous wastes, toxic substances, adverse environmental conditions, etc.) that would make the property less valuable, and has assumed that there are no such conditions and makes no guarantees or warranties, express or implied. The appraiser will not be responsible for any such conditions that do exist or for any engineering or testing that might be required to discover whether such conditions exist. Because the appraiser is not an expert in the field of environmental hazards, this appraisal report must not be considered as an environmental assessment of the property.

6. The appraiser has based his or her appraisal report and valuation conclusion for an appraisal that is subject to satisfactory completion, repairs, or alterations on the assumption that the completion, repairs, or alterations of the subject property will be performed in a professional manner.

Appraiser's Certification

The Appraiser's Certification contained within the URAR form (page 5 of the form) satisfies the minimum requirement of USPAP and then expands the certification statements to a more specific and greater level. Examples of those statements include (but are not limited to):

- Specific methodology used in the assignment and, unless otherwise indicated, that the cost approach was not developed
- Analysis and reporting of offerings and any current sales agreement of the subject property
- Research, verification, analysis, and reporting of prior sales of the comparable data
- Process of selecting and analyzing comparable sales data
- Techniques for adjusting comparable sales
- Competency in the assignment

Due to the preprinted and expanded language in the Appraiser's Certification contained in this form (as well as other forms), appraisers should be very familiar with the certification's content and meaning **prior to** affixing their signature. **No content in the certification may be deleted or modified.** However, to accommodate required certifications mentioned in the general provisions and certain disclosures required by USPAP, as discussed in Chapter 1, an "Additional Certifications" page may need to be added to the report. Items that may need to be added for USPAP compliance include:

- Any services as an appraiser, or in any other capacity, regarding the subject property performed within the prior three-year period immediately proceeding acceptance of the assignment (see note on page 78)
- Specific name(s) of individuals not signing the certification who provided significant professional assistance in the assignment
- Any fees, commissions, or things of value that were paid by the appraiser in connection with procurement of the assignment

It should be noted that certification statement #17 states the appraiser does not have any current or prospective personal interest or bias regarding the subject property or the parties involved in the transaction. Therefore, since this certification statement cannot be modified or deleted, an appraiser must **not** accept an assignment for which this certification statement **cannot** be answered truthfully as it is printed in the form. Obviously, in compliance with the ETHICS RULE of USPAP, an appraiser must **not** perform an appraisal with bias at any time.

The signature section immediately following the certification will be discussed later in this chapter. (See sample of Certification section on following pages)

Subject

Turning attention to Page 1 of the URAR form, reporting commences with the general identification of the subject property. This section is a combination of identifying elements of the subject property and specifics regarding the appraisal assignment. Much of the information contained in this section is fairly straightforward. However, there are some specific reporting requirements that should be specifically mentioned and must be observed by the appraiser.

The purpose of this summary appraisal report is to provide the lender/client with an accurate, and adequately supported, opinion of the market value of the subject property.			
Property Address	City	State	Zip Code
Borrower	Owner of Public Record	County	
Legal Description			
Assessor's Parcel #	Tax Year	R.E. Taxes $	
Neighborhood Name	Map Reference	Census Tract	
Occupant ☐ Owner ☐ Tenant ☐ Vacant	Special Assessments $	☐ PUD HOA $	☐ per year ☐ per month
Property Rights Appraised ☐ Fee Simple ☐ Leasehold ☐ Other (describe)			
Assignment Type ☐ Purchase Transaction ☐ Refinance Transaction ☐ Other (describe)			
Lender/Client	Address		
Is the subject property currently offered for sale or has it been offered for sale in the twelve months prior to the effective date of this appraisal? ☐ Yes ☐ No			
Report data source(s) used, offering price(s), and date(s).			

Uniform Residential Appraisal Report   File

APPRAISER'S CERTIFICATION: The Appraiser certifies and agrees that:

1. I have, at a minimum, developed and reported this appraisal in accordance with the scope of work requirements stated in this appraisal report.

2. I performed a complete visual inspection of the interior and exterior areas of the subject property. I reported the condition of the improvements in factual, specific terms. I identified and reported the physical deficiencies that could affect the livability, soundness, or structural integrity of the property.

3. I performed this appraisal in accordance with the requirements of the Uniform Standards of Professional Appraisal Practice that were adopted and promulgated by the Appraisal Standards Board of The Appraisal Foundation and that were in place at the time this appraisal report was prepared.

4. I developed my opinion of the market value of the real property that is the subject of this report based on the sales comparison approach to value. I have adequate comparable market data to develop a reliable sales comparison approach for this appraisal assignment. I further certify that I considered the cost and income approaches to value but did not develop them, unless otherwise indicated in this report.

5. I researched, verified, analyzed, and reported on any current agreement for sale for the subject property, any offering for sale of the subject property in the twelve months prior to the effective date of this appraisal, and the prior sales of the subject property for a minimum of three years prior to the effective date of this appraisal, unless otherwise indicated in this report.

6. I researched, verified, analyzed, and reported on the prior sales of the comparable sales for a minimum of one year prior to the date of sale of the comparable sale, unless otherwise indicated in this report.

7. I selected and used comparable sales that are locationally, physically, and functionally the most similar to the subject property.

8. I have not used comparable sales that were the result of combining a land sale with the contract purchase price of a home that has been built or will be built on the land.

9. I have reported adjustments to the comparable sales that reflect the market's reaction to the differences between the subject property and the comparable sales.

10. I verified, from a disinterested source, all information in this report that was provided by parties who have a financial interest in the sale or financing of the subject property.

11. I have knowledge and experience in appraising this type of property in this market area.

12. I am aware of, and have access to, the necessary and appropriate public and private data sources, such as multiple listing services, tax assessment records, public land records and other such data sources for the area in which the property is located.

13. I obtained the information, estimates, and opinions furnished by other parties and expressed in this appraisal report from reliable sources that I believe to be true and correct.

14. I have taken into consideration the factors that have an impact on value with respect to the subject neighborhood, subject property, and the proximity of the subject property to adverse influences in the development of my opinion of market value. I have noted in this appraisal report any adverse conditions (such as, but not limited to, needed repairs, deterioration, the presence of hazardous wastes, toxic substances, adverse environmental conditions, etc.) observed during the inspection of the subject property or that I became aware of during the research involved in performing this appraisal. I have considered these adverse conditions in my analysis of the property value, and have reported on the effect of the conditions on the value and marketability of the subject property.

15. I have not knowingly withheld any significant information from this appraisal report and, to the best of my knowledge, all statements and information in this appraisal report are true and correct.

16. I stated in this appraisal report my own personal, unbiased, and professional analysis, opinions, and conclusions, which are subject only to the assumptions and limiting conditions in this appraisal report.

17. I have no present or prospective interest in the property that is the subject of this report, and I have no present or prospective personal interest or bias with respect to the participants in the transaction. I did not base, either partially or completely, my analysis and/or opinion of market value in this appraisal report on the race, color, religion, sex, age, marital status, handicap, familial status, or national origin of either the prospective owners or occupants of the subject property or of the present owners or occupants of the properties in the vicinity of the subject property or on any other basis prohibited by law.

18. My employment and/or compensation for performing this appraisal or any future or anticipated appraisals was not conditioned on any agreement or understanding, written or otherwise, that I would report (or present analysis supporting) a predetermined specific value, a predetermined minimum value, a range or direction in value, a value that favors the cause of any party, or the attainment of a specific result or occurrence of a specific subsequent event (such as approval of a pending mortgage loan application).

19. I personally prepared all conclusions and opinions about the real estate that were set forth in this appraisal report. If I relied on significant real property appraisal assistance from any individual or individuals in the performance of this appraisal or the preparation of this appraisal report, I have named such individual(s) and disclosed the specific tasks performed in this appraisal report. I certify that any individual so named is qualified to perform the tasks. I have not authorized anyone to make a change to any item in this appraisal report; therefore, any change made to this appraisal is unauthorized and I will take no responsibility for it.

20. I identified the lender/client in this appraisal report who is the individual, organization, or agent for the organization that ordered and will receive this appraisal report.

Uniform Residential Appraisal Report   File #

21. The lender/client may disclose or distribute this appraisal report to: the borrower; another lender at the request of the borrower; the mortgagee or its successors and assigns; mortgage insurers; government sponsored enterprises; other secondary market participants; data collection or reporting services; professional appraisal organizations; any department, agency, or instrumentality of the United States; and any state, the District of Columbia, or other jurisdictions; without having to obtain the appraiser's or supervisory appraiser's (if applicable) consent. Such consent must be obtained before this appraisal report may be disclosed or distributed to any other party (including, but not limited to, the public through advertising, public relations, news, sales, or other media).

22. I am aware that any disclosure or distribution of this appraisal report by me or the lender/client may be subject to certain laws and regulations. Further, I am also subject to the provisions of the Uniform Standards of Professional Appraisal Practice that pertain to disclosure or distribution by me.

23. The borrower, another lender at the request of the borrower, the mortgagee or its successors and assigns, mortgage insurers, government sponsored enterprises, and other secondary market participants may rely on this appraisal report as part of any mortgage finance transaction that involves any one or more of these parties.

24. If this appraisal report was transmitted as an "electronic record" containing my "electronic signature," as those terms are defined in applicable federal and/or state laws (excluding audio and video recordings), or a facsimile transmission of this appraisal report containing a copy or representation of my signature, the appraisal report shall be as effective, enforceable and valid as if a paper version of this appraisal report were delivered containing my original hand written signature.

25. Any intentional or negligent misrepresentation(s) contained in this appraisal report may result in civil liability and/or criminal penalties including, but not limited to, fine or imprisonment or both under the provisions of Title 18, United States Code, Section 1001, et seq., or similar state laws.

SUPERVISORY APPRAISER'S CERTIFICATION: The Supervisory Appraiser certifies and agrees that:

Property Address

Identify the subject property by its complete property address and legal description; a post office box number is **not** acceptable. Per UAD requirements, address information entered must conform to the *United States Postal Service (USPS) address standards in Publication 28* – Postal Addressing Standards for complete addresses.

The following address information must be entered:

- Street number
- Street name (including direction indicator such as N., W., etc.; suffix such as St., Ave., Dr, etc.; post-directional indicator such as NW, SE, etc.; and unit number, when applicable)
- City
- USPS two-letter state or territory abbreviation
- 5-digit ZIP Code or ZIP+4 code (either with or without the dash)

Owner of Public Record

Enter the owner's name as listed in public records. If the seller is not the owner of public record, the appraiser should explain the results of his research in detail. In some cases, for example, a seller purchasing the property via land contract may not be the owner of record. In other cases, there may be an issue with public records or placement of a prior transfer on record.

Legal Description

Enter the legal description of the property. The four types of legal descriptions are: Lot and block system, geodetic survey, government survey system, and metes and bounds system. Include an addendum to the appraisal report that fully describes or simply refers to the subject property's location in the public records when the legal description is lengthy.

Assessor's Parcel Number

Enter the parcel number assigned by the local tax assessor. The parcel number(s) should be in the same format used by the taxing agency, including all spaces and dashes as applicable. If no parcel number is available, enter 'None'. Multiple parcel numbers should be separated by a semicolon.

Tax Year/Real Estate Taxes

Enter the year using four digits and the annual sum of all taxes (not including special assessments, in whole dollars only. For example: If the annual real estate tax is $849.90, the tax would be entered on the form as $850.

Neighborhood Name

Neighborhood name refers to the name of the subdivision or the commonly known local neighborhood designation. If the subject property is in a planned unit development, **enter the name of the development**. If there is no recognized neighborhood name, **enter the common name used by residents of the area to reference the neighborhood**.

Census Tract

Enter the Census Track number. Census tract numbers commonly have four digits and may have a two-digit decimal suffix. Where the basic census tract number is less than four digits, the Census Bureau includes leading zeros except when displaying numbers on maps or printed reports. To uniquely identify a census tract, a two-digit state code and three-digit county code precedes the four- or six-digit census tract number. The Census Bureau has an Internet resource guide for locating census information.

Occupant

The appraiser must **indicate, by placing an X in the appropriate checkbox, whether the subject property is occupied by the owner or a tenant, or is vacant as of the effective date of the appraisal**. Only one selection is permitted. For properties that are comprised of one unit with an accessory unit, the selection must reflect the occupancy status of the main unit.

Special Assessments

The appraiser should **enter any special assessment applicable to the subject property**. It must be expressed as an annual or annualized amount in whole dollars. If there is more than one special assessment, enter the annualized sum of all special assessments. If there are no special assessments applicable to the subject property, enter the numeral zero (0).

Homeowners Association (HOA) Fees

The appraiser must **enter all applicable homeowners association (HOA) fees in whole dollars associated with the subject property**. Additionally, the appraiser must select the appropriate checkbox to indicate if the amount is payable per year or per month. Only one selection is permitted. If the amount is paid on a different frequency (e.g., bi-monthly or semi-annually), it must be normalized as either per year or per month for reporting.

If there are multiple fees assessed, such as for an HOA and a master association, the appraiser must first convert the fees to the appropriate frequency (if necessary) and then report the total of all fees in this data field. For instance, if the property is subject to a monthly HOA fee and a quarterly master association fee, the quarterly fee must be converted to a monthly fee and added to the monthly HOA fee. If there are no HOA fees applicable to the subject property, enter the numeral zero (0).

Assignment Type

The appraiser must **indicate the transaction type for the assignment – Purchase, Refinance, or Other – by placing an X in the appropriate checkbox**. Only one selection is permitted. If 'Other' is selected, a description must be provided.

Lender/Client

The appraiser must **enter the name of the lender**. Any applicable AMC name should only be entered in the Appraiser Certification Section (discussed later in this chapter).

Current and/or Prior Offering of the Subject Property

The final obligation of the Subject section of the report form requires the appraiser to **disclose any prior offering of the property in the 12 months prior to the effective date of the appraisal by indicating so in the appropriate checkbox**.

If the answer is **No**, the data source(s) used must be provided.

If the answer is **Yes**, the following information is required:

- Days on Market (DOM) – The appraiser must enter the DOM for the subject property (Numeric to 4 digits). **DOM** is defined as *the total number of continuous days from the date that a property is listed or advertised for sale through the date that it is taken off the market or contracted for sale*. DOM applies not only to properties that are listed in a Multiple Listing Service (MLS), but also applies to properties marketed for sale outside an MLS. If the subject property was not individually listed or advertised for sale, enter zero (0). If the DOM is unknown, enter 'Unk'.

- Offering Price(s) – The appraiser must report the original offering price and a history of price changes, if any, in whole dollars only.

- Offering Date(s) – The appraiser must report the date(s) that the property was offered for sale in MM/DD/YYYY format.

- Data Source(s) Used – The appraiser must report the data source(s) used to obtain the offering information. If the data source is MLS, the appraiser must enter the abbreviated MLS organization name, followed by a pound sign (#), and the specific listing identifier.

If the subject property was offered For Sale by Owner (FSBO), or otherwise marketed for sale outside of an MLS, the appraiser must report the original offering price; history of price changes, if any; and the date(s) the property was offered for sale, etc., to the extent that this information is known or available to the appraiser in the normal course of business.

EXAMPLES (IF YES):

DOM150;Subject property was offered for sale on 03/01/2010 for $200,000. The data source is MRIS#12345AB.

DOMUnk;Subject property was listed for sale by owner for $200,000. The data source is a public source.

EXAMPLE (IF NO):

MRIS MLS

Contract

This section of the URAR requires several responses when a purchase transaction has been indicated in the Subject section as the Assignment Type. The appraiser must first **indicate if he did or did not analyze the contract for sale, and then go on to report pertinent specified information regarding the transaction**.

C O N T R A C T	I ☐ did ☐ did not analyze the contract for sale for the subject purchase transaction. Explain the results of the analysis of the contract for sale or why the analysis was not performed.
	Contract Price $ Date of Contract Is the property seller the owner of public record? ☐ Yes ☐ No Data Source(s)
	Is there any financial assistance (loan charges, sale concessions, gift or downpayment assistance, etc.) to be paid by any party on behalf of the borrower? ☐ Yes ☐ No If Yes, report the total dollar amount and describe the items to be paid.

Analysis of the Contract for the Purchase Transaction

The first question in this section **requires a response affirming if the appraiser did or did not analyze the sales contract by placing an X in the appropriate checkbox.**

Next, the appraiser must **indicate the type of sale for this transaction from the dropdown list of available choices.** The appraiser must start at the top of the list and select the *first* sale type that applies. Only one selection is permitted. The valid sale types are as follows:

SALE TYPE
REO sale
Short sale
Court ordered sale
Estate sale
Relocation sale
Non-arms length sale
Arms length sale

Once a valid sale type has been chosen, the results will be inserted in the blank space on the second line of the section; immediately following on this line, provide an explanation of the results of the analysis of the contract or why the analysis was not performed.

EXAMPLE:

Arms length sale;(Description of the appraiser's analysis of the sales contract)*

*The semicolon will automatically be inserted in this and other fields.

Contract Price/ Date of Contract/Property Seller

- Contract price must be the same as the sales price for the subject property in the Sales Comparison Approach section and must be stated in whole dollars only.
- The contract date must be stated in DD/MM/YYYY format.
- The appraiser must **indicate 'Yes' or 'No' as to if the seller is the owner of public record, if the "Assignment Type" is a purchase transaction.**

A discussion should have already taken place in the Subject section if there is a disparity.

Financial Assistance

The appraiser must **indicate 'Yes' or 'No' if the "Assignment Type" is a purchase transaction.** Financial assistance or concessions paid by any party on behalf of the borrower include both monetary and non-monetary items, including below-market-rate mortgage financing, gifts of personal property, payment of property taxes and/or HOA dues for a period of time, etc.

If **No** is selected, **a zero (0) must be entered in the dollar amount field.**

If **Yes** is selected, **enter the total dollar amount of all financial assistance** (loan charges, sale concessions, gift or down payment assistance, etc.) paid by any party on behalf of the borrower, including any closing costs or other payments from the seller or other third party. If the appraiser is not able to determine a dollar amount for all or part of the financial assistance, the number must reflect the total known dollar amount. Leave this field blank if the entire financial assistance amount is unknown. If there is any unknown financial assistance amount, the text *'There is a financial assistance amount that is unknown'* will appear in this field. Next, the **appraiser must provide a description of the items being paid.**

EXAMPLES:

$5000;There is a financial assistance amount that is unknown.;Down payment assistance, plus furniture of unknown value.

$5000;;Down payment assistance.

Neighborhood

This section should reflect the area surrounding the subject property. The appraiser must observe neighborhood characteristics and surrounding properties to make determinations that will be incorporated into the valuation of the subject property.

Note: Race and the racial composition of the neighborhood are not appraisal factors.					
Neighborhood Characteristics	**One-Unit Housing Trends**		**One-Unit Housing**	**Present Land Use %**	
Location ☐ Urban ☐ Suburban ☐ Rural	Property Values ☐ Increasing ☐ Stable ☐ Declining		PRICE AGE	One-Unit %	
Built-Up ☐ Over 75% ☐ 25–75% ☐ Under 25%	Demand/Supply ☐ Shortage ☐ In Balance ☐ Over Supply		$ (000) (yrs)	2-4 Unit %	
Growth ☐ Rapid ☐ Stable ☐ Slow	Marketing Time ☐ Under 3 mths ☐ 3–6 mths ☐ Over 6 mths		Low	Multi-Family %	
Neighborhood Boundaries			High	Commercial %	
			Pred.	Other %	
Neighborhood Description					
Market Conditions (including support for the above conclusions)					

Neighborhood Characteristics

Indicate the location, built-up, and growth. "**Location**" refers to *the type of area surrounding the subject property*. While this point is often the topic of great discussion among appraisers, most agree that "**Urban**" refers to *a city*, "**Suburban**" refers to *an area adjacent to a city*, and "Rural" refers to *the country or beyond the suburban area*. "**Built-Up**" is *the percentage of available land that has been improved*. Land that could not be developed (e.g., due to a large preservation reserve or state park) would not be considered available land. "**Growth**" refers to the *growth rate*. If many lots are available, the growth rate may be rapid, stable, or slow. If *the neighborhood is fully developed*, "**Stable**" is the appropriate designation for the checkbox. Only one response is permitted in each field.

One-Unit Housing Trends

Determining the appropriate reporting responses requires significant analysis leading to the appraiser's conclusions during appraisal development. Comparing houses that have been sold and resold in recent years can be an effective way to determine market trends. To determine the status of supply and demand in the neighborhood, compare the number of houses sold to the number of houses listed for sale in a recent time period.

The appraiser must **indicate whether property values for one-unit housing in the subject's neighborhood are increasing, stable, or declining**. Next, the appraiser must **indicate whether the demand/supply of one-unit housing in the subject property's neighborhood is in shortage, in balance, or over supply**. Finally, the appraiser must **indicate whether the marketing time for one-unit housing is under 3 mths, 3-6 mths, or over 6 mths**. Only one selection is permitted for these categories.

One-Unit Housing Age/Price

The appraisal report must **indicate the age range and predominant age of properties in the subject neighborhood**. The age range must reflect the oldest and newest ages for similar types of properties. The appraiser can state the predominant age as a single figure, or as a range if that is more appropriate, and should select properties that represent the age range and predominant age, rather than merely relying on the same properties used to illustrate the price range and predominant price.

The age of a property should be within the general age range of the neighborhood. Normally, neighborhoods are developed over a relatively narrow span of time so that most dwelling units will fall within a particular age range. A property that has an age outside of the general age range must receive special consideration. Unless there is strong evidence of long-term neighborhood stability, a new dwelling in an old neighborhood will carry some marginal risk. Conversely, an old dwelling in a newly developed area is generally acceptable if renovation will result in its conforming to the neighborhood.

Neighborhood Boundaries

Neighborhood boundaries can be identified by various physical characteristics including (but not limited to) streets, bodies of water, and other natural boundaries defining the subject neighborhood from another. The appraiser should **provide an outline of the neighborhood boundaries**, which should be clearly delineated using 'North', 'South', 'East', and 'West'.

Reference in this section to a map or other addendum as the only example of the neighborhood boundaries is **unacceptable**.

Neighborhood Description

Typically, dwellings best maintain their value when situated in neighborhoods consisting of other similar dwellings. However, some typical factors of a mixed-use neighborhood (e.g., easy access to employment centers and a high level of community activity) can actually enhance the property's market value through increased buyer demand. Urban neighborhoods also frequently reflect a blend of residential and non-residential land uses—including residential multi-family properties, other properties used to provide commercial services (e.g., grocery and other neighborhood stores) in support of the local neighborhood, industrial properties, etc.

When different land uses and property types are present in a neighborhood, it is a neighborhood characteristic the appraiser needs to take into consideration when performing the neighborhood analysis and defining the neighborhood boundaries. To ensure any positive or negative effects of the mixed land uses are reflected in the sales comparison analysis, the appraiser should select comparable sales from the same neighborhood whenever possible.

Market Conditions

The appraiser should **explain any changes that might influence the marketability of the properties in the neighborhood**.

For Example

 The appraiser must comment if there is market resistance to a neighborhood because of the known presence of an environmental hazard.

If a property is located in a neighborhood with vacant or boarded-up properties that affect the value and/or marketability of other properties in the neighborhood, the appraiser must address these conditions in his analysis and appraisal report. He must use comparable sales from the same neighborhood (whenever possible) to ensure any effect of the vacant or boarded-up properties is taken into consideration in the development of the opinion of market value for the subject property. The appraiser should also address the reasons for the vacancies or boarded-up properties in factual terms (by providing data related to such things as demand/supply, foreclosure rates, tax sales, etc.) and discuss how this factor affects the market value and marketability of the property being appraised and other properties in the neighborhood.

◇ **Note:** Development of a valuation conclusion based—either partially or completely—on the sex, race, color, religion, handicap, national origin, or familial status (or any other factor that local, state, or federal law has designated as being discriminatory) of either the prospective owners or occupants of the subject property or the present owners or occupants of the properties in the vicinity of the subject property is **prohibited**.

Site

The Site section allows the appraiser to report the physical and legal characteristics of the property.

Important factors pertaining to the subject lot include topography, shape, size, and drainage. Drainage must be away from the improvements to avoid collection of water in or around them. Steep slopes are generally unfavorable conditions because they may cause erosion, difficulty in maintaining a lawn, and difficult access to the property or a garage. In some areas where this is common, the appraiser may need to include expanded commentary regarding the condition.

Dimensions		Area	Shape		View		
Specific Zoning Classification		Zoning Description					
Zoning Compliance ☐ Legal ☐ Legal Nonconforming (Grandfathered Use) ☐ No Zoning ☐ Illegal (describe)							
Is the highest and best use of the subject property as improved (or as proposed per plans and specifications) the present use? ☐ Yes ☐ No If No, describe							

Utilities	Public	Other (describe)		Public	Other (describe)	Off-site Improvements—Type	Public	Private
Electricity	☐	☐	Water	☐	☐	Street	☐	☐
Gas	☐	☐	Sanitary Sewer	☐	☐	Alley	☐	☐
FEMA Special Flood Hazard Area ☐ Yes ☐ No FEMA Flood Zone			FEMA Map #			FEMA Map Date		
Are the utilities and off-site improvements typical for the market area? ☐ Yes ☐ No If No, describe								
Are there any adverse site conditions or external factors (easements, encroachments, environmental conditions, land uses, etc.)? ☐ Yes ☐ No If Yes, describe								

Dimensions

The appraiser should **list all dimensions of the site beginning with the frontage**. If the shape of the site is irregular, a sound suggestion is to show the boundary dimensions by attaching a property survey, site plan, plat, or legal description as an addenda. *Do not list site area on the dimensions line.*

Area

For sites/parcels that have an area of less than one acre, the size must be reported in square feet. For sites/parcels that have an area of one acre or greater, the size must be reported in acreage to two decimal places. The unit of measure must be indicated as either 'sf' for square feet or 'ac' for acres. **A numeric value must be entered, followed by the appropriate unit of measure. The total size of the entire site/parcel must be entered.** No other data is permitted.

Area less than one acre – whole numbers only (no comma) + sf

Area equal to one acre or more – numeric to 2 decimals + ac

EXAMPLES:

27840 sf

3.40 ac

Shape

The appraiser should **describe the shape of the site** (e.g., triangular, square, rectangular, irregular, flag lot).

View

In the view category, the appraiser must **select from the dropdown list an appropriate rating**, and then **up to two view factors from a second dropdown list.**

The appraiser must provide *one* of the ratings from the list below to describe the overall effect on value and marketability of the view factors associated with the subject property.

ABBREVIATED ENTRY	OVERALL VIEW RATING
N	Neutral
B	Beneficial
A	Adverse

The appraiser must also provide *at least one, but not more than two*, view factor(s) from the list below to provide details about the overall view rating selected above.

ABBREVIATED ENTRY	VIEW FACTOR
Wtr	Water View
Pstl	Pastoral View
Woods	Woods View
Prk	Park View
Glfvw	Golf Course View
CtySky	City View Skyline View
Mtn	Mountain View
Res	Residential View
CtyStr	City Street View
Ind	Industrial View
PwrLn	Power Lines
LtdSght	Limited Sight
See Instruction Below	Other – Appraiser to enter a description of the view*

*Other: If a view factor not on this list materially affects the value of the subject property, the appraiser must enter a description of the view associated with the property (see second example below). The description entered must allow a reader of the appraisal report to understand what the view associated with the property actually is. Descriptors such as 'None', 'N/A', 'Typical', 'Average', etc., are unacceptable. Descriptions should be entered carefully because the same text will be represented in both the Site section and the comparable sales grid for the subject property. The text must fit in the allowable space.

Examples:

B;Mtn;Wtr

A;RRtracks [example of appraiser-entered 'Other' description]

Specific Zoning Category

Enter the specific zoning classification used by the local municipality or jurisdiction (e.g., R-1). If there is no zoning, indicate as such.

Zoning Description

Describe what the specific classification means. Include a general statement describing what the zoning permits (e.g., R-1 = Residential-Single Family). If there is no zoning, the appraiser should describe the prevalent use of sites in the neighborhood.

Zoning Compliance

Select he appropriate checkbox for zoning compliance. If the current use is in compliance with the current zoning ordinances by marking "Legal". If the existing property does not comply with current zoning regulations (e.g., use, lot size, improvement size, off street parking) but is accepted by the local zoning authority, the appraiser should mark "Legal Non-Conforming". If there is no zoning, indicate as such. When the improvements do not conform and is not a grandfathered use or has been granted a variance, the appraiser should mark "Illegal". Additional commentary should be provided by the appraiser when the zoning is anything other than "Legal".

Highest and Best Use

Indicate the highest and best use of the site as improved or as proposed and completed in relation to the neighborhood and current market conditions. If the current use represents the highest and best use, mark "Yes". If it does not, mark "No" and provide an explanation.

Utilities

The appraiser must **indicate for each utility whether it is 'Public' and/or 'Other'**. Utilities include electricity, gas, water, and sanitary sewer. The appraiser must also enter a description if 'Other' is indicated. If the utility is not present, enter 'None' in the description field.

Street/Alley

Briefly describe the off-site improvements under "Type" and **enter road surface material and mark "Public" or "Private"**.

For Example

An appraiser may enter the following information: "Street: Asphalt; Public," "Alley: None."

Public refers to an improvement dedicated to and accepted by a unit of government—not including a homeowners association.

FEMA Information

There are several reporting requirements relative to this category. If the property is within a Special Flood Hazard Area, mark "Yes"; otherwise, mark "No". A copy of the flood map panel is required by most lenders. The FEMA Zone designations, such as zones "A" (a special flood hazard area) and "V" (a coastal area), require flood insurance and are considered a Special Flood Hazard Area. Zones "B", "C", and "X" are not. The appraiser must **enter the FEMA Map number and map date**. There are some (usually isolated) areas of the country that are not mapped by FEMA. If it is not shown on any map, the appraiser should specify "not mapped."

Adverse Site Conditions or External Conditions

Finally, the appraiser must **indicate if the utilities and off-site improvements are typical for the area as well as the presence of adverse site conditions or external conditions**, such as easements (including surface, sub-surface, and overhead), encroachments, or environmental issues affecting the property value.

Improvements

The Improvements Section of the URAR form is at the bottom of Page 1. Again, much of this information is fairly direct, but must be reported with very specific designators and descriptions. Here is where the UAD becomes somewhat different and possibly tedious for even seasoned appraisal professionals.

General Description	Foundation	Exterior Description	materials/condition	Interior	materials/condition
Units ☐ One ☐ One with Accessory Unit	☐ Concrete Slab ☐ Crawl Space	Foundation Walls		Floors	
# of Stories	☐ Full Basement ☐ Partial Basement	Exterior Walls		Walls	
Type ☐ Det. ☐ Att. ☐ S-Det./End Unit	Basement Area sq. ft.	Roof Surface		Trim/Finish	
☐ Existing ☐ Proposed ☐ Under Const.	Basement Finish %	Gutters & Downspouts		Bath Floor	
Design (Style)	☐ Outside Entry/Exit ☐ Sump Pump	Window Type		Bath Wainscot	
Year Built	Evidence of ☐ Infestation	Storm Sash/Insulated		Car Storage ☐ None	
Effective Age (Yrs)	☐ Dampness ☐ Settlement	Screens		☐ Driveway # of Cars	
Attic ☐ None	Heating ☐ FWA ☐ HWBB ☐ Radiant	Amenities	☐ Woodstove(s) #	Driveway Surface	
☐ Drop Stair ☐ Stairs	☐ Other Fuel	☐ Fireplace(s) #	☐ Fence	☐ Garage # of Cars	
☐ Floor ☐ Scuttle	Cooling ☐ Central Air Conditioning	☐ Patio/Deck	☐ Porch	☐ Carport # of Cars	
☐ Finished ☐ Heated	☐ Individual ☐ Other	☐ Pool	☐ Other	☐ Att. ☐ Det. ☐ Built-in	
Appliances ☐Refrigerator ☐Range/Oven ☐Dishwasher ☐Disposal ☐Microwave ☐Washer/Dryer ☐Other (describe)					
Finished area **above** grade contains: Rooms Bedrooms Bath(s) Square Feet of Gross Living Area Above Grade					
Additional features (special energy efficient items, etc.)					
Describe the condition of the property (including needed repairs, deterioration, renovations, remodeling, etc.).					
Are there any physical deficiencies or adverse conditions that affect the livability, soundness, or structural integrity of the property? ☐ Yes ☐ No If Yes, describe					
Does the property generally conform to the neighborhood (functional utility, style, condition, use, construction, etc.)? ☐ Yes ☐ No If No, describe					

Number of Stories

The appraiser must **indicate the number of stories, numerically to two decimal places**, for the subject property. Do not use any designators or descriptors, such as 'one story' or 'one story and a half.'

EXAMPLES:

1.00 (One story)

1.50 (One and one-half story)

2.00 (Two story)

Design

The appraiser should **enter an appropriate architectural design (style) type descriptor** that best describes the subject property. Valid descriptions include, but are not limited to, 'Colonial,' 'Rambler,' 'Georgian,' 'Farmhouse'. Do not use descriptors such as 'Brick,' '2 stories,' 'Average,' 'Conventional,' or 'Typical' as these are not architectural styles. Design style names may vary by locality. The appraiser should report the name of the design style that is applicable within the local market area.

Year Built

The appraiser must **indicate the year the subject property was built**. If it is unknown or unavailable to the appraiser within the normal course of business, the appraiser must estimate the year the subject property was built.

Year Built – 4-digit number, yyyy

Estimation of Year Built – A tilde (~) must be placed before the estimated year built

EXAMPLES:

1978

~1950

Basement Area and Finish

If a basement exists, the appraiser must **indicate the basement size in square feet and the percentage of the basement that is finished**. If there is no basement, enter zero (0) in both fields.

Basement Area – Numeric to 5 digits, whole numbers only

Basement Finish – Numeric to 3 digits, whole numbers only

Heating/Cooling

The appraiser should **select the heating and/or cooling types**. If there is no heating or cooling source, the appraiser should indicate 'Other' and enter 'None' in the description.

Amenities

The appraiser should **select the appropriate checkbox(es) to indicate the amenities available**. The appraiser should enter zero (0) in the appropriate space if there are no fireplaces or woodstoves. The appraiser should enter 'None' in the appropriate space if there is no patio/deck, pool, fence, porch, or other amenity.

Exterior Description

The exterior description is fairly brief at first glance. This section requires the appraiser to **state the material type of several common exterior components**. However, the appraiser's reporting diligence may be amplified when considering the other required reporting element: Condition of the exterior components. Here, the appraiser must rate the condition of the improvements (e.g., fair, average, good) and then discuss any adverse or atypical condition in later comment areas or in the report.

Interior

Reporting of the interior finishes is similar to the exterior description in that this section requires the appraiser to **report the finish materials as well as the condition of the finishes** (e.g., fair, average, good). Responses in this section may be mixed with some properties (e.g., some bath floors are tile while others are sheet vinyl). In such case, additional commentary should be provided by the appraiser. Also, the type of materials should be defined, if possible, such as the type of tile or wallboard.

Car Storage

The appraiser must **indicate whether the subject property has a driveway, garage, and/or carport**, or has no car storage. If the subject property has a driveway, garage, and/or carport, the appraiser must enter the number of spaces for each type of car storage; if none, enter zero (0).

Appliances

Appliances included with the property should be noted here. The appraiser should **note if the appliances are built-in or considered personal property**, but included in the real property appraisal.

Finished Area – Rooms/Bedrooms/Baths

The appraiser must **enter the total number of finished rooms and bedrooms above grade numerically**, using **whole numbers only**.

For baths, the appraiser must **enter the total number of full baths and partial baths above grade numerically to two decimal places**. A three-quarter bath is to be counted as a full bath in all cases. Quarter baths (baths that feature only a toilet) are not to be included in the bathroom count. The number of full and half baths must be entered, separated by a period. The full bath count is represented to the left of the period. The half bath count is represented to the right of the period.

EXAMPLE:

3.2 indicates three full baths and two half baths above grade.

Above Grade Gross Living Area

The appraiser must **enter the total square footage of the above grade living area numerically to five digits in whole numbers**.

Property Condition

The appraiser must provide the following information:

Overall Condition Rating – The appraiser must **select one of the following ratings that best describes the overall condition of the subject property or unit**. For condominium properties, the rating must reflect the overall condition for the individual unit being appraised. Only one selection is permitted. The rating for the subject property must match the overall condition rating that is reported in the Sales Comparison Approach section.

- C1
- C2
- C3
- C4
- C5
- C6

The following definitions apply to the ratings:

C1 The improvements have been very recently constructed and have not previously been occupied. The entire structure and all components are new and the dwelling features no physical depreciation.*

Note: Newly constructed improvements that feature recycled materials and/or components can be considered new dwellings provided that the dwelling is placed on a 100% new foundation and the recycled materials and the recycled components have been rehabilitated/re-manufactured into like-new condition. Recently constructed improvements that have not been previously occupied are not considered "new" if they have any significant physical depreciation (i.e., newly constructed dwellings that have been vacant for an extended period of time without adequate maintenance or upkeep).

C2 The improvements feature no deferred maintenance, little or no physical depreciation, and require no repairs. Virtually all building components are new or have been recently repaired, refinished, or rehabilitated. All outdated components and finishes have been updated and/or replaced with components that meet current standards. Dwellings in this category either are almost new or have been recently completely renovated and are similar in condition to new construction.

C3 The improvements are well maintained and feature limited physical depreciation due to normal wear and tear. Some components, but not every major building component, may be updated or recently rehabilitated. The structure has been well maintained.

C4 The improvements feature some minor deferred maintenance and physical deterioration due to normal wear and tear. The dwelling has been adequately maintained and requires only minimal repairs to building components/mechanical systems and cosmetic repairs. All major building components have been adequately maintained and are functionally adequate.

C5 The improvements feature obvious deferred maintenance and are in need of some significant repairs. Some building components need repairs, rehabilitation, or updating. The functional utility and overall livability is somewhat diminished due to condition, but the dwelling remains useable and functional as a residence.

C6 The improvements have substantial damage or deferred maintenance with deficiencies or defects that are severe enough to affect the safety, soundness, or structural integrity of the improvements. The improvements are in need of substantial repairs and rehabilitation, including many or most major components.

The appraiser must **indicate 'Yes' or 'No' if there has been any material work done to the kitchen(s) or bathroom(s) in the prior 15 years**.

- *If No*, the statement: 'No updates in the prior 15 years' must be provided.

- *If Yes*, additional information for kitchens and bathrooms must be provided.

Kitchen(s) and Bathroom(s) – Level of Work Completed and Timeframes – The appraiser must identify any work completed in the kitchen(s) and bathroom(s) along with the timeframes in which the work was completed. The appraiser must select one of the values from the lists below for both the kitchen(s) and the bathroom(s).

Level of Work Completed:

- Not updated
- Updated
- Remodeled

Timeframes:

- Less than one year ago
- One to five years ago
- Six to ten years ago
- Eleven to fifteen years ago
- Timeframe unknown

Timeframes represent the time period in which the majority of the improvements were completed.

A **description of the condition of the subject property improvements must be provided** by the appraiser.

EXAMPLES:

C4;No updates in the prior 15 years;[enter description of property condition]

C3;Kitchen-updated-less than one year ago;Bathrooms-remodeled-one to five years ago;[enter description of property condition]

C2;Kitchen-not updated;Bathrooms-remodeled-less than one year ago;[enter description of property condition]

Sales Comparison Approach

The Sales Comparison Approach section of the URAR report is the subject of most of Page 2 and has numerous fields with very specific criteria for filling in the form. Some of these items are on dropdown lists identical to what has already been illustrated, or part of lists that will be introduced in this section. As well, data entered on the form must be specific to the standards that will be discussed.

There are ___ comparable properties currently offered for sale in the subject neighborhood ranging in price from $ ___ to $ ___ .				
There are ___ comparable sales in the subject neighborhood within the past twelve months ranging in sale price from $ ___ to $ ___ .				

FEATURE	SUBJECT	COMPARABLE SALE # 1	COMPARABLE SALE # 2	COMPARABLE SALE # 3
Address				
Proximity to Subject				
Sale Price	$	$	$	$
Sale Price/Gross Liv. Area	$ sq. ft.	$ sq. ft.	$ sq. ft.	$ sq. ft.
Data Source(s)				
Verification Source(s)				

VALUE ADJUSTMENTS	DESCRIPTION	DESCRIPTION	+(-) $ Adjustment	DESCRIPTION	+(-) $ Adjustment	DESCRIPTION	+(-) $ Adjustment
Sale or Financing Concessions							
Date of Sale/Time							
Location							
Leasehold/Fee Simple							
Site							
View							
Design (Style)							
Quality of Construction							
Actual Age							
Condition							
Above Grade Room Count	Total Bdrms. Baths	Total Bdrms. Baths		Total Bdrms. Baths		Total Bdrms. Baths	
Gross Living Area	sq. ft.	sq. ft.		sq. ft.		sq. ft.	
Basement & Finished Rooms Below Grade							
Functional Utility							
Heating/Cooling							
Energy Efficient Items							
Garage/Carport							
Porch/Patio/Deck							
Net Adjustment (Total)		☐ + ☐ -	$	☐ + ☐ -	$	☐ + ☐ -	$
Adjusted Sale Price of Comparables		Net Adj. % Gross Adj. %	$	Net Adj. % Gross Adj. %	$	Net Adj. % Gross Adj. %	$

I ☐ did ☐ did not research the sale or transfer history of the subject property and comparable sales. If not, explain

My research ☐ did ☐ did not reveal any prior sales or transfers of the subject property for the three years prior to the effective date of this appraisal.

Data source(s)

My research ☐ did ☐ did not reveal any prior sales or transfers of the comparable sales for the year prior to the date of sale of the comparable sale.

Data source(s)

Report the results of the research and analysis of the prior sale or transfer history of the subject property and comparable sales (report additional prior sales on page 3).

ITEM	SUBJECT	COMPARABLE SALE # 1	COMPARABLE SALE # 2	COMPARABLE SALE # 3
Date of Prior Sale/Transfer				
Price of Prior Sale/Transfer				
Data Source(s)				
Effective Date of Data Source(s)				

Analysis of prior sale or transfer history of the subject property and comparable sales

Summary of Sales Comparison Approach

Indicated Value by Sales Comparison Approach $

(left margin, vertical text: SALES COMPARISON APPROACH)

Current Comparable Offerings and Sales

This information is typically gathered from MLS data and possibly other sources.

Address

The appraiser must **enter the subject property address and the address for each comparable sale**. The information is the same as the "Property Address" data field in the Subject section. Likely, most appraisal software applications will populate this area automatically for the subject property using information previously input. Comparable sales should be entered in the same manner.

Proximity of Comparable Sales to the Subject

The appraiser must **enter the proximity of the comparable sales to the subject property, expressed as a distance in miles**. The distance between the subject property and each comparable property is to be measured using a *straight line* between the properties. The direction of the comparable property in relation to the subject property must be expressed.

If the address for a comparable property is not found by the appraiser's mapping program, the appraiser must choose a location on the map as close as possible to the address of the comparable property to derive an accurate distance calculation.

The method to report the proximity of the comparable sale to the subject is: Numeric to two decimal places + '(the word) miles' + Directional

EXAMPLE:

1.75 miles NW

Sale Price of the Comparable

The appraiser must **enter the sale price of the subject property, when applicable, and each comparable property**. The sale price for the subject property *must match* the contract price reported in the Contract section. If any of the comparable properties sold for a price that was not in whole dollars, the appraiser must round the sales price to the nearest dollar. If any of the comparable properties is a listing or pending sale, the appraiser must enter the offering price or contract price as applicable.

Data Sources

The appraiser must provide the data source(s) utilized to obtain the data for each comparable sale. When using MLS as the data source, the MLS organization acronym or abbreviation followed by '#' and the listing number must be reported. If the appraiser utilizes additional data sources that do not fit into this data field, they must be provided in the Comments section or Addenda in the appraisal report.

Additionally, the appraiser must **provide the DOM (numerically to four digits) for each comparable sale for the latest time period that the property was listed or advertised for sale**. DOM is defined as the total number of continuous days from the date that a property is listed or advertised for sale until the date that it is taken off the market or sold. DOM applies not only to properties that are listed in the MLS, but also applies to properties marketed for sale outside the MLS. If the comparable property was not individually listed or advertised for sale, enter zero (0). If the DOM is unknown, enter 'Unk'.

EXAMPLES:

MRIS#AA123456789;DOM 220

MRIS#BB123456789;DOM Unk

Sales or Financing Concessions

This field is comprised of two lines used to report the sale type, financing type, and any concessions. The information must be entered on line 1 and line 2 as indicated.

Line 1

The appraiser must **indicate the sale type for each comparable property**. If more than one sale type applies to the comparable property, the appraiser must start at the top of the list and identify the first sale type that applies. The valid values are:

Abbreviated Entry	Sale Type
REO	REO sale
Short	Short sale
CrtOrd	Court ordered sale
Estate	Estate sale
Relo	Relocation sale
NonArm	Non-arms length sale
ArmLth	Arms length sale
Listing	Listing

Line 2

The appraiser must **enter the financing type from the list below and the total amount of concessions, if any, for each settled sale**. If there are no sales or financing concessions, enter zero (0).

Abbreviated Entry	Financing Type
FHA	FHA
VA	VA
Conv	Conventional
Seller	Seller
Cash	Cash
RH	USDA – Rural housing
See Instruction Below	Other – Appraiser to enter a description of the financing type*

*Other: If the financing type is not on this list, the appraiser must enter a description of the financing type. The text must fit in the allowable space.

 Note: Below-market financing can have an impact on market values and, therefore, is of particular importance. A variety of government programs, such as state and local bond programs, provide below-market financing. The appraiser must indicate if sales transactions with below-market financing are used for comparable sales.

EXAMPLE:

Line 1: ArmLth
Line 2: FHA;5000

Date of Sale

For comparable properties being reported, the appraiser must **identify the status of the sale from the dropdown list with the following options:**

Status Type
Active
Contract
Expired
Withdrawn
Settled sale

- If the comparable property is an **active** listing, the appraiser must specify 'Active'.
- If the comparable property is **under contract**, or **an expired** or **withdrawn** listing, the appraiser must first indicate the date status type using the abbreviations below followed by the corresponding contract, expiration, or withdrawal date in mm/yy format. Use 'c' for contract, 'w' for withdrawn listings, and 'e' for expired listings.

Abbreviated Entry	Date Status Type
c	Contract Date
s	Settlement Date
w	Withdrawn Date
e	Expiration Date

EXAMPLES:

Active listing: Active

Contract: c04/10

Expired listing: e04/10

Withdrawn listing: w04/10

Settled sale (contract date known): s04/10;c02/10

Settled sale (contract date unknown): s04/10;Unk

Location

The appraiser must **choose one of these ratings from the dropdown to describe the overall effect on value and marketability of the location factor(s) associated with the subject property and each comparable property**. The abbreviation for the rating must be entered.

Abbreviated Entry	Overall View Rating
N	Neutral
B	Beneficial
A	Adverse

The appraiser must also **select at least one, but not more than two, location factor(s) from the dropdown list below**. If two factors are entered, separate them with a semicolon. The abbreviation for the factor must be entered, with the exception of 'Other'.

Abbreviated Entry	Location Factor
Res	Residential
Ind	Industrial
Comm	Commercial
BsyRd	Busy Road
WtrFr	Water Front
GlfCse	Golf Course
AdjPrk	Adjacent to Park
AdjPwr	Adjacent to Power Lines
Lndfl	Landfill
PubTrn	Public Transportation
See Instruction Below	Other – Appraiser to enter a description of the location*

*Other: If a location factor not on this list materially affects the value of the property, the appraiser must enter a description of the location associated with the property. The description entered must allow a reader of the appraisal report to understand the location factor(s) that is associated with the property. Descriptors such as 'None', 'N/A', 'Typical', 'Average', etc., are unacceptable. The text must fit in the allowable space.

EXAMPLE:

B;AdjPrk;WtrFr

Site

Similar to the information entered in the Site information, **the site area in the sales comparison approach must be entered following the same requirements**.

For sites/parcels that have an area of *less than one acre, the size must be reported in square feet*. For sites/parcels that have an *area of one acre or greater, the size must be reported in acreage to two decimal places*. The unit of measure must be indicated as either 'sf' for square feet or 'ac' for acres. A numeric value must be entered followed by the appropriate unit of measure. The total size of the entire site/parcel must be entered. No other data is permitted in this field.

EXAMPLES:

6400 sf

3.40 ac

View

View, in the sales comparison approach is also entered the same way as in the Site section and uses the same dropdown choices for overall view rating and view factors.

The appraiser must **provide one of the ratings from the list below to describe the overall effect on value and marketability of the view factor(s) associated with the subject property and each comparable property**.

Abbreviated Entry	Overall View Rating
N	Neutral
B	Beneficial
A	Adverse

The appraiser must also **provide at least one, but not more than two, view factor(s) from the list below to provide details about the overall view rating selected above**.

Abbreviated Entry	View Factor
Wtr	Water View
Pstl	Pastoral View
Woods	Woods View
Prk	Park View
Glfvw	Golf Course View
CtySky	City View Skyline View
Mtn	Mountain View
Res	Residential View
CtyStr	City Street View
Ind	Industrial View
PwrLn	Power Lines
LtdSght	Limited Sight
See Instruction Below	Other – Appraiser to enter a description of the view*

*Other: If a view factor not on this list materially affects the value of the property, the appraiser must enter a description of the view associated with the property (see second example below). Descriptions should be entered carefully because the text will be represented in both the Site Section and the Sales Comparison Approach section for the subject property. The description entered must allow a reader of the appraisal report to understand what the view is that is associated with the property. Descriptors such as 'None', 'N/A', 'Typical', 'Average', etc., are unacceptable. The text must fit in the allowable space.

EXAMPLE:

B;Mtn;Wtr

A;RRtracks [example of appraiser-entered 'Other' description]

Quality of Construction

Quality of construction uses a rating system similar to property condition. The appraiser must **select one quality rating from the list below for the subject property and each comparable property**. The appraiser must indicate the quality rating that best describes the overall quality of the property. *Any one choice is permitted.*

- Q1
- Q2
- Q3
- Q4
- Q5
- Q6

Qualtiy ratings are defined as follows:

Q1 Dwellings with this quality rating are usually unique structures that are individually designed by an architect for a specified user. Such residences typically are constructed from detailed architectural plans and specifications and feature an exceptionally high level of workmanship and exceptionally high-grade materials throughout the interior and exterior of the structure.. The design features exceptionally high-quality exterior refinements and ornamentation, and exceptionally high-quality interior refinements. The workmanship, materials, and finishes throughout the dwelling are exceptionally high quality.

Q2 Dwellings with this quality rating are often custom designed for construction on an individual property owner's site. However, dwellings in this quality grade are also found in high-quality tract developments featuring residences constructed from individual plans or from highly modified or upgraded plans. The design features detailed, high-quality exterior ornamentation, high-quality interior refinements, and detail. The workmanship, materials, and finishes throughout the dwelling are generally of high or very high quality.

Q3 Dwellings with this quality rating are residences of higher quality built from individual or readily available designer plans in above-standard residential tract developments or on an individual property owner's site. The design includes significant exterior ornamentation and interiors that are well finished. The workmanship exceeds acceptable standards and many materials and finishes throughout the dwelling have been upgraded from "stock" standards.

Q4 Dwellings with this quality rating meet or exceed the requirements of applicable building codes. Standard or modified standard building plans are utilized and the design includes adequate fenestration and some exterior ornamentation and interior refinements. Materials, workmanship, finish, and equipment are of stock or builder grade and may feature some upgrades.

Q5 Dwellings with this quality rating feature economy of construction and basic functionality as main considerations. Such dwellings feature plain design using readily available or basic floor plans featuring minimal fenestration and basic finishes with minimal exterior ornamentation and limited interior detail. These dwellings meet minimum building codes and are constructed with inexpensive, stock materials with limited refinements and upgrades.

Q6 Dwellings with this quality rating are of basic quality and lower cost; some may not be suitable for year-round occupancy. Such dwellings are often built with simple plans or without plans, often utilizing the lowest quality building materials. Such dwellings are often built or expanded by persons who are professionally unskilled or possess only minimal construction skills. Electrical, plumbing, and other mechanical systems and equipment may be minimal or non-existent. Older dwellings may feature one or more substandard or non-conforming additions to the original structure.

Unique UAD Reporting Requirements

The following describes the UAD reporting requirements that affect the Sales Comparison Sections of Single Family reporting forms (1004 and 2055) and Condominium reporting forms (1073 and 1075), which include expanded instructions and requirements for reporting the Design (style) of the subject and comparable sales and the details regarding garage or car storage for the subject and comparable sales.

Single Family Forms (1004 and 2055)

Design (Style)

Describe the architectural design for the subject and comparable properties including the type of attachment and the number of stories.

Reporting Format:

Attachment Type – Select one of the following from the specified list:

Abbreviated Entry	Attachment Type
AT	Attached Structure, use for row and townhomes that share multiple communal walls
DT	Detached Structure, does not share any communal walls, floor, or ceiling with another property
SD	Semi-detached structure, use for end-unit row and townhomes as well as duplexes

Number of Stories – Enter a number up to 2 decimal places.

Description of Style – Enter a brief description of the style of the property.

- The PDF creator will display the input in the proper order.
- For Number of Stories, only display a number after the decimal point if it exceeds zero. There should be no spaces before or after the semicolon.
- The maximum number of characters permitted before the semicolon is 6.

Examples:

DT1.75;CapeCod

AT2;IntTwnhse

SD3.5;Duplex

Condominium Forms (1073 and 1075)

Design (Style)

Provide the attachment type, the number of levels and the architectural design for the subject property and each comparable property.

Reporting Format:

Attachment Types – Select one value from the specified list below:

Abbreviated Entry	Attachment Type
DT	Detached Structure, does not share any communal walls, floor, or ceiling with another property
RT	Row or Townhouse - One in a row of identical houses or having a common wall; attached to another unit via common wall
GR	Garden - Structure is 1-3 stories tall, contains units with communal walls, floors, and/or ceilings
MR	Mid-Rise - Structure is 4-7 stories tall, contains units with communal walls, floors, and/or ceilings
HR	High Rise -Structure is 8+ stories tall, contains units with communal walls, floors, and/or ceilings
O	Other

Number of Levels –Indicate the attachment type of the property followed by the number of levels within the condominium unit. The number of levels should be displayed in whole numbers.

Description of Style - Enter a brief description of the style of the property.

• The PDF creator will populate the selected text from the specified list for 'Attachment Type', followed by the 'Number of Levels', and the 'Description of Style'.

• A semicolon is used to separate the number of levels from the Description of the style.

• No semicolon should be used between the Attachment Type and the Number of Levels.

EXAMPLES:

DT1L;SitecondoRamb

RT3L;Twnhse

GR1L;Garden

MR1L;Midrise

HR2L;Penthouse

Actual Age

The appraiser must **report the actual age of the subject property and each comparable property**. For new construction that is less than one year old, enter zero (0). Do not enter any additional information such as 'years' or other descriptors. If the actual age is unknown, enter the estimated age.

This is similar to the information provided in the Improvement section.

Actual Age – Numeric to three digits, whole numbers only

Estimation of Actual Age – A tilde (~) must be placed before the actual age

EXAMPLES:

18

~150

Condition

The appraiser must **select one overall condition rating for the subject property and each comparable property using the C1-C6 condition rating as was used in the Improvements section of the report.** (See pages 66 and 67) The overall condition rating selected for the subject property must match the overall condition rating that was reported in the Improvements section so that it is consistent throughout the appraisal report. Any one choice is permitted.

Above Grade Room Count/Gross Living Area

The process here also mirrors that in the Improvements section of the report for the subject property. Here, the appraiser must **enter the total number of rooms as well as the number of bedrooms and bathrooms for the subject property and each comparable property**. The appraiser must also **enter the gross living area for the subject property and each comparable property**. The appraiser must follow the same standards outlined in the **Improvements section** (see page 64) under "Finished Area Above Grade" and "Square Feet of Gross Living Area Above Grade."

The format for reporting the information is as follows:

# of Rooms – Numeric to two digits, whole numbers only

# of Bedrooms – Numeric to two digits, whole numbers only

# of Bath(s) – Numeric to two decimal places

Separate full bath count from half bath count with a period (.), nn.nn

Gross Living Area – Numeric to five digits, whole numbers only

Basement and Finished Rooms Below Grade

The appraiser must **report the information for both the subject and each comparable property using the following format:**

Line 1

- **Total square footage of the property improvements below grade** – If there is no basement, enter zero (0). No other information may be entered.
- **Finished square footage of the property improvements below grade, if applicable.** Do not indicate a percent finished.
- **The type of access to the basement, if applicable.** The allowable values are 'Walk-out' (wo), 'Walk-up' (wu), or 'Interior only' (in), which must be abbreviated on the appraisal report form to fit in the available space.

Line 2

The appraiser must report the number of each type of finished rooms in the basement on Line 2 of this data field. The room type descriptors are:

Abbreviated Entry	Room Type
rr	Recreation Room
br	Bedroom
ba	Bathroom
o	Other

The appraiser must enter zero (0) if there are no rooms of a particular type.

Line 1: Finished Square Footage – Numeric to five digits, whole numbers only

Line 1: Basement Access – Appraiser must select one value from the specified list (values wo, wu, or in)

Line 2: Room Count/Type – Numeric to one digit*

*For bathrooms, the format is n.n – full baths separated from half baths with a period (.).

> **EXAMPLES:**
>
> **Line 1:** 1000sf750sfwu (1,000 square foot basement, 750 square foot finished, walk-up access)
>
> **Line 2:** 1rr1br1.0ba2o (1 recreation room, 1 bedroom, 1 full bath, 2 rooms – other)

Energy Efficient Items

The appraiser must **enter any energy efficient items for the subject property and each comparable property.** If there are no energy efficient items, enter 'None'.

Garage/Carport

The appraiser should **indicate the type of parking and number of spaces for each type identified for the subject property and each comparable property.**

Reporting Format:

Utilize the below abbreviations, in the order that they are listed, preceded by the number of parking spaces without spaces or delimiters.

- If there is no off-street parking, the appraiser should enter "None".
- Include all parking types if all types are present.

Abbreviated Entry	Parking Type
ga	Attached Garage
gd	Detached Garage
gbi	Built-in Garage
cp	Carport
dw	Driveway

EXAMPLES:

2ga2dw

1ga2gd1dw

1cp

1ga1gd1gbi1cp2dw

None

Garage/Carport (for Condominiums)

Indicate the **type of parking and number of spaces for each type identified for the subject property and each comparable property.**

Reporting Format:

Use the illustrated abbreviations preceded by the number of parking spaces without spaces or delimiters between the types.

- Use the additional space, as needed, for a text description.
- The PDF creator shall render a delimiter in the form of a semicolon (;) and insert the delimiter prior to the text description.
- Attributes such as assigned and owned may be noted within the text description.
- If there is no off-street parking, enter "None".
- Include all parking types if all types are present.

Abbreviated Entry	Parking Type
g	Garage
cv	Covered
op	Open

EXAMPLES:

2g

1g1cv

1cv

None

None;street permit

1g1cv;1 Owned

2g1cv1op;1a 2ow

**Note: In the last example, the appraiser should note the use of any additional abbreviations within the report so that the reader can interpret the entry.

Adjustments in the Sales Comparison Approach

Adjustments to comparable properties (+/-) are made *in whole dollars only*. If a feature or aspect of the subject property differs from a feature or aspect of a comparable property and the appraiser determines that no adjustment is warranted, the appraiser must **enter a zero (0) in the adjustment line.** The zero (0) will indicate to the reader/user of the report that the appraiser considered the difference and determined that no adjustment should be made.

When the features for the subject and comparable sale(s) are the same and no adjustment is warranted, leave the field blank - do not enter or default to zero.

Net Adjustment is the sum of all adjustments. If there are no adjustments, the net adjustment value must be zero (0).

Prior Sales of the Subject and Comparable Properties

In this portion of the Sales Comparison Approach section, there are various statements that require a response and certain information that must be provided.

USPAP does not reference or obligate an appraiser to research or analyze prior sales of comparable properties. However, Fannie Mae and Freddie Mac guidelines require research and analysis of comparable sales by the appraiser and, thus, compliance with the COMPETENCY RULE of USPAP regarding these guidelines is required, which would not be fulfilled without research and analysis of the comparable sales.

As a final note, prior sales include other transfers, such as non-arm's length transactions, transfers between related parties, transfers related to foreclosure, etc. Refer to USPAP FAQs for further guidance on the issue.

My research did/did not reveal any prior sales or transfers...

The appraiser must **select the appropriate checkbox** and insert an "x" to indicate either 'did' or 'did not' for this statement. Only one response is permitted for each statement.

Date of Prior Sale/Transfer

The appraiser must **report the date(s) of prior sale(s) or transfer(s) of the subject property for the three years prior to the effective date of the appraisal using MM/DD/YYYY format**. The appraiser must report the date(s) of the prior sale(s) or transfer(s) of any comparable property during the twelve months prior to its date of sale.

If more than one prior transfer of the subject property or any of the comparable sale(s) occurred within the applicable time period, the additional transfer(s) must be listed and reported in the "Analysis of Prior Sale or Transfer History of the Subject Property and Comparable Sales" field.

Price of Prior Sale/Transfer

The appraiser must **report the price(s) of prior sale(s) or transfer(s) of the subject property for the three years prior to the effective date of the appraisal in *whole dollars only***. The appraiser must report the price(s) of the prior sale(s) or transfer(s) of any comparable property during the twelve months prior to its date of sale.

If more than one prior transfer of the subject property or any of the comparable sales occurred within the applicable time period, the additional transfer(s) must be listed and reported in the "Analysis of Prior Sale or Transfer History of the Subject Property and Comparable Sales" field.

Data Source(s), Effective Date of Data Source(s) – *Prior Sales*

The appraiser must **enter the data source(s) and effective date(s) of the data source(s) associated with the prior transfer(s) of each property.**

If the data source is an MLS, the appraiser must enter the abbreviated MLS organization name, followed by a pound sign (#) and the specific listing identifier.

Data Source(s) – Text

Effective Date of Data Source(s) – MM/DD/YYYY

Indicated Value by the Sales Comparison Approach

The appraiser must **enter the reconciled value of the Sales Comparison Approach *in whole dollars*.**

Reconciliation

In this step, the appraiser considers the indications produced in his reconciliation of the data analyzed and must report three specific fields in this section of the report.

Indicated Value by:	Sales Comparison Approach $	Income Approach $	Cost Approach (if developed) $

R E C O N C I L I A T I O N

This appraisal is made ☐ "as is", ☐ subject to completion per plans and specifications on the basis of a hypothetical condition that the improvements have been completed, ☐ subject to the following repairs or alterations on the basis of a hypothetical condition that the repairs or alterations have been completed, or ☐ subject to the following required inspection based on the extraordinary assumption that the condition or deficiency does not require alteration or repair:

Based on a complete visual inspection of the interior and exterior areas of the subject property, defined scope of work, statement of assumptions and limiting conditions, and appraiser's certification, my (our) opinion of the market value, as defined, of the real property that is the subject of this report is $ _____ , as of _____ , which is the date of inspection and the effective date of this appraisal.

This appraisal is made 'as is', subject to completion...

The appraiser must **select and insert an "x" in either the 'as is' or at least one of the 'subject to' checkboxes**. If any of the 'subject to' checkboxes are selected, provide a description.

My (our) opinion of the market value...

The appraiser must **enter the value of the subject property**. The value of the subject property **must match the appraised value of the subject property in the Appraiser Certification section**.

Date of Inspection and Effective Date of Appraisal

The appraiser must **enter the date of the inspection in MM/DD/YYYY format**, which is also the effective date of the appraisal.

Appraiser's Certification

The information that must be completed for the Appraiser's Certification is located on Page 6 of the URAR form.

```
APPRAISER                                    SUPERVISORY APPRAISER (ONLY IF REQUIRED)

Signature_____            Signature_____
Name _____            Name _____
Company Name _____            Company Name _____
Company Address_____            Company Address_____

Telephone Number _____            Telephone Number _____
Email Address_____            Email Address_____
Date of Signature and Report_____            Date of Signature _____
Effective Date of Appraisal _____            State Certification # _____
State Certification #_____            or State License # _____
or State License # _____            State _____
or Other (describe) _____ State #__         Expiration Date of Certification or License _____
State _____
Expiration Date of Certification or License _____   SUBJECT PROPERTY

ADDRESS OF PROPERTY APPRAISED                ☐ Did not inspect subject property
                                             ☐ Did inspect exterior of subject property from street
_____               Date of Inspection _____
_____            ☐ Did inspect interior and exterior of subject property
APPRAISED VALUE OF SUBJECT PROPERTY $ _____    Date of Inspection _____
LENDER/CLIENT
Name _____            COMPARABLE SALES
Company Name _____
Company Address_____            ☐ Did not inspect exterior of comparable sales from street
_____            ☐ Did inspect exterior of comparable sales from street
Email Address_____               Date of Inspection _____
```

Freddie Mac Form 70 March 2005   Page 6 of 6   Fannie Mae Form 1004 March 2005

◇ **Note:** It should be specifically noted, as was discussed in Chapter 1, effective January 1, 2012, per the 2012-2013 Edition of USPAP, the Appraiser's Certification must include a statement regarding prior services to the subject property performed as an appraiser or in any other capacity within the three-year period immediately preceding acceptance of the assignment. Appraisers must assure that the disclosure is included in any preprinted form, or expand the certification in addenda to include the required disclosure.

In the final reconciliation, appraisers must:

- Reconcile the reasonableness and reliability of each applicable approach to value.
- Reconcile the reasonableness and validity of the indicated values.
- Reconcile the reasonableness of available data.
- Select and report the approach or approaches that were given the most weight.

Commentary should elaborate on the logic used and relevance of the data, as well as the approaches developed.

The UAD Requirements are as follows:

State Certification # or State License # – (Appraiser and Supervisory Appraiser if required)

The appraiser and supervisory appraiser (if applicable) must **enter their license or certification number(s) as they appear on the Appraisal Subcommittee (ASC) website, http://www.asc.gov**, unless otherwise mandated by state law or regulation. If the jurisdiction does not provide license numbers for trainees and a trainee performs the appraisal, the term "trainee" must be entered in the (Appraiser Certification Section) "or Other (describe)" field. If there is no supervisory appraiser, leave the field blank; do not make any entry (such as N/A or none).

Expiration Date of Certification or License – (Appraiser and Supervisory Appraiser if required)

The appraiser and supervisory appraiser (if applicable) must **enter the expiration date of their license or certification number(s) in MM/DD/YYYY format**. If there is no supervisory appraiser, leave the field blank; do not make any entry (such as N/A or none).

Lender/Client

The appraiser must **enter the name of the appraisal management company (AMC)** in this field if the appraisal is ordered through an AMC. If no AMC is involved, 'No AMC' must be entered.

Income Approach

The Income Approach on the URAR form for single-family properties is **reported using the gross rent multiplier (GRM) method and only when the approach is necessary for credible results**. This section is very abbreviated and found toward the bottom of Page 3 of the form.

Fannie Mae and Freddie Mac do **not** accept appraisals that rely singularly on the income approach as an indicator of market value. This is an important point for the appraiser when considering the final reconciliation of value.

There are no specified UAD requirements for reporting the income approach.

I	Total gross monthly rent $	X gross rent multiplier (GRM)	= $	Indicated value by the Income Approach
N	Comments on income approach including reconciliation of the GRM			
C				
O				
M				
E				

Cost Approach

The Cost Approach section is located in the lower half of Page 3 of the form. There are limited circumstances for which the cost approach would be applicable in an appraisal assignment of a small residential income property. One of those instances would be when the subject property is a new or proposed construction.

Further, Fannie Mae or Freddie Mac do **not** require development or reporting of the cost approach, except in assignments of manufactured housing. As well, the approach may not be relied upon as a final indicator of value. However, many clients request or require the cost approach be completed. If such is the case, the appraiser **must comply with the request or requirement if agreed to with the client.**

The final reconciliation of value should **include comments regarding the development and reporting of the cost approach and its applicability as an indicator of value.**

COST APPROACH TO VALUE (not required by Fannie Mae)				
Provide adequate information for the lender/client to replicate the below cost figures and calculations.				
Support for the opinion of site value (summary of comparable land sales or other methods for estimating site value)				
ESTIMATED ☐ REPRODUCTION OR ☐ REPLACEMENT COST NEW	OPINION OF SITE VALUE..			= $
Source of cost data	Dwelling	Sq. Ft. @ $	....	=$
Quality rating from cost service Effective date of cost data		Sq. Ft. @ $	....	=$
Comments on Cost Approach (gross building area calculations, depreciation, etc.)				
	Garage/Carport	Sq. Ft. @ $	....	=$
	Total Estimate of Cost-New		....	= $
	Less Physical	Functional	External	
	Depreciation			=$( )
	Depreciated Cost of Improvements..........................			=$
	"As-is" Value of Site Improvements.........................			=$
Estimated Remaining Economic Life (HUD and VA only) Years	Indicated Value By Cost Approach..........................			=$

Required Exhibits

There are several exhibits that are **required** to be attached to the URAR form.

- An exterior building sketch that indicates the dimensions.

    If the floor plan is atypical or functionally obsolete, thus limiting the market appeal for the property in comparison to competitive properties in the neighborhood, a floor plan sketch is required.

- Calculations demonstrating how the estimate for gross living area is derived.

- A street map that shows the location of the subject property and of all comparables that the appraiser used.

- Clear, descriptive, original photographs showing the front, back, and a street scene of the subject property and the front of each comparable sale.

The subject and all comparables must be appropriately identified. Acceptable photographs include clear, descriptive, original images from photographs or electronic images, copies of photographs from an MLS, or copies from the appraiser's files.

- Interior photographs that must, at a minimum, include:
    - The kitchen
    - All bathrooms
    - Main living area
    - Examples of physical deterioration, if present
    - Examples of recent updates, such as restoration, remodeling, and renovation, if present
- Any other pertinent information related to the property.
- Any other data—as an attachment or addendum to the appraisal report form—that are necessary to provide an adequately supported opinion of market value.

Case Study

The URAR is the most common reporting form employed for appraising residential properties for use by a lender client. While Fannie Mae and Freddie Mac developed the reporting form, many others within the real property lending industry have also adopted use of the form, such as FHA and VA, as well as smaller primary lenders.

For lending entities other than Fannie Mae or Freddie Mac, there are likely (other than specific client requirements) no defined style or formatting requirements. The selected sections illustrated in this case study are excerpted from an appraisal report that was not developed following UAD guidelines.

Identify the fields that do not comply with UAD requirements and determine the appropriate response that would be in compliance.

 Note: It should be noted that there are likely other fields in the remainder of the report, not illustrated here, that might not be in compliance, as well.

SUBJECT SECTION

SUBJECT			
Property Address 123 Main Street	City Defiance	State OH	Zip Code 43512-3312
Borrower John and Jane Doe	Owner of Public Record John and Jane Doe	County Defiance	
Legal Description Lot G PT, Indian Addition			
Assessor's Parcel # Q014574004702	Tax Year 2009	R.E. Taxes $ 976.22	
Neighborhood Name Indian Addition	Map Reference See attached	Census Tract 9587.00	
Occupant [X] Owner ☐ Tenant ☐ Vacant	Special Assessments $ 0.00	☐ PUD HOA $	☐ per year ☐ per month
Property Rights Appraised [X] Fee Simple ☐ Leasehold ☐ Other (describe)			
Assignment Type ☐ Purchase Transaction [X] Refinance Transaction ☐ Other (describe)			
Lender/Client Any Bank and Trust Company	Address 987 Clinton St., Defiance, OH 43512		
Is the subject property currently offered for sale or has it been offered for sale in the twelve months prior to the effective date of this appraisal? ☐ Yes [X] No			
Report data source(s) used, offering price(s), and date(s). Per owner and MLS, the subject has not been listed for sale within the past year.			

_____

_____

_____

_____

_____

_____

_____

_____

_____

_____

_____

_____

_____

SITE SECTION

Dimensions 45' x 100' approximately	Area 4500 sq. ft. approximately	Shape Irregular-cul-de-sac	View Residential

Specific Zoning Classification Residential — Zoning Description Residential

Zoning Compliance [X] Legal [ ] Legal Nonconforming (Grandfathered Use) [ ] No Zoning [ ] Illegal (describe)

Is the highest and best use of the subject property as improved (or as proposed per plans and specifications) the present use? [X] Yes [ ] No If No, describe.

Utilities	Public	Other (describe)		Public	Other (describe)	Off-site Improvements—Type	Public	Private
Electricity	[X]		Water	[X]		Street Asphalt	[X]	[ ]
Gas	[X]		Sanitary Sewer	[X]		Alley None	[ ]	[ ]

FEMA Special Flood Hazard Area [ ] Yes [X] No FEMA Flood Zone C FEMA Map # 3901440005D FEMA Map Date 03/04/1985

Are the utilities and off-site improvements typical for the market area? [X] Yes [ ] No If No, describe.

Are there any adverse site conditions or external factors (easements, encroachments, environmental conditions, land uses, etc.)? [ ] Yes [X] No If Yes, describe. Standard utility easements, with no adverse conditions or apparent encroachments noted. Flood hazard information is subject to verification by the client's surveyor, and is not to be relied upon with respect to flood insurance determinations.

IMPROVEMENT SECTION

GENERAL DESCRIPTION		FOUNDATION		EXTERIOR DESCRIPTION materials/condition		INTERIOR materials/condition	
Units [X] One [ ] One with Accessory Unit		[X] Concrete Slab [X] Crawl Space		Foundation Walls Concrete/avg		Floors Carpet,vnl/avg.gd	
# of Stories One		[ ] Full Basement [ ] Partial Basement		Exterior Walls Vinyl/avg		Walls Plas,pan,DW/avg	
Type [X] Det. [ ] Att. [ ] S-Det./End Unit		Basement Area sq. ft.		Roof Surface Asphalt/avg		Trim/Finish Pntd.wood/avg	
[X] Existing [ ] Proposed [ ] Under Const.		Basement Finish %		Gutters & Downspouts Aluminum/avg		Bath Floor Vinyl/avg	
Design (Style) Ranch		[ ] Outside Entry/Exit [ ] Sump Pump		Window Type Vinyl DH, slide/avg		Bath Wainscot Fiberglass/avg	
Year Built 1954		Evidence of [ ] Infestation		Storm Sash/Insulated Yes/avg		Car Storage [ ] None	
Effective Age (Yrs) 15 years		[ ] Dampness [ ] Settlement		Screens Yes/avg		[X] Driveway # of Cars 2	
Attic [ ] None		Heating [X] FWA [ ] HWBB [ ] Radiant		Amenities [ ] WoodStove(s) #		Driveway Surface Concrete	
[ ] Drop Stair [ ] Stairs		[ ] Other Fuel Gas		[ ] Fireplace(s) # [ ] Fence		[ ] Garage # of Cars	
[ ] Floor [X] Scuttle		Cooling [ ] Central Air Conditioning		[X] Patio/Deck Conc. [X] Porch OP		[ ] Carport # of Cars	
[ ] Finished [ ] Heated		[ ] Individual [ ] Other		[ ] Pool [X] Other Shed		[ ] Att. [ ] Det. [ ] Built-in	
Appliances [ ] Refrigerator [ ] Range/Oven		[ ] Dishwasher [ ] Disposal [ ] Microwave		[ ] Washer/Dryer [ ] Other (describe)			

Finished area above grade contains: 6 Rooms 3 Bedrooms 1 Bath(s) 1,344 Square Feet of Gross Living Area Above Grade

Additional features (special energy efficient items, etc.). Decorative fireplaces and a shed are considered to be personal property and are not valued. Electric hot water tank, 100 amp electrical box.

Market Conditions Addendum

The Market Conditions Addendum is required to accompany the URAR form for all appraisals for use by Fannie Mae and Freddie Mac. The form is more formally known as Fannie Mae Form 1004MC and Freddie Mac Form 71. A reproduction of the form can be found in the Appendix of this text.

While the reporting format may exceed the level common in many residential appraisal assignments, the analysis required to develop the appraiser's opinions should not be entirely new. Correctly analyzing most of these factors is embedded in the appraiser's obligation in compliance with Standards Rule 1-3 of USPAP.

Guidelines for Using the Market Conditions Addendum

The Market Conditions Addendum form is intended to provide the lender with a clear and accurate understanding of the market trends and conditions prevalent in the subject neighborhood. The form provides the appraiser with a structured format to report the data and to more easily identify current market trends and conditions. The appraiser's conclusions are to be reported in the "Neighborhood" section of the appraisal report.

Fannie Mae and Freddie Mac recognize that all of the requested data elements for analysis are not equally available in all markets. In some markets, it may not be possible to retrieve the total number of comparable active listings from earlier periods. If this is the case, the appraiser must explain the attempt to obtain such information. Also, there may be markets in which the data is available in terms of an "average" as opposed to a "median." In this case, the appraiser needs to note that his analysis has been based on an "average" representation of the data. Regardless of whether all requested information is available, the appraiser must provide support for his conclusions regarding market trends and conditions.

Inventory Analysis Section

The Inventory Analysis section assists the appraiser in analyzing important supply and demand factors in order to reach a conclusion regarding housing trends and market conditions. When completing this section, the appraiser must **include the comparable data that reflects the total pool of comparable properties from which a buyer may select a property in order to analyze the sales activity and the local housing supply**. One of the tools used to monitor these trends is the absorption rate. The **absorption rate** is *the rate at which properties for sale have been or can be sold (marketed) within a given area*. To determine the absorption rate, the appraiser divides the total number of settled sales by the timeframe being analyzed. The months of housing supply is based on the total listings for the applicable period divided by the absorption rate.

Inventory Analysis	Prior 7–12 Months	Prior 4–6 Months	Current – 3 Months	Overall Trend		
Total # of Comparable Sales (Settled)				☐ Increasing	☐ Stable	☐ Declining
Absorption Rate (Total Sales/Months)				☐ Increasing	☐ Stable	☐ Declining
Total # of Comparable Active Listings				☐ Declining	☐ Stable	☐ Increasing
Months of Housing Supply (Total Listings/Ab.Rate)				☐ Declining	☐ Stable	☐ Increasing

For Example

Step 1: Calculate the absorption rate. If there were 60 sales during a six-month period (e.g., "Prior 7 – 12 Months" column), the absorption rate is 10 sales per month (60 ÷ 6).

Step 2: Calculate the months of housing supply. If there are 240 active listings, there is a 24-month supply of homes on the market (240 active sales ÷ 10 sales per month). This may support the appraiser's conclusion that there is an over-supply of homes on the market. Anomalies in the data, such as seasonal markets, new construction, or other factors, must be addressed in the form.

Median Sale & List Price, DOM, List/Sale Ratio Section

The appraiser must **analyze additional trends, including the changes in median prices and days on the market (DOM) for both sales and listings, as well as a change in list-to-sales price ratios.**

Median Sale & List Price, DOM, Sale/List %	Prior 7–12 Months	Prior 4–6 Months	Current – 3 Months	Overall Trend		
Median Comparable Sale Price				☐ Increasing	☐ Stable	☐ Declining
Median Comparable Sales Days on Market				☐ Declining	☐ Stable	☐ Increasing
Median Comparable List Price				☐ Increasing	☐ Stable	☐ Declining
Median Comparable Listings Days on Market				☐ Declining	☐ Stable	☐ Increasing
Median Sale Price as % of List Price				☐ Increasing	☐ Stable	☐ Declining
Seller-(developer, builder, etc.) paid financial assistance prevalent? ☐ Yes ☐ No				☐ Declining	☐ Stable	☐ Increasing

For Example

If the median comparable sale prices are $300,000, $295,000, and $305,000 for their respective time periods, the overall trend for the prior 12 months is relatively "stable."

Overall Trend Section

The Overall Trend section is designed to reflect potential positive trends, neutral trends, or negative trends in inventory, median sale and list price, days on market, list-to- sale price ratio, and seller concessions.

For Example

An increase in the absorption rate is generally viewed as a positive trend, whereas a decrease in the absorption rate may be viewed as a negative trend. Furthermore, a decrease in the number of days on the market, either sales or listings, more than likely represents an overall positive trend.

Seller Concessions

The Market Conditions Addendum also provides a section for comments on the prevalence of seller concessions and the trend in seller concessions for the past 12 months. The change in seller concessions within the market provides the lender with additional insight into current market conditions. The appraiser should **consider and report on seller-paid (or third-party) costs.**

Explain in detail the seller concessions trends for the past 12 months (e.g., seller contributions increased from 3% to 5%, increasing use of buydowns, closing costs, condo fees, options, etc.).

For Example

These items include, but are not limited to, mortgage payments, points and fees, and in condominium or cooperative projects, items such as homeowners' association fees and guaranteed rental programs.

◇ **Important:** Seller concessions must be carefully analyzed by the appraiser, since excessive concessions often lead to inflated property values.

Foreclosure Sales and Summary/Analysis of Data

The **presence and extent of foreclosure/REO sales are worthy of comment when analyzing market data and must be reported on the form.** The form also allows for the appraiser to **summarize the data and provide other data analysis or additional information**, such as analysis of pending sales, which over time can show a market trend.

&ANALYSIS	
Are foreclosure sales (REO sales) a factor in the market? ☐ Yes ☐ No If yes, explain (including the trends in listings and sales of foreclosed properties).	
Cite data sources for above information.	
Summarize the above information as support for your conclusions in the Neighborhood section of the appraisal report form. If you used any additional information, such as an analysis of pending sales and/or expired and withdrawn listings, to formulate your conclusions, provide both an explanation and support for your conclusions.	

Summary

1. At the direction of the Federal Housing Finance Agency, Fannie Mae and Freddie Mac have developed the Uniform Appraisal Dataset (UAD). According to Fannie Mae, the Uniform Appraisal Dataset defines all fields required for an appraisal submission for specific appraisal forms and standardizes definitions and responses for a key subset of fields to enhance data quality and promote consistency. The purpose of UAD is to improve the quality and consistency of appraisal data on loans delivered to Fannie Mae and Freddie Mac.

2. The UAD is a component of the Uniform Mortgage Data Program (UMDP). The purpose of the UMDP is for Fannie Mae and Freddie Mac to combine their efforts to implement uniform appraisal and other loan delivery data standards, including a joint appraisal data delivery system for single-family loans they purchase.

3. The Uniform Collateral Data Portal (UCDP) collects and submits electronic appraisal data via a web application. The Uniform Loan Delivery Dataset (ULDD) leverages the industry-recognized MISMO® (Mortgage Industry Standards Maintenance Organization) standard which is a loan delivery dataset. MISMO is the leading technology standards development body for residential and commercial real estate finance industries. Its mission is to benefit industry participants and consumers of mortgage and investment products.

4. The UAD defines the required fields only for appraisal submission to Fannie Mae and Freddie Mac on four specific appraisal forms: The URAR (Uniform Residential Appraisal Report) for single-family residential property when there is an interior and exterior inspection, the 2055 single-family exterior inspection only form, and forms for condominiums using either an interior and exterior inspection, or an exterior inspection only.

5. The URAR report form is considered an *Appraisal Report* designed to report an appraisal of a one-unit property or a one-unit property with an accessory unit; including a unit in a planned unit development (PUD), based on an *interior and exterior inspection* of the subject property. This report form is not designed to report an appraisal of a manufactured home or a unit in a condominium or cooperative project.

6. The Market Conditions Addendum is required to accompany the URAR form for all appraisals for use by Fannie Mae and Freddie Mac (and others). The form is more formally known as Fannie Mae Form 1004MC and Freddie Mac Form 71, and is intended to provide the lender with a clear and accurate understanding of the market trends and conditions prevalent in the subject neighborhood.

Chapter Quiz

1. *The Uniform Residential Appraisal Report form*

    a. can be considered a general purpose reporting form.

    b. is limited to the use for loans through Fannie Mae.

    c. may be used for condominiums and manufactured homes.

    d. was developed in collaboration of Fannie Mae and Freddie Mac.

2. *Which of these is required to accompany the URAR for Fannie Mae, Freddie Mac, and some other lending industry participants?*

    a. copy of the appraiser's license certification

    b. interior photos of the comparable properties

    c. Market Conditions Addendum

    d. zoning map of the subject neighborhood

3. *Which is most important to appraisers in how they report appraisals for Fannie Mae and Freddie Mac?*

    a. Mortgage Industry Standards Maintenance Organization

    b. Uniform Appraisal Dataset

    c. Uniform Collateral Data Portal

    d. Uniform Loan Delivery Dataset

4. *Which type of property would NOT require application of the UAD criteria for reporting?*

    a. condominium

    b. duplex

    c. one-unit property with an accessory unit

    d. single-family dwelling

5. *Which occurrence could cause the appraiser's certification in the URAR to be expanded with additional certification statements in compliance with USPAP?*

    a. change in scope of work from that originally planned

    b. lack of geographic competency

    c. prior services performed by the appraiser in past three years

    d. specific techniques for adjusting comparable sales

6. *Which address element is in compliance with the United States Postal Service standards?*

    a. Minneapolis, Minn.

    b. Minneapolis, Minnesota

    c. Minneapolis, MN

    d. Minneapolis, Mnsta.

7. *Which is an acceptable method for reporting the prior listing of the subject property in compliance with UAD requirements?*

    a. DOM150;Subject property was listed on 07/15/2011 for $100,000. The data source is SMLS#1224

    b. 150 DOM; SMLS #1224 - The subject property was listed for $100,000 on 7/15/2011

    c. Offered at $100,000 for 150 days per SMLS #1224

    d. The subject property was listed on 07/15/2011 for $100,000;150 DOM; SMLS #1224

8. *If the subject site is 110' x 225', how should the site area be reported in compliance with UAD requirements?*

    a. 24750 sf

    b. 24,750 square feet

    c. 0.5682 ac

    d. 0.57

9. *A site being reported in compliance with the UAD that is 300' x 475' should be stated as having what area in the site section of the URAR report form?*

    a. 142500 sf

    b. 142,500 sf

    c. 3.27 ac

    d. 3.2714 ac

10. *If the view from a property is market preferred and looks out upon a park and woods, how would the view information be formatted in compliance of the UAD?*

    a. A;Wds;Prk

    b. B;Woods;Prk

    c. Good;Woods;Park

    d. P;Woods;Park

11. *If a dwelling has two full baths, two half baths and a room with only a toilet, how is the bathroom count reported in compliance with the UAD?*

    a. 02/50x2/25

    b. 2.25

    c. 2 ½ + ¼

    d. 2.2

12. *What condition rating is entered that represents this definition?*

    "The improvements are well maintained and feature limited physical depreciation due to normal wear and tear. Some components, but not every major building component, may be updated or recently rehabilitated. The structure has been well maintained."

    a.   C1
    b.   C2
    c.   C3
    d.   C4

13. *To satisfy UAD requirements, an appraiser must indicate if there has been any material work done to the kitchen or baths within how many years prior?*

    a.   5
    b.   10
    c.   15
    d.   20

14. *Which is NOT a specific required photo exhibit that always must accompany the URAR form?*

    a.   bathrooms
    b.   electrical service
    c.   kitchen
    d.   physical deterioration

15. *For the Market Conditions Addendum form, if the absorption rate is 12 sales per month and there is currently an inventory of 60 active listings, how many months supply is present in the market?*

    a.   3
    b.   5
    c.   7
    d.   9

Appendix A: Case Studies

Appendix Case Study 1

Note: Race and the racial composition of the neighborhood are not appraisal factors.										
Neighborhood Characteristics			**One-Unit Housing Trends**				**One-Unit Housing**		**Present Land Use %**	
Location ☐ Urban	☐ Suburban	☐ Rural	Property Values ☐ Increasing	☐ Stable	☐ Declining		PRICE $ (000)	AGE (yrs)	One-Unit	%
Built-Up ☐ Over 75%	☐ 25-75%	☐ Under 25%	Demand/Supply ☐ Shortage	☐ In Balance	☐ Over Supply		$ (000)	(yrs)	2-4 Unit	%
Growth ☐ Rapid	☐ Stable	☐ Slow	Marketing Time ☐ Under 3 mths	☐ 3-6 mths	☐ Over 6 mths		Low		Multi-Family	%
Neighborhood Boundaries							High		Commercial	%
							Pred.		Other	%
Neighborhood Description										
Market Conditions (including support for the above conclusions)										

The subject property is located in the Stearns Subdivision in Washington Township. Stearns Subdivision is bounded by County Road 8 to the north, Washington Road to the east, Clearview Road to the south, and National Highway to the west. The development, which was introduced to the market approximately two years ago, has a total of 28 residential building lots. To date, six lots have sold. However, only four houses have been built in the subdivision. The developer has reduced the prices of all lots by 20% since their initial offering to spur activity, although only one lot has sold since the reduction three months ago. The existing houses range in value from $150,000 to $220,000 for the newest (one year old) house, with most valued at the lower part of that range. One of the lower-end existing homes is currently on the market for $150,000. It has between listed for approximately nine months, but is among 27 competing listings. The multiple listing service indicates that six similar properties have sold in the past year.

The subdivision is suburban to the City of Fairwell, which is the county seat. Most employers are located in or just outside of Fairwell. The subject's school district, Washington-Fairwell Local Schools, is located about five miles away. Students are provided transportation by bus. Two major factories in Fairwell have recently reduced their workforce, and another factory is rumored to be in poor operating circumstances. Interest rates have risen recently with projected escalation probable.

Using the information from this scenario, complete the Neighborhood Data portion of the URAR form.

Appendix Case Study 2

Calculate the Gross Living Area of the following floor plan sketch to be communicated in the appraisal report.

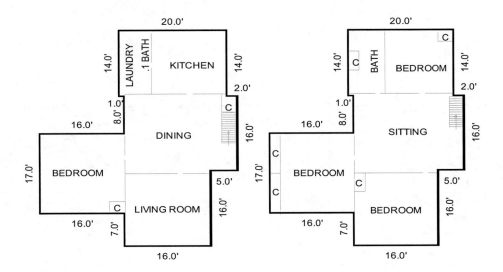

_____

_____

_____

_____

_____

_____

_____

_____

_____

Appendix Case Study 3

A three-unit residential dwelling located on a single lot is being appraised. The subject is located in an area designated as R-4, Medium Density Residential by the local zoning ordinances. The zoning designation allows for dwellings containing up to two units per lot. However, the use existed prior to zoning being imposed. The final value opinion is conditioned, using an extraordinary assumption regarding the continued permissibility of the use to zoning.

Using this information, write a narrative commentary regarding the zoning and the extraordinary assumption.

_____

_____

_____

_____

_____

_____

_____

_____

_____

_____

_____

_____

_____

_____

_____

_____

Appendix Case Study 4

A single-family dwelling that has been used for many years as a rental property is being appraised. The property owner has revealed that the subject currently rents for $300 per month. The rent has not been raised for about 8 years, primarily due to the tenant having rented the house for over 12 years and being a low maintenance tenant. Market research of several very similar rental properties indicates that market rent for such a property currently would be $450 per month.

Using this information, write a narrative commentary regarding the current lease terms as it relates to current market data. The comment should clarify and support the use of the higher market rent in developing a value indication by the Income Approach.

Appendix B: Sample Forms

Uniform Residential Appraisal Report

File #

The purpose of this summary appraisal report is to provide the lender/client with an accurate, and adequately supported, opinion of the market value of the subject property.

SUBJECT

Property Address		City		State	Zip Code

Borrower   Owner of Public Record   County

Legal Description

Assessor's Parcel #   Tax Year   R.E. Taxes $

Neighborhood Name   Map Reference   Census Tract

Occupant ☐ Owner ☐ Tenant ☐ Vacant   Special Assessments $ ☐ PUD   HOA $ ☐ per year ☐ per month

Property Rights Appraised ☐ Fee Simple ☐ Leasehold ☐ Other (describe)

Assignment Type ☐ Purchase Transaction ☐ Refinance Transaction ☐ Other (describe)

Lender/Client   Address

Is the subject property currently offered for sale or has it been offered for sale in the twelve months prior to the effective date of this appraisal? ☐ Yes ☐ No

Report data source(s) used, offering price(s), and date(s).

CONTRACT

I ☐ did ☐ did not analyze the contract for sale for the subject purchase transaction. Explain the results of the analysis of the contract for sale or why the analysis was not performed.

Contract Price $ Date of Contract   Is the property seller the owner of public record? ☐ Yes ☐ No   Data Source(s)

Is there any financial assistance (loan charges, sale concessions, gift or downpayment assistance, etc.) to be paid by any party on behalf of the borrower? ☐ Yes ☐ No
If Yes, report the total dollar amount and describe the items to be paid.

NEIGHBORHOOD

Note: Race and the racial composition of the neighborhood are not appraisal factors.

Neighborhood Characteristics			One-Unit Housing Trends				One-Unit Housing		Present Land Use %	
Location ☐ Urban	☐ Suburban	☐ Rural	Property Values ☐ Increasing	☐ Stable	☐ Declining		PRICE	AGE	One-Unit	%
Built-Up ☐ Over 75%	☐ 25–75%	☐ Under 25%	Demand/Supply ☐ Shortage	☐ In Balance	☐ Over Supply		$ (000)	(yrs)	2-4 Unit	%
Growth ☐ Rapid	☐ Stable	☐ Slow	Marketing Time ☐ Under 3 mths	☐ 3–6 mths	☐ Over 6 mths		Low		Multi-Family	%
Neighborhood Boundaries							High		Commercial	%
							Pred.		Other	%

Neighborhood Description

Market Conditions (including support for the above conclusions)

SITE

Dimensions   Area   Shape   View

Specific Zoning Classification   Zoning Description

Zoning Compliance ☐ Legal ☐ Legal Nonconforming (Grandfathered Use) ☐ No Zoning ☐ Illegal (describe)

Is the highest and best use of the subject property as improved (or as proposed per plans and specifications) the present use? ☐ Yes ☐ No If No, describe

Utilities	Public	Other (describe)		Public	Other (describe)	Off-site Improvements—Type	Public	Private
Electricity	☐	☐	Water	☐	☐	Street	☐	☐
Gas	☐	☐	Sanitary Sewer	☐	☐	Alley	☐	☐

FEMA Special Flood Hazard Area ☐ Yes ☐ No FEMA Flood Zone   FEMA Map #   FEMA Map Date

Are the utilities and off-site improvements typical for the market area? ☐ Yes ☐ No If No, describe

Are there any adverse site conditions or external factors (easements, encroachments, environmental conditions, land uses, etc.)? ☐ Yes ☐ No If Yes, describe

IMPROVEMENTS

General Description		Foundation		Exterior Description	materials/condition	Interior	materials/condition
Units ☐ One ☐ One with Accessory Unit		☐ Concrete Slab ☐ Crawl Space		Foundation Walls		Floors	
# of Stories		☐ Full Basement ☐ Partial Basement		Exterior Walls		Walls	
Type ☐ Det. ☐ Att. ☐ S-Det./End Unit		Basement Area	sq. ft.	Roof Surface		Trim/Finish	
☐ Existing ☐ Proposed ☐ Under Const.		Basement Finish	%	Gutters & Downspouts		Bath Floor	
Design (Style)		☐ Outside Entry/Exit ☐ Sump Pump		Window Type		Bath Wainscot	
Year Built		Evidence of ☐ Infestation		Storm Sash/Insulated		Car Storage ☐ None	
Effective Age (Yrs)		☐ Dampness ☐ Settlement		Screens		☐ Driveway # of Cars	
Attic ☐ None		Heating ☐ FWA ☐ HWBB ☐ Radiant		Amenities ☐ Woodstove(s) #		Driveway Surface	
☐ Drop Stair ☐ Stairs		☐ Other	Fuel	☐ Fireplace(s) # ☐ Fence		☐ Garage # of Cars	
☐ Floor ☐ Scuttle		Cooling ☐ Central Air Conditioning		☐ Patio/Deck ☐ Porch		☐ Carport # of Cars	
☐ Finished ☐ Heated		☐ Individual ☐ Other		☐ Pool ☐ Other		☐ Att. ☐ Det. ☐ Built-in	

Appliances ☐ Refrigerator ☐ Range/Oven ☐ Dishwasher ☐ Disposal ☐ Microwave ☐ Washer/Dryer ☐ Other (describe)

Finished area **above** grade contains: Rooms   Bedrooms   Bath(s)   Square Feet of Gross Living Area Above Grade

Additional features (special energy efficient items, etc.)

Describe the condition of the property (including needed repairs, deterioration, renovations, remodeling, etc.).

Are there any physical deficiencies or adverse conditions that affect the livability, soundness, or structural integrity of the property? ☐ Yes ☐ No If Yes, describe

Does the property generally conform to the neighborhood (functional utility, style, condition, use, construction, etc.)? ☐ Yes ☐ No If No, describe

Uniform Residential Appraisal Report

File # _____

| There are | _____ comparable properties currently offered for sale in the subject neighborhood ranging in price from $ _____ | | to $ _____ | . |
| There are | _____ comparable sales in the subject neighborhood within the past twelve months ranging in sale price from $ _____ | | to $ _____ | . |

FEATURE	SUBJECT	COMPARABLE SALE # 1		COMPARABLE SALE # 2		COMPARABLE SALE # 3	
Address							
Proximity to Subject							
Sale Price	$		$		$		$
Sale Price/Gross Liv. Area	$ sq. ft.	$ sq. ft.		$ sq. ft.		$ sq. ft.	
Data Source(s)							
Verification Source(s)							
VALUE ADJUSTMENTS	DESCRIPTION	DESCRIPTION	+(-) $ Adjustment	DESCRIPTION	+(-) $ Adjustment	DESCRIPTION	+(-) $ Adjustment
Sale or Financing Concessions							
Date of Sale/Time							
Location							
Leasehold/Fee Simple							
Site							
View							
Design (Style)							
Quality of Construction							
Actual Age							
Condition							
Above Grade	Total Bdrms. Baths	Total Bdrms. Baths		Total Bdrms. Baths		Total Bdrms. Baths	
Room Count							
Gross Living Area	sq. ft.	sq. ft.		sq. ft.		sq. ft.	
Basement & Finished Rooms Below Grade							
Functional Utility							
Heating/Cooling							
Energy Efficient Items							
Garage/Carport							
Porch/Patio/Deck							
Net Adjustment (Total)		☐ + ☐ -	$	☐ + ☐ -	$	☐ + ☐ -	$
Adjusted Sale Price of Comparables		Net Adj. % Gross Adj. %	$	Net Adj. % Gross Adj. %	$	Net Adj. % Gross Adj. %	$

SALES COMPARISON APPROACH

I ☐ did ☐ did not research the sale or transfer history of the subject property and comparable sales. If not, explain

My research ☐ did ☐ did not reveal any prior sales or transfers of the subject property for the three years prior to the effective date of this appraisal.
Data source(s)

My research ☐ did ☐ did not reveal any prior sales or transfers of the comparable sales for the year prior to the date of sale of the comparable sale.
Data source(s)

Report the results of the research and analysis of the prior sale or transfer history of the subject property and comparable sales (report additional prior sales on page 3).

ITEM	SUBJECT	COMPARABLE SALE # 1	COMPARABLE SALE # 2	COMPARABLE SALE # 3
Date of Prior Sale/Transfer				
Price of Prior Sale/Transfer				
Data Source(s)				
Effective Date of Data Source(s)				

Analysis of prior sale or transfer history of the subject property and comparable sales

Summary of Sales Comparison Approach

Indicated Value by Sales Comparison Approach $ _____

RECONCILIATION

Indicated Value by: Sales Comparison Approach $ _____   Cost Approach (if developed) $ _____   Income Approach (if developed) $ _____

This appraisal is made ☐ "as is", ☐ subject to completion per plans and specifications on the basis of a hypothetical condition that the improvements have been completed, ☐ subject to the following repairs or alterations on the basis of a hypothetical condition that the repairs or alterations have been completed, or ☐ subject to the following required inspection based on the extraordinary assumption that the condition or deficiency does not require alteration or repair:

Based on a complete visual inspection of the interior and exterior areas of the subject property, defined scope of work, statement of assumptions and limiting conditions, and appraiser's certification, my (our) opinion of the market value, as defined, of the real property that is the subject of this report is $ _____ , as of _____ , which is the date of inspection and the effective date of this appraisal.

97

Uniform Residential Appraisal Report

File #

ADDITIONAL COMMENTS

COST APPROACH TO VALUE (not required by Fannie Mae)

Provide adequate information for the lender/client to replicate the below cost figures and calculations.

Support for the opinion of site value (summary of comparable land sales or other methods for estimating site value)

ESTIMATED ☐ REPRODUCTION OR ☐ REPLACEMENT COST NEW	OPINION OF SITE VALUE .... = $
Source of cost data	Dwelling Sq. Ft. @ $ .... =$
Quality rating from cost service Effective date of cost data	Sq. Ft. @ $ .... =$
Comments on Cost Approach (gross living area calculations, depreciation, etc.)	Garage/Carport Sq. Ft. @ $ .... =$
	Total Estimate of Cost-New .... = $
	Less Physical Functional External
	Depreciation =$( )
	Depreciated Cost of Improvements.. =$
	"As-is" Value of Site Improvements... =$
Estimated Remaining Economic Life (HUD and VA only) Years	Indicated Value By Cost Approach .... =$

INCOME APPROACH TO VALUE (not required by Fannie Mae)

Estimated Monthly Market Rent $ X Gross Rent Multiplier = $ Indicated Value by Income Approach

Summary of Income Approach (including support for market rent and GRM)

PROJECT INFORMATION FOR PUDs (if applicable)

Is the developer/builder in control of the Homeowners' Association (HOA)? ☐ Yes ☐ No Unit type(s) ☐ Detached ☐ Attached

Provide the following information for PUDs ONLY if the developer/builder is in control of the HOA and the subject property is an attached dwelling unit.

Legal name of project

Total number of phases Total number of units Total number of units sold

Total number of units rented Total number of units for sale Data source(s)

Was the project created by the conversion of an existing building(s) into a PUD? ☐ Yes ☐ No If Yes, date of conversion

Does the project contain any multi-dwelling units? ☐ Yes ☐ No Data source(s)

Are the units, common elements, and recreation facilities complete? ☐ Yes ☐ No If No, describe the status of completion.

Are the common elements leased to or by the Homeowners' Association? ☐ Yes ☐ No If Yes, describe the rental terms and options.

Describe common elements and recreational facilities

Uniform Residential Appraisal Report

File #

This report form is designed to report an appraisal of a one-unit property or a one-unit property with an accessory unit; including a unit in a planned unit development (PUD). This report form is not designed to report an appraisal of a manufactured home or a unit in a condominium or cooperative project.

This appraisal report is subject to the following scope of work, intended use, intended user, definition of market value, statement of assumptions and limiting conditions, and certifications. Modifications, additions, or deletions to the intended use, intended user, definition of market value, or assumptions and limiting conditions are not permitted. The appraiser may expand the scope of work to include any additional research or analysis necessary based on the complexity of this appraisal assignment. Modifications or deletions to the certifications are also not permitted. However, additional certifications that do not constitute material alterations to this appraisal report, such as those required by law or those related to the appraiser's continuing education or membership in an appraisal organization, are permitted.

SCOPE OF WORK: The scope of work for this appraisal is defined by the complexity of this appraisal assignment and the reporting requirements of this appraisal report form, including the following definition of market value, statement of assumptions and limiting conditions, and certifications. The appraiser must, at a minimum: (1) perform a complete visual inspection of the interior and exterior areas of the subject property, (2) inspect the neighborhood, (3) inspect each of the comparable sales from at least the street, (4) research, verify, and analyze data from reliable public and/or private sources, and (5) report his or her analysis, opinions, and conclusions in this appraisal report.

INTENDED USE: The intended use of this appraisal report is for the lender/client to evaluate the property that is the subject of this appraisal for a mortgage finance transaction.

INTENDED USER: The intended user of this appraisal report is the lender/client.

DEFINITION OF MARKET VALUE: The most probable price which a property should bring in a competitive and open market under all conditions requisite to a fair sale, the buyer and seller, each acting prudently, knowledgeably and assuming the price is not affected by undue stimulus. Implicit in this definition is the consummation of a sale as of a specified date and the passing of title from seller to buyer under conditions whereby: (1) buyer and seller are typically motivated; (2) both parties are well informed or well advised, and each acting in what he or she considers his or her own best interest; (3) a reasonable time is allowed for exposure in the open market; (4) payment is made in terms of cash in U. S. dollars or in terms of financial arrangements comparable thereto; and (5) the price represents the normal consideration for the property sold unaffected by special or creative financing or sales concessions* granted by anyone associated with the sale.

*Adjustments to the comparables must be made for special or creative financing or sales concessions. No adjustments are necessary for those costs which are normally paid by sellers as a result of tradition or law in a market area; these costs are readily identifiable since the seller pays these costs in virtually all sales transactions. Special or creative financing adjustments can be made to the comparable property by comparisons to financing terms offered by a third party institutional lender that is not already involved in the property or transaction. Any adjustment should not be calculated on a mechanical dollar for dollar cost of the financing or concession but the dollar amount of any adjustment should approximate the market's reaction to the financing or concessions based on the appraiser's judgment.

STATEMENT OF ASSUMPTIONS AND LIMITING CONDITIONS: The appraiser's certification in this report is subject to the following assumptions and limiting conditions:

1. The appraiser will not be responsible for matters of a legal nature that affect either the property being appraised or the title to it, except for information that he or she became aware of during the research involved in performing this appraisal. The appraiser assumes that the title is good and marketable and will not render any opinions about the title.

2. The appraiser has provided a sketch in this appraisal report to show the approximate dimensions of the improvements. The sketch is included only to assist the reader in visualizing the property and understanding the appraiser's determination of its size.

3. The appraiser has examined the available flood maps that are provided by the Federal Emergency Management Agency (or other data sources) and has noted in this appraisal report whether any portion of the subject site is located in an identified Special Flood Hazard Area. Because the appraiser is not a surveyor, he or she makes no guarantees, express or implied, regarding this determination.

4. The appraiser will not give testimony or appear in court because he or she made an appraisal of the property in question, unless specific arrangements to do so have been made beforehand, or as otherwise required by law.

5. The appraiser has noted in this appraisal report any adverse conditions (such as needed repairs, deterioration, the presence of hazardous wastes, toxic substances, etc.) observed during the inspection of the subject property or that he or she became aware of during the research involved in performing this appraisal. Unless otherwise stated in this appraisal report, the appraiser has no knowledge of any hidden or unapparent physical deficiencies or adverse conditions of the property (such as, but not limited to, needed repairs, deterioration, the presence of hazardous wastes, toxic substances, adverse environmental conditions, etc.) that would make the property less valuable, and has assumed that there are no such conditions and makes no guarantees or warranties, express or implied. The appraiser will not be responsible for any such conditions that do exist or for any engineering or testing that might be required to discover whether such conditions exist. Because the appraiser is not an expert in the field of environmental hazards, this appraisal report must not be considered as an environmental assessment of the property.

6. The appraiser has based his or her appraisal report and valuation conclusion for an appraisal that is subject to satisfactory completion, repairs, or alterations on the assumption that the completion, repairs, or alterations of the subject property will be performed in a professional manner.

Uniform Residential Appraisal Report

File #

APPRAISER'S CERTIFICATION: The Appraiser certifies and agrees that:

1. I have, at a minimum, developed and reported this appraisal in accordance with the scope of work requirements stated in this appraisal report.

2. I performed a complete visual inspection of the interior and exterior areas of the subject property. I reported the condition of the improvements in factual, specific terms. I identified and reported the physical deficiencies that could affect the livability, soundness, or structural integrity of the property.

3. I performed this appraisal in accordance with the requirements of the Uniform Standards of Professional Appraisal Practice that were adopted and promulgated by the Appraisal Standards Board of The Appraisal Foundation and that were in place at the time this appraisal report was prepared.

4. I developed my opinion of the market value of the real property that is the subject of this report based on the sales comparison approach to value. I have adequate comparable market data to develop a reliable sales comparison approach for this appraisal assignment. I further certify that I considered the cost and income approaches to value but did not develop them, unless otherwise indicated in this report.

5. I researched, verified, analyzed, and reported on any current agreement for sale for the subject property, any offering for sale of the subject property in the twelve months prior to the effective date of this appraisal, and the prior sales of the subject property for a minimum of three years prior to the effective date of this appraisal, unless otherwise indicated in this report.

6. I researched, verified, analyzed, and reported on the prior sales of the comparable sales for a minimum of one year prior to the date of sale of the comparable sale, unless otherwise indicated in this report.

7. I selected and used comparable sales that are locationally, physically, and functionally the most similar to the subject property.

8. I have not used comparable sales that were the result of combining a land sale with the contract purchase price of a home that has been built or will be built on the land.

9. I have reported adjustments to the comparable sales that reflect the market's reaction to the differences between the subject property and the comparable sales.

10. I verified, from a disinterested source, all information in this report that was provided by parties who have a financial interest in the sale or financing of the subject property.

11. I have knowledge and experience in appraising this type of property in this market area.

12. I am aware of, and have access to, the necessary and appropriate public and private data sources, such as multiple listing services, tax assessment records, public land records and other such data sources for the area in which the property is located.

13. I obtained the information, estimates, and opinions furnished by other parties and expressed in this appraisal report from reliable sources that I believe to be true and correct.

14. I have taken into consideration the factors that have an impact on value with respect to the subject neighborhood, subject property, and the proximity of the subject property to adverse influences in the development of my opinion of market value. I have noted in this appraisal report any adverse conditions (such as, but not limited to, needed repairs, deterioration, the presence of hazardous wastes, toxic substances, adverse environmental conditions, etc.) observed during the inspection of the subject property or that I became aware of during the research involved in performing this appraisal. I have considered these adverse conditions in my analysis of the property value, and have reported on the effect of the conditions on the value and marketability of the subject property.

15. I have not knowingly withheld any significant information from this appraisal report and, to the best of my knowledge, all statements and information in this appraisal report are true and correct.

16. I stated in this appraisal report my own personal, unbiased, and professional analysis, opinions, and conclusions, which are subject only to the assumptions and limiting conditions in this appraisal report.

17. I have no present or prospective interest in the property that is the subject of this report, and I have no present or prospective personal interest or bias with respect to the participants in the transaction. I did not base, either partially or completely, my analysis and/or opinion of market value in this appraisal report on the race, color, religion, sex, age, marital status, handicap, familial status, or national origin of either the prospective owners or occupants of the subject property or of the present owners or occupants of the properties in the vicinity of the subject property or on any other basis prohibited by law.

18. My employment and/or compensation for performing this appraisal or any future or anticipated appraisals was not conditioned on any agreement or understanding, written or otherwise, that I would report (or present analysis supporting) a predetermined specific value, a predetermined minimum value, a range or direction in value, a value that favors the cause of any party, or the attainment of a specific result or occurrence of a specific subsequent event (such as approval of a pending mortgage loan application).

19. I personally prepared all conclusions and opinions about the real estate that were set forth in this appraisal report. If I relied on significant real property appraisal assistance from any individual or individuals in the performance of this appraisal or the preparation of this appraisal report, I have named such individual(s) and disclosed the specific tasks performed in this appraisal report. I certify that any individual so named is qualified to perform the tasks. I have not authorized anyone to make a change to any item in this appraisal report; therefore, any change made to this appraisal is unauthorized and I will take no responsibility for it.

20. I identified the lender/client in this appraisal report who is the individual, organization, or agent for the organization that ordered and will receive this appraisal report.

100

Uniform Residential Appraisal Report

File #

21. The lender/client may disclose or distribute this appraisal report to: the borrower; another lender at the request of the borrower; the mortgagee or its successors and assigns; mortgage insurers; government sponsored enterprises; other secondary market participants; data collection or reporting services; professional appraisal organizations; any department, agency, or instrumentality of the United States; and any state, the District of Columbia, or other jurisdictions; without having to obtain the appraiser's or supervisory appraiser's (if applicable) consent. Such consent must be obtained before this appraisal report may be disclosed or distributed to any other party (including, but not limited to, the public through advertising, public relations, news, sales, or other media).

22. I am aware that any disclosure or distribution of this appraisal report by me or the lender/client may be subject to certain laws and regulations. Further, I am also subject to the provisions of the Uniform Standards of Professional Appraisal Practice that pertain to disclosure or distribution by me.

23. The borrower, another lender at the request of the borrower, the mortgagee or its successors and assigns, mortgage insurers, government sponsored enterprises, and other secondary market participants may rely on this appraisal report as part of any mortgage finance transaction that involves any one or more of these parties.

24. If this appraisal report was transmitted as an "electronic record" containing my "electronic signature," as those terms are defined in applicable federal and/or state laws (excluding audio and video recordings), or a facsimile transmission of this appraisal report containing a copy or representation of my signature, the appraisal report shall be as effective, enforceable and valid as if a paper version of this appraisal report were delivered containing my original hand written signature.

25. Any intentional or negligent misrepresentation(s) contained in this appraisal report may result in civil liability and/or criminal penalties including, but not limited to, fine or imprisonment or both under the provisions of Title 18, United States Code, Section 1001, et seq., or similar state laws.

SUPERVISORY APPRAISER'S CERTIFICATION: The Supervisory Appraiser certifies and agrees that:

1. I directly supervised the appraiser for this appraisal assignment, have read the appraisal report, and agree with the appraiser's analysis, opinions, statements, conclusions, and the appraiser's certification.

2. I accept full responsibility for the contents of this appraisal report including, but not limited to, the appraiser's analysis, opinions, statements, conclusions, and the appraiser's certification.

3. The appraiser identified in this appraisal report is either a sub-contractor or an employee of the supervisory appraiser (or the appraisal firm), is qualified to perform this appraisal, and is acceptable to perform this appraisal under the applicable state law.

4. This appraisal report complies with the Uniform Standards of Professional Appraisal Practice that were adopted and promulgated by the Appraisal Standards Board of The Appraisal Foundation and that were in place at the time this appraisal report was prepared.

5. If this appraisal report was transmitted as an "electronic record" containing my "electronic signature," as those terms are defined in applicable federal and/or state laws (excluding audio and video recordings), or a facsimile transmission of this appraisal report containing a copy or representation of my signature, the appraisal report shall be as effective, enforceable and valid as if a paper version of this appraisal report were delivered containing my original hand written signature.

APPRAISER

Signature_____

Name _____

Company Name _____

Company Address_____

_____

Telephone Number _____

Email Address_____

Date of Signature and Report_____

Effective Date of Appraisal _____

State Certification #_____

or State License # _____

or Other (describe) _____ State # _____

State _____

Expiration Date of Certification or License _____

ADDRESS OF PROPERTY APPRAISED

_____

_____

APPRAISED VALUE OF SUBJECT PROPERTY $ _____

LENDER/CLIENT

Name _____

Company Name _____

Company Address_____

_____

Email Address_____

SUPERVISORY APPRAISER (ONLY IF REQUIRED)

Signature _____

Name_____

Company Name _____

Company Address_____

_____

Telephone Number _____

Email Address_____

Date of Signature _____

State Certification #_____

or State License # _____

State _____

Expiration Date of Certification or License _____

SUBJECT PROPERTY

☐ Did not inspect subject property

☐ Did inspect exterior of subject property from street

Date of Inspection _____

☐ Did inspect interior and exterior of subject property

Date of Inspection _____

COMPARABLE SALES

☐ Did not inspect exterior of comparable sales from street

☐ Did inspect exterior of comparable sales from street

Date of Inspection _____

101

Market Conditions Addendum to the Appraisal Report   File No.

The purpose of this addendum is to provide the lender/client with a clear and accurate understanding of the market trends and conditions prevalent in the subject neighborhood. This is a required addendum for all appraisal reports with an effective date on or after April 1, 2009.

Property Address		City		State	ZIP Code
Borrower					

Instructions: The appraiser must use the information required on this form as the basis for his/her conclusions, and must provide support for those conclusions, regarding housing trends and overall market conditions as reported in the Neighborhood section of the appraisal report form. The appraiser must fill in all the information to the extent it is available and reliable and must provide analysis as indicated below. If any required data is unavailable or is considered unreliable, the appraiser must provide an explanation. It is recognized that not all data sources will be able to provide data for the shaded areas below; if it is available, however, the appraiser must include the data in the analysis. If data sources provide the required information as an average instead of the median, the appraiser should report the available figure and identify it as an average. Sales and listings must be properties that compete with the subject property, determined by applying the criteria that would be used by a prospective buyer of the subject property. The appraiser must explain any anomalies in the data, such as seasonal markets, new construction, foreclosures, etc.

Inventory Analysis	Prior 7–12 Months	Prior 4–6 Months	Current – 3 Months	Overall Trend		
Total # of Comparable Sales (Settled)				☐ Increasing	☐ Stable	☐ Declining
Absorption Rate (Total Sales/Months)				☐ Increasing	☐ Stable	☐ Declining
Total # of Comparable Active Listings				☐ Declining	☐ Stable	☐ Increasing
Months of Housing Supply (Total Listings/Ab.Rate)				☐ Declining	☐ Stable	☐ Increasing
Median Sale & List Price, DOM, Sale/List %	Prior 7–12 Months	Prior 4–6 Months	Current – 3 Months	Overall Trend		
Median Comparable Sale Price				☐ Increasing	☐ Stable	☐ Declining
Median Comparable Sales Days on Market				☐ Declining	☐ Stable	☐ Increasing
Median Comparable List Price				☐ Increasing	☐ Stable	☐ Declining
Median Comparable Listings Days on Market				☐ Declining	☐ Stable	☐ Increasing
Median Sale Price as % of List Price				☐ Increasing	☐ Stable	☐ Declining
Seller-(developer, builder, etc.) paid financial assistance prevalent? ☐ Yes ☐ No				☐ Declining	☐ Stable	☐ Increasing

Explain in detail the seller concessions trends for the past 12 months (e.g., seller contributions increased from 3% to 5%, increasing use of buydowns, closing costs, condo fees, options, etc.).

Are foreclosure sales (REO sales) a factor in the market? ☐ Yes ☐ No If yes, explain (including the trends in listings and sales of foreclosed properties).

Cite data sources for above information.

Summarize the above information as support for your conclusions in the Neighborhood section of the appraisal report form. If you used any additional information, such as an analysis of pending sales and/or expired and withdrawn listings, to formulate your conclusions, provide both an explanation and support for your conclusions.

If the subject is a unit in a condominium or cooperative project , complete the following: Project Name:

Subject Project Data	Prior 7-12 Months	Prior 4-6 Months	Current – 3 Months	Overall Trend		
Total # of Comparable Sales (Settled)				☐ Increasing	☐ Stable	☐ Declining
Absorption Rate (Total Sales/Months)				☐ Increasing	☐ Stable	☐ Declining
Total # of Active Comparable Listings				☐ Declining	☐ Stable	☐ Increasing
Months of Unit Supply (Total Listings/Ab. Rate)				☐ Declining	☐ Stable	☐ Increasing

Are foreclosure sales (REO sales) a factor in the project? ☐ Yes ☐ No If yes, indicate the number of REO listings and explain the trends in listings and sales of foreclosed properties.

Summarize the above trends and address the impact on the subject unit and project.

Signature		Signature	
Appraiser Name		Supervisory Appraiser Name	
Company Name		Company Name	
Company Address		Company Address	
State License/Certification #	State	State License/Certification #	State
Email Address		Email Address	

Freddie Mac Form 71   March 2009   Page 1 of 1   Fannie Mae Form 1004MC   March 2009

Manufactured Home Appraisal Report

File #

The purpose of this summary appraisal report is to provide the lender/client with an accurate, and adequately supported, opinion of the market value of the subject property.

SUBJECT

Property Address		City	State	Zip Code
Borrower		Owner of Public Record	County	

Legal Description

Assessor's Parcel #		Tax Year	R.E. Taxes $
Neighborhood Name		Map Reference	Census Tract

Occupant ☐ Owner ☐ Tenant ☐ Vacant   Project Type (if applicable) ☐ PUD ☐ Condominium ☐ Cooperative ☐ Other (describe)

Special Assessments $ HOA $ ☐ per year ☐ per month

Property Rights Appraised ☐ Fee Simple ☐ Leasehold ☐ Other (describe)

Assignment Type ☐ Purchase Transaction ☐ Refinance Transaction ☐ Other (describe)

Lender/Client   Address

Is the subject property currently offered for sale or has it been offered for sale in the twelve months prior to the effective date of this appraisal? ☐ Yes ☐ No

Report data source(s) used, offering price(s), and date(s).

CONTRACT

Manufactured homes located in either a condominium or cooperative project require the appraiser to inspect the project and complete the Project Information section of the Individual Condominium Unit Appraisal Report or the Individual Cooperative Interest Appraisal Report and attach it as an addendum to this report.

I ☐ did ☐ did not analyze the contract for sale for the subject purchase transaction. Explain the results of the analysis of the contract for sale or why the analysis was not performed.

Contract Price $ Date of Contract   Is the property seller the owner of public record? ☐ Yes ☐ No Data Source(s)

Is there any financial assistance (loan charges, sale concessions, gift or downpayment assistance, etc.) to be paid by any party on behalf of the borrower? ☐ Yes ☐ No
If Yes, report the total dollar amount and describe the items to be paid.

I ☐ did ☐ did not analyze the manufacturer's invoice. Explain the results of the analysis of the manufacturer's invoice or why the analysis was not performed.

Retailer's Name (New Construction)

NEIGHBORHOOD

Note: Race and the racial composition of the neighborhood are not appraisal factors.

Neighborhood Characteristics			Manufactured Housing Trends				Manufactured Housing		Present Land Use %	
Location ☐ Urban	☐ Suburban	☐ Rural	Property Values ☐ Increasing	☐ Stable	☐ Declining		PRICE	AGE	One-Unit	%
Built-Up ☐ Over 75%	☐ 25–75%	☐ Under 25%	Demand/Supply ☐ Shortage	☐ In Balance	☐ Over Supply		$ (000)	(yrs)	2-4 Unit	%
Growth ☐ Rapid	☐ Stable	☐ Slow	Marketing Time ☐ Under 3 mths	☐ 3–6 mths	☐ Over 6 mths		Low		Multi-Family	%
Neighborhood Boundaries							High		Commercial	%
							Pred.		Other	%

Neighborhood Description

Market Conditions (including support for the above conclusions)

SITE

Dimensions	Area	Shape	View

Specific Zoning Classification   Zoning Description

Zoning Compliance ☐ Legal ☐ Legal Nonconforming (Grandfathered Use) ☐ No Zoning ☐ Illegal (describe)

Is the highest and best use of the subject property as improved (or as proposed per plans and specifications) the present use? ☐ Yes ☐ No If No, describe

Utilities	Public	Other (describe)		Public	Other (describe)	Off-site Improvements—Type	Public	Private
Electricity	☐	☐	Water	☐	☐	Street	☐	☐
Gas	☐	☐	Sanitary Sewer	☐	☐	Alley	☐	☐

FEMA Special Flood Hazard Area ☐ Yes ☐ No FEMA Flood Zone   FEMA Map #   FEMA Map Date

Are the utilities and off-site improvements typical for the market area? ☐ Yes ☐ No If No, describe

Is the site size, shape and topography generally conforming to and acceptable in the market area? ☐ Yes ☐ No If No, explain

Is there adequate vehicular access to the subject property? ☐ Yes ☐ No If No, describe

Is the street properly maintained? ☐ Yes ☐ No If No, describe

Are there any adverse site conditions or external factors (easements, encroachments, environmental conditions, land uses, etc.)? ☐ Yes ☐ No If Yes, describe

HUD DATA PLATE

The HUD Data Plate/Compliance Certificate is located on the interior of the subject and contains, among other things, the manufacturer's name, trade/model name, year manufactured and serial number. The HUD Certification Label is located on the exterior of each section of the home.

Is the HUD Data Plate/Compliance Certificate attached to the dwelling? ☐ Yes ☐ No If Yes, identify the location. If No, provide the data source(s) for the HUD Data Plate/Compliance Certificate information.

Is a HUD Certification Label attached to the exterior of each section of the dwelling? ☐ Yes ☐ No If No, provide the data source(s) for the HUD Certification Label #'s

Manufacturer's Serial #(s)/VIN #(s)

HUD Certification Label #(s)

Manufacturer's Name	Trade/Model	Date of Manufacture

Do the Wind, Roof Load, and Thermal Zones meet the minimum HUD requirements for the location of the subject property? ☐ Yes ☐ No If No, explain

103

Manufactured Home Appraisal Report

File #

General Description	Foundation	Exterior Description materials/condition	Interior materials/condition
# of Units ☐ One ☐ Additions	☐ Poured Concrete ☐ Concrete Runners	Skirting	Floors
# of Stories ☐ 1 ☐ 2 ☐ Other	☐ Block & Pier ☐ Other-att. description	Exterior Walls	Walls
Design (Style)	☐ Full Basement ☐ Partial Basement	Roof Surface	Trim/Finish
# of Sections ☐ 1 ☐ 2 ☐ 3	Basement Area sq. ft.	Gutters & Downspouts	Bath Floor
☐ Other	Basement Finish %	Window Type	Bath Wainscot
Type ☐ Det. ☐ Att. ☐ S-Det./End Unit	☐ Outside Entry/Exit ☐ Sump Pump	Storm Sash/Insulated	Car Storage ☐ None
☐ Existing ☐ Proposed ☐ Under Const.	Evidence of ☐ Infestation	Screens	☐ Driveway # of Cars
Year Built Effective Age (Yrs)	☐ Dampness ☐ Settlement	Doors	Driveway Surface
Attic ☐ None	Heating ☐ FWA ☐ HWBB ☐ Radiant	Amenities ☐ WoodStove(s) #	☐ Garage # of Cars
☐ Drop Stair ☐ Stairs	☐ Other Fuel	☐ Fireplace(s) # ☐ Fence	☐ Carport # of Cars
☐ Floor ☐ Scuttle	Cooling ☐ Central Air Conditioning	☐ Patio/Deck ☐ Porch	☐ Attached ☐ Detached
☐ Finished ☐ Heated	☐ Individual ☐ Other	☐ Pool ☐ Other	☐ Built-in

Appliances ☐Refrigerator ☐Range/Oven ☐Dishwasher ☐Disposal ☐Microwave ☐Washer/Dryer ☐Other (describe)

Finished area **above** grade contains: Rooms   Bedrooms   Bath(s)   Square Feet of Gross Living Area Above Grade

Describe any additions or modifications (decks, rooms, remodeling, etc.)

Installer's Name   Date Installed   Model Year

Is the manufactured home attached to a permanent foundation system? ☐ Yes ☐ No If No, describe the foundation sytem and the manner of attachment.

Have the towing hitch, wheels, and axles been removed? ☐ Yes ☐ No If No, explain

Is the manufactured home permanently connected to a septic tank or sewage system and other utilities? ☐ Yes ☐ No If No, explain

Does the dwelling have sufficient gross living area and room dimensions to be acceptable to the market? ☐ Yes ☐ No If No, explain

Additional features (special energy efficient items, non-realty items, etc.)

The appraiser must rate the quality of construction for the subject unit based on objective criteria (such as N.A.D.A. Manufactured Housing Appraisal Guide®, Marshall & Swift Residential Cost Handbook®, or other published cost service). The appraiser must also report the source used for this quality of construction rating determination.

Quality ☐ Poor ☐ Fair ☐ Average ☐ Good ☐ Excellent   Identify source of quality rating

Describe the condition of the property (including needed repairs, deterioration, renovations, remodeling, etc.).

Are there any physical deficiencies or adverse conditions that affect the livability, soundness, or structural integrity of the property? ☐ Yes ☐ No If Yes, describe

Does the property generally conform to the neighborhood (functional utility, style, condition, use, construction, etc.)? ☐ Yes ☐ No If No, describe

Provide adequate information for the lender/client to replicate the below cost figures and calculations.

Support for the opinion of site value (summary of comparable land sales or other methods for estimating site value)

ESTIMATED ☐ REPRODUCTION OR ☐ REPLACEMENT COST NEW

Source of cost data   Effective date of cost data   Quality rating from cost service

OPINION OF SITE VALUE		$	Exterior Dimensions of the Subject Unit		
Section One	Sq. ft. @ $	$	X	=	Sq. ft.
Section Two	Sq. ft. @ $	$	X	=	Sq. ft.
Section Three	Sq. ft. @ $	$	X	=	Sq. ft.
Section Four	Sq. ft. @ $	$	X	=	Sq. ft.
		$	Total Gross Living Area:		Sq. ft.
		$	Other Data Identification		
		$	N.A.D.A. Data Identification Info: Edition Mo: Yr:		
Sub-total:		$	MH State: Region: Size: ft. x ft.		
Cost Multiplier (if applicable):		x	Gray pg. White pg. Black SVS pg.		
Modified Sub-total:			15 years and older Conversion Chart pg. Yellow pg.		
Physical Depreciation or Condition Modifier:			Comments		
Functional Obsolescence (not used for N.A.D.A.):					
External Depreciation or State Location Modifier:					
Delivery, Installation, and Setup (not used for N.A.D.A.):		$			
Other Depreciated Site Improvements:		$			
Market Value of Subject Site (as supported above):		$			
Indicated Value by Cost Approach:		$	Estimated Remaining Economic Life (HUD and VA only) Years		

Summary of Cost Approach

104

Manufactured Home Appraisal Report

File #

| There are | comparable properties currently offered for sale in the subject neighborhood ranging in price from $ | | to $ | | . |

| There are | comparable sales in the subject neighborhood within the past twelve months ranging in sale price from $ | | to $ | | . |

FEATURE	SUBJECT	COMPARABLE SALE # 1		COMPARABLE SALE # 2		COMPARABLE SALE # 3	
Address							
Proximity to Subject							
Sale Price	$		$		$		$
Sale Price/Gross Liv. Area	$ sq. ft.	$ sq. ft.		$ sq. ft.		$ sq. ft.	
Manufactured Home		☐ Yes ☐ No		☐ Yes ☐ No		☐ Yes ☐ No	
Data Source(s)							
Verification Source(s)							
VALUE ADJUSTMENTS	DESCRIPTION	DESCRIPTION	+(-) $ Adjustment	DESCRIPTION	+(-) $ Adjustment	DESCRIPTION	+(-) $ Adjustment
Sale or Financing Concessions							
Date of Sale/Time							
Location							
Leasehold/Fee Simple							
Site							
View							
Design (Style)							
Quality of Construction							
Actual Age							
Condition							
Above Grade	Total Bdrms. Baths	Total Bdrms. Baths		Total Bdrms. Baths		Total Bdrms. Baths	
Room Count							
Gross Living Area	sq. ft.	sq. ft.		sq. ft.		sq. ft.	
Basement & Finished Rooms Below Grade							
Functional Utility							
Heating/Cooling							
Energy Efficient Items							
Garage/Carport							
Porch/Patio/Deck							
Net Adjustment (Total)		☐ + ☐ -	$	☐ + ☐ -	$	☐ + ☐ -	$
Adjusted Sale Price of Comparables		Net Adj. % Gross Adj. %	$	Net Adj. % Gross Adj. %	$	Net Adj. % Gross Adj. %	$

I ☐ did ☐ did not research the sale or transfer history of the subject property and comparable sales. If not, explain

My research ☐ did ☐ did not reveal any prior sales or transfers of the subject property for the three years prior to the effective date of this appraisal.

Data source(s)

My research ☐ did ☐ did not reveal any prior sales or transfers of the comparable sales for the year prior to the date of sale of the comparable sale.

Data source(s)

Report the results of the research and analysis of the prior sale or transfer history of the subject property and comparable sales (report additional prior sales on page 4).

ITEM	SUBJECT	COMPARABLE SALE # 1	COMPARABLE SALE # 2	COMPARABLE SALE # 3
Date of Prior Sale/Transfer				
Price of Prior Sale/Transfer				
Data Source(s)				
Effective Date of Data Source(s)				

Analysis of prior sale or transfer history of the subject property and comparable sales

Summary of Sales Comparison Approach

Indicated Value by Sales Comparison Approach $

| Indicated Value by: | Sales Comparison Approach $ | Cost Approach $ | Income Approach (if developed) $ |

This appraisal is made ☐ "as is", ☐ subject to completion per plans and specifications on the basis of a hypothetical condition that the improvements have been completed, ☐ subject to the following repairs or alterations on the basis of a hypothetical condition that the repairs or alterations have been completed, or ☐ subject to the following required inspection based on the extraordinary assumption that the condition or deficiency does not require alteration or repair.

Based on a complete visual inspection of the interior and exterior areas of the subject property, defined scope of work, statement of assumptions and limiting conditions, and appraiser's certification, my (our) opinion of the market value, as defined, of the real property that is the subject of this report is

$, as of , which is the date of inspection and the effective date of this appraisal.

105

Manufactured Home Appraisal Report

File #

ADDITIONAL COMMENTS

INCOME

INCOME APPROACH TO VALUE (not required by Fannie Mae.)

Estimated Monthly Market Rent $ _____ X Gross Rent Multiplier _____ = $ _____ Indicated Value by Income Approach

Summary of Income Approach (including support for market rent and GRM)

PROJECT INFORMATION FOR PUDs (if applicable)

PUD INFORMATION

Is the developer/builder in control of the Homeowners' Association (HOA)? ☐ Yes ☐ No   Unit type(s) ☐ Detached ☐ Attached

Provide the following information for PUDs ONLY if the developer/builder is in control of the HOA and the subject property is an attached dwelling unit.

Legal name of project

Total number of phases	Total number of units	Total number of units sold
Total number of units rented	Total number of units for sale	Data source(s)

Was the project created by the conversion of existing building(s) into a PUD? ☐ Yes ☐ No If Yes, date of conversion

Does the project contain any multi-dwelling units? ☐ Yes ☐ No Data source(s)

Are the units, common elements, and recreation facilities complete? ☐ Yes ☐ No If No, describe the status of completion.

Are the common elements leased to or by the Homeowners' Association? ☐ Yes ☐ No If Yes, describe the rental terms and options.

Describe common elements and recreational facilities.

Freddie Mac Form 70B   March 2005   Page 4 of 7   Fannie Mae Form 1004C March 2005

Manufactured Home Appraisal Report

File #

This report form is designed to report an appraisal of a one-unit manufactured home; including a manufactured home in a planned unit development (PUD). A Manufactured home located in either a condominium or cooperative project requires the appraiser to inspect the project and complete the project information section of the Individual Condominium Unit Appraisal Report or the Individual Cooperative Interest Appraisal Report and attach it as an addendum to this report.

This appraisal report is subject to the following scope of work, intended use, intended user, definition of market value, statement of assumptions and limiting conditions, and certifications. Modifications, additions, or deletions to the intended use, intended user, definition of market value, or assumptions and limiting conditions are not permitted. The appraiser may expand the scope of work to include any additional research or analysis necessary based on the complexity of this appraisal assignment. Modifications or deletions to the certifications are also not permitted. However, additional certifications that do not constitute material alterations to this appraisal report, such as those required by law or those related to the appraiser's continuing education or membership in an appraisal organization, are permitted.

SCOPE OF WORK: The scope of work for this appraisal is defined by the complexity of this appraisal assignment and the reporting requirements of this appraisal report form, including the following definition of market value, statement of assumptions and limiting conditions, and certifications. The appraiser must, at a minimum: (1) perform a complete visual inspection of the interior and exterior areas of the subject property, (2) inspect the neighborhood, (3) inspect each of the comparable sales from at least the street, (4) research, verify, and analyze data from reliable public and/or private sources, and (5) report his or her analysis, opinions, and conclusions in this appraisal report.

INTENDED USE: The intended use of this appraisal report is for the lender/client to evaluate the property that is the subject of this appraisal for a mortgage finance transaction.

INTENDED USER: The intended user of this appraisal report is the lender/client.

DEFINITION OF MARKET VALUE: The most probable price which a property should bring in a competitive and open market under all conditions requisite to a fair sale, the buyer and seller, each acting prudently, knowledgeably and assuming the price is not affected by undue stimulus. Implicit in this definition is the consummation of a sale as of a specified date and the passing of title from seller to buyer under conditions whereby: (1) buyer and seller are typically motivated; (2) both parties are well informed or well advised, and each acting in what he or she considers his or her own best interest; (3) a reasonable time is allowed for exposure in the open market; (4) payment is made in terms of cash in U. S. dollars or in terms of financial arrangements comparable thereto; and (5) the price represents the normal consideration for the property sold unaffected by special or creative financing or sales concessions* granted by anyone associated with the sale.

*Adjustments to the comparables must be made for special or creative financing or sales concessions. No adjustments are necessary for those costs which are normally paid by sellers as a result of tradition or law in a market area; these costs are readily identifiable since the seller pays these costs in virtually all sales transactions. Special or creative financing adjustments can be made to the comparable property by comparisons to financing terms offered by a third party institutional lender that is not already involved in the property or transaction. Any adjustment should not be calculated on a mechanical dollar for dollar cost of the financing or concession but the dollar amount of any adjustment should approximate the market's reaction to the financing or concessions based on the appraiser's judgment.

STATEMENT OF ASSUMPTIONS AND LIMITING CONDITIONS: The appraiser's certification in this report is subject to the following assumptions and limiting conditions:

1. The appraiser will not be responsible for matters of a legal nature that affect either the property being appraised or the title to it, except for information that he or she became aware of during the research involved in performing this appraisal. The appraiser assumes that the title is good and marketable and will not render any opinions about the title.

2. The appraiser has provided a sketch in this appraisal report to show approximate dimensions of the improvements. The sketch is included only to assist the reader in visualizing the property and understanding the appraiser's determination of its size.

3. The appraiser has examined the available flood maps that are provided by the Federal Emergency Management Agency (or other data sources) and has noted in this appraisal report whether any portion of the subject site is located in an identified Special Flood Hazard Area. Because the appraiser is not a surveyor, he or she makes no guarantees, express or implied, regarding this determination.

4. The appraiser will not give testimony or appear in court because he or she made an appraisal of the property in question, unless specific arrangements to do so have been made beforehand, or as otherwise required by law.

5. The appraiser has noted in this appraisal report any adverse conditions (such as needed repairs, deterioration, the presence of hazardous wastes, toxic substances, etc.) observed during the inspection of the subject property or that he or she became aware of during the research involved in performing this appraisal. Unless otherwise stated in this appraisal report, the appraiser has no knowledge of any hidden or unapparent physical deficiencies or adverse conditions of the property (such as, but not limited to, needed repairs, deterioration, the presence of hazardous wastes, toxic substances, adverse environmental conditions, etc.) that would make the property less valuable, and has assumed that there are no such conditions and makes no guarantees or warranties, express or implied. The appraiser will not be responsible for any such conditions that do exist or for any engineering or testing that might be required to discover whether such conditions exist. Because the appraiser is not an expert in the field of environmental hazards, this appraisal report must not be considered as an environmental assessment of the property.

6. The appraiser has based his or her appraisal report and valuation conclusion for an appraisal that is subject to satisfactory completion, repairs, or alterations on the assumption that the completion, repairs, or alterations of the subject property will be performed in a professional manner.

107

Manufactured Home Appraisal Report

File #

APPRAISER'S CERTIFICATION: The Appraiser certifies and agrees that:

1. I have, at a minimum, developed and reported this appraisal in accordance with the scope of work requirements stated in this appraisal report.

2. I performed a complete visual inspection of the interior and exterior areas of the subject property. I reported the condition of the improvements in factual, specific terms. I identified and reported the physical deficiencies that could affect the livability, soundness, or structural integrity of the property.

3. I performed this appraisal in accordance with the requirements of the Uniform Standards of Professional Appraisal Practice that were adopted and promulgated by the Appraisal Standards Board of The Appraisal Foundation and that were in place at the time this appraisal report was prepared.

4. I developed my opinion of the market value of the real property that is the subject of this report based on the sales comparison approach to value. I also developed the cost approach to value as support for the sales comparison approach. I have adequate comparable market and cost data to develop reliable sales comparison and cost approaches for this appraisal assignment. I further certify that I considered the income approach to value but did not develop it, unless otherwise indicated in this report.

5. I researched, verified, analyzed, and reported on any current agreement for sale for the subject property, any offering for sale of the subject property in the twelve months prior to the effective date of this appraisal, and the prior sales of the subject property for a minimum of three years prior to the effective date of this appraisal, unless otherwise indicated in this report.

6. I researched, verified, analyzed, and reported on the prior sales of the comparable sales for a minimum of one year prior to the date of sale of the comparable sale, unless otherwise indicated in this report.

7. I selected and used comparable sales that are locationally, physically, and functionally the most similar to the subject property.

8. I have not used comparable sales that were the result of combining a land sale with the contract purchase price of a home that has been built or will be built on the land.

9. I have reported adjustments to the comparable sales that reflect the market's reaction to the differences between the subject property and the comparable sales.

10. I verified, from a disinterested source, all information in this report that was provided by parties who have a financial interest in the sale or financing of the subject property.

11. I have knowledge and experience in appraising this type of property in this market area.

12. I am aware of, and have access to, the necessary and appropriate public and private data sources, such as multiple listing services, tax assessment records, public land records and other such data sources for the area in which the property is located.

13. I obtained the information, estimates, and opinions furnished by other parties and expressed in this appraisal report from reliable sources that I believe to be true and correct.

14. I have taken into consideration the factors that have an impact on value with respect to the subject neighborhood, subject property, and the proximity of the subject property to adverse influences in the development of my opinion of market value. I have noted in this appraisal report any adverse conditions (such as, but not limited to, needed repairs, deterioration, the presence of hazardous wastes, toxic substances, adverse environmental conditions, etc.) observed during the inspection of the subject property or that I became aware of during the research involved in performing this appraisal. I have considered these adverse conditions in my analysis of the property value, and have reported on the effect of the conditions on the value and marketability of the subject property.

15. I have not knowingly withheld any significant information from this appraisal report and, to the best of my knowledge, all statements and information in this appraisal report are true and correct.

16. I stated in this appraisal report my own personal, unbiased, and professional analysis, opinions, and conclusions, which are subject only to the assumptions and limiting conditions in this appraisal report.

17. I have no present or prospective interest in the property that is the subject of this report, and I have no present or prospective personal interest or bias with respect to the participants in the transaction. I did not base, either partially or completely, my analysis and/or opinion of market value in this appraisal report on the race, color, religion, sex, age, marital status, handicap, familial status, or national origin of either the prospective owners or occupants of the subject property or of the present owners or occupants of the properties in the vicinity of the subject property or on any other basis prohibited by law.

18. My employment and/or compensation for performing this appraisal or any future or anticipated appraisals was not conditioned on any agreement or understanding, written or otherwise, that I would report (or present analysis supporting) a predetermined specific value, a predetermined minimum value, a range or direction in value, a value that favors the cause of any party, or the attainment of a specific result or occurrence of a specific subsequent event (such as approval of a pending mortgage loan application).

19. I personally prepared all conclusions and opinions about the real estate that were set forth in this appraisal report. If I relied on significant real property appraisal assistance from any individual or individuals in the performance of this appraisal or the preparation of this appraisal report, I have named such individual(s) and disclosed the specific tasks performed in this appraisal report. I certify that any individual so named is qualified to perform the tasks. I have not authorized anyone to make a change to any item in this appraisal report; therefore, any change made to this appraisal is unauthorized and I will take no responsibility for it.

20. I identified the lender/client in this appraisal report who is the individual, organization, or agent for the organization that ordered and will receive this appraisal report.

Manufactured Home Appraisal Report   File

21. The lender/client may disclose or distribute this appraisal report to: the borrower; another lender at the request of the borrower; the mortgagee or its successors and assigns; mortgage insurers; government sponsored enterprises; other secondary market participants; data collection or reporting services; professional appraisal organizations; any department, agency, or instrumentality of the United States; and any state, the District of Columbia, or other jurisdictions; without having to obtain the appraiser's or supervisory appraiser's (if applicable) consent. Such consent must be obtained before this appraisal report may be disclosed or distributed to any other party (including, but not limited to, the public through advertising, public relations, news, sales, or other media).

22. I am aware that any disclosure or distribution of this appraisal report by me or the lender/client may be subject to certain laws and regulations. Further, I am also subject to the provisions of the Uniform Standards of Professional Appraisal Practice that pertain to disclosure or distribution by me.

23. The borrower, another lender at the request of the borrower, the mortgagee or its successors and assigns, mortgage insurers, government sponsored enterprises, and other secondary market participants may rely on this appraisal report as part of any mortgage finance transaction that involves any one or more of these parties.

24. If this appraisal report was transmitted as an "electronic record" containing my "electronic signature," as those terms are defined in applicable federal and/or state laws (excluding audio and video recordings), or a facsimile transmission of this appraisal report containing a copy or representation of my signature, the appraisal report shall be as effective, enforceable and valid as if a paper version of this appraisal report were delivered containing my original hand written signature.

25. Any intentional or negligent misrepresentation(s) contained in this appraisal report may result in civil liability and/or criminal penalties including, but not limited to, fine or imprisonment or both under the provisions of Title 18, United States Code, Section 1001, et seq., or similar state laws.

SUPERVISORY APPRAISER'S CERTIFICATION: The Supervisory Appraiser certifies and agrees that:

1. I directly supervised the appraiser for this appraisal assignment, have read the appraisal report, and agree with the appraiser's analysis, opinions, statements, conclusions, and the appraiser's certification.

2. I accept full responsibility for the contents of this appraisal report including, but not limited to, the appraiser's analysis, opinions, statements, conclusions, and the appraiser's certification.

3. The appraiser identified in this appraisal report is either a sub-contractor or an employee of the supervisory appraiser (or the appraisal firm), is qualified to perform this appraisal, and is acceptable to perform this appraisal under the applicable state law.

4. This appraisal report complies with the Uniform Standards of Professional Appraisal Practice that were adopted and promulgated by the Appraisal Standards Board of The Appraisal Foundation and that were in place at the time this appraisal report was prepared.

5. If this appraisal report was transmitted as an "electronic record" containing my "electronic signature," as those terms are defined in applicable federal and/or state laws (excluding audio and video recordings), or a facsimile transmission of this appraisal report containing a copy or representation of my signature, the appraisal report shall be as effective, enforceable and valid as if a paper version of this appraisal report were delivered containing my original hand written signature.

APPRAISER

Signature _____
Name _____
Company Name _____
Company Address _____
_____
Telephone Number _____
Email Address _____
Date of Signature and Report _____
Effective Date of Appraisal _____
State Certification # _____
or State License # _____
or Other _____
State _____
Expiration Date of Certification or License _____

ADDRESS OF PROPERTY APPRAISED
_____
_____

APPRAISED VALUE OF SUBJECT PROPERTY $ _____
LENDER/CLIENT
Name _____
Company Name _____
Company Address _____
Email Address _____

SUPERVISORY APPRAISER (ONLY IF REQUIRED)

Signature _____
Name _____
Company Name _____
Company Address _____
_____
Telephone Number _____
Email Address _____
Date Signature _____
State Certification # _____
or State License # _____
State _____
Expiration Date of Certification or License _____

SUBJECT PROPERTY
☐ Did not inspect subject property
☐ Did inspect exterior of subject property from street
   Date of Inspection _____
☐ Did inspect interior and exterior of subject property
   Date of Inspection _____

COMPARABLE SALES
☐ Did not inspect exterior of comparable sales from street
☐ Did inspect exterior of comparable sales from street
   Date of Inspection _____

Exterior-Only Inspection Residential Appraisal Report   File

The purpose of this summary appraisal report is to provide the lender/client with an accurate, and adequately supported, opinion of the market value of the subject property.

SUBJECT

Property Address		City	State	Zip Code

Borrower _____ Owner of Public Record _____ County _____

Legal Description

Assessor's Parcel # _____ Tax Year _____ R.E. Taxes $ _____

Neighborhood Name _____ Map Reference _____ Census Tract _____

Occupant ☐ Owner ☐ Tenant ☐ Vacant   Special Assessments $ _____ ☐ PUD   HOA $ _____ ☐ per year ☐ per month

Property Rights Appraised ☐ Fee Simple ☐ Leasehold ☐ Other (describe)

Assignment Type ☐ Purchase Transaction ☐ Refinance Transaction ☐ Other (describe)

Lender/Client _____ Address _____

Is the subject property currently offered for sale or has it been offered for sale in the twelve months prior to the effective date of this appraisal? ☐ Yes ☐ No

Report data source(s) used, offering price(s), and date(s).

CONTRACT

I ☐ did ☐ did not analyze the contract for sale for the subject purchase transaction. Explain the results of the analysis of the contract for sale or why the analysis was not performed.

Contract Price $ _____ Date of Contract _____ Is the property seller the owner of public record? ☐Yes ☐No Data Source(s) _____

Is there any financial assistance (loan charges, sale concessions, gift or downpayment assistance, etc.) to be paid by any party on behalf of the borrower? ☐ Yes ☐ No
If Yes, report the total dollar amount and describe the items to be paid.

NEIGHBORHOOD

Note: Race and the racial composition of the neighborhood are not appraisal factors.

Neighborhood Characteristics	One-Unit Housing Trends	One-Unit Housing	Present Land Use %
Location ☐ Urban ☐ Suburban ☐ Rural	Property Values ☐ Increasing ☐ Stable ☐ Declining	PRICE AGE	One-Unit ____%
Built-Up ☐ Over 75% ☐ 25–75% ☐ Under 25%	Demand/Supply ☐ Shortage ☐ In Balance ☐ Over Supply	$ (000) (yrs)	2-4 Unit ____%
Growth ☐ Rapid ☐ Stable ☐ Slow	Marketing Time ☐ Under 3 mths ☐ 3–6 mths ☐ Over 6 mths	Low	Multi-Family ____%
Neighborhood Boundaries		High	Commercial ____%
		Pred.	Other ____%

Neighborhood Description

Market Conditions (including support for the above conclusions)

SITE

Dimensions _____ Area _____ Shape _____ View _____

Specific Zoning Classification _____ Zoning Description _____

Zoning Compliance ☐ Legal ☐ Legal Nonconforming (Grandfathered Use) ☐ No Zoning ☐ Illegal (describe)

Is the highest and best use of the subject property as improved (or as proposed per plans and specifications) the present use? ☐ Yes ☐ No If No, describe

Utilities	Public	Other (describe)		Public	Other (describe)	Off-site Improvements—Type	Public	Private
Electricity	☐	☐	Water	☐	☐	Street	☐	☐
Gas	☐	☐	Sanitary Sewer	☐	☐	Alley	☐	☐

FEMA Special Flood Hazard Area ☐ Yes ☐ No   FEMA Flood Zone _____ FEMA Map # _____ FEMA Map Date _____

Are the utilities and off-site improvements typical for the market area? ☐ Yes ☐ No If No, describe

Are there any adverse site conditions or external factors (easements, encroachments, environmental conditions, land uses, etc.)? ☐ Yes ☐ No If Yes, describe

IMPROVEMENTS

Source(s) Used for Physical Characteristics of Property ☐ Appraisal Files ☐ MLS ☐ Assessment and Tax Records ☐ Prior Inspection ☐ Property Owner
☐ Other (describe) _____ Data Source(s) for Gross Living Area

General Description	General Description	Heating / Cooling	Amenities	Car Storage
Units ☐One ☐One with Accessory Unit	☐Concrete Slab ☐Crawl Space	☐ FWA ☐ HWBB	☐ Fireplace(s) #	☐ None
# of Stories	☐Full Basement ☐ Finished	☐ Radiant	☐ Woodstove(s) #	☐ Driveway # of Cars
Type ☐Det. ☐Att. ☐S-Det./End Unit	☐Partial Basement ☐Finished	☐ Other	☐ Patio/Deck	Driveway Surface
☐Existing ☐ Proposed ☐ Under Const.	Exterior Walls	Fuel	☐ Porch	☐ Garage # of Cars
Design (Style)	Roof Surface	☐ Central Air Conditioning	☐ Pool	☐ Carport # of Cars
Year Built	Gutters & Downspouts	☐ Individual	☐ Fence	☐ Attached ☐ Detached
Effective Age (Yrs)	Window Type	☐ Other	☐ Other	☐Built-in

Appliances ☐Refrigerator ☐Range/Oven ☐Dishwasher ☐Disposal ☐Microwave ☐Washer/Dryer ☐Other (describe)

Finished area **above** grade contains: Rooms _____ Bedrooms _____ Bath(s) _____ Square Feet of Gross Living Area Above Grade

Additional features (special energy efficient items, etc.).

Describe the condition of the property and data source(s) (including apparent needed repairs, deterioration, renovations, remodeling, etc.).

Are there any apparent physical deficiencies or adverse conditions that affect the livability, soundness, or structural integrity of the property? ☐ Yes ☐ No
If Yes, describe

Does the property generally conform to the neighborhood (functional utility, style, condition, use, construction, etc.)? ☐ Yes ☐ No If No, describe

110

Exterior-Only Inspection Residential Appraisal Report

File #

There are	comparable properties currently offered for sale in the subject neighborhood ranging in price from $		to $	.
There are	comparable sales in the subject neighborhood within the past twelve months ranging in sale price from $		to $	.

SALES COMPARISON APPROACH

FEATURE	SUBJECT	COMPARABLE SALE # 1		COMPARABLE SALE # 2		COMPARABLE SALE # 3	
Address							
Proximity to Subject							
Sale Price	$		$		$		$
Sale Price/Gross Liv. Area	$ sq. ft.	$ sq. ft.		$ sq. ft.		$ sq. ft.	
Data Source(s)							
Verification Source(s)							
VALUE ADJUSTMENTS	DESCRIPTION	DESCRIPTION	+(-) $ Adjustment	DESCRIPTION	+(-) $ Adjustment	DESCRIPTION	+(-) $ Adjustment
Sale or Financing Concessions							
Date of Sale/Time							
Location							
Leasehold/Fee Simple							
Site							
View							
Design (Style)							
Quality of Construction							
Actual Age							
Condition							
Above Grade Room Count	Total | Bdrms. | Baths	Total | Bdrms. | Baths		Total | Bdrms. | Baths		Total | Bdrms. | Baths	
Gross Living Area	sq. ft.	sq. ft.		sq. ft.		sq. ft.	
Basement & Finished Rooms Below Grade							
Functional Utility							
Heating/Cooling							
Energy Efficient Items							
Garage/Carport							
Porch/Patio/Deck							
Net Adjustment (Total)		☐ + ☐ -	$	☐ + ☐ -	$	☐ + ☐ -	$
Adjusted Sale Price of Comparables		Net Adj. % Gross Adj. %	$	Net Adj. % Gross Adj. %	$	Net Adj. % Gross Adj. %	$

I ☐ did ☐ did not research the sale or transfer history of the subject property and comparable sales. If not, explain

My research ☐ did ☐ did not reveal any prior sales or transfers of the subject property for the three years prior to the effective date of this appraisal.

Data source(s)

My research ☐ did ☐ did not reveal any prior sales or transfers of the comparable sales for the year prior to the date of sale of the comparable sale.

Data source(s)

Report the results of the research and analysis of the prior sale or transfer history of the subject property and comparable sales (report additional prior sales on page 3).

ITEM	SUBJECT	COMPARABLE SALE # 1	COMPARABLE SALE # 2	COMPARABLE SALE # 3
Date of Prior Sale/Transfer				
Price of Prior Sale/Transfer				
Data Source(s)				
Effective Date of Data Source(s)				

Analysis of prior sale or transfer history of the subject property and comparable sales

Summary of Sales Comparison Approach

Indicated Value by Sales Comparison Approach $

RECONCILIATION

Indicated Value by: Sales Comparison Approach $ Cost Approach (if developed) $ Income Approach (if developed) $

This appraisal is made ☐ "as is", ☐ subject to completion per plans and specifications on the basis of a hypothetical condition that the improvements have been completed, ☐ subject to the following repairs or alterations on the basis of a hypothetical condition that the repairs or alterations have been completed, or ☐ subject to the following required inspection based on the extraordinary assumption that the condition or deficiency does not require alteration or repair:

Based on a visual inspection of the exterior areas of the subject property from at least the street, defined scope of work, statement of assumptions and limiting conditions, and appraiser's certification, my (our) opinion of the market value, as defined, of the real property that is the subject of this report is
$, as of   , which is the date of the inspection and the effective date of this appraisal.

Exterior-Only Inspection Residential Appraisal Report   File

ADDITIONAL COMMENTS

(blank lined area)

COST APPROACH TO VALUE (not required by Fannie Mae)

Provide adequate information for the lender/client to replicate the below cost figures and calculations.

Support for the opinion of site value (summary of comparable land sales or other methods for estimating site value)

COST APPROACH

ESTIMATED ☐ REPRODUCTION OR ☐ REPLACEMENT COST NEW	OPINION OF SITE VALUE...= $
Source of cost data	Dwelling Sq. Ft. @ $ ....=$
Quality rating from cost service Effective date of cost data	Sq. Ft. @ $ ....=$
Comments on Cost Approach (gross living area calculations, depreciation, etc.)	
	Garage/Carport Sq. Ft. @ $ ....=$
	Total Estimate of Cost-New ....= $
	Less Physical Functional External
	Depreciation =$( )
	Depreciated Cost of Improvements.........................=$
	"As-is" Value of Site Improvements.......................=$
Estimated Remaining Economic Life (HUD and VA only) Years	Indicated Value By Cost Approach................................=$

INCOME APPROACH TO VALUE (not required by Fannie Mae)

INCOME

Estimated Monthly Market Rent $ X Gross Rent Multiplier   = $ Indicated Value by Income Approach

Summary of Income Approach (including support for market rent and GRM)

PROJECT INFORMATION FOR PUDs (if applicable)

PUD INFORMATION

Is the developer/builder in control of the Homeowners' Association (HOA)? ☐ Yes ☐ No   Unit type(s) ☐ Detached ☐ Attached

Provide the following information for PUDs ONLY if the developer/builder is in control of the HOA and the subject property is an attached dwelling unit.

Legal name of project

Total number of phases   Total number of units   Total number of units sold

Total number of units rented   Total number of units for sale   Data source(s)

Was the project created by the conversion of an existing building(s) into a PUD? ☐ Yes ☐ No   If Yes, date of conversion

Does the project contain any multi-dwelling units? ☐ Yes ☐ No   Data source(s)

Are the units, common elements, and recreation facilities complete? ☐ Yes ☐ No   If No, describe the status of completion.

Are the common elements leased to or by the Homeowners' Association? ☐ Yes ☐ No   If Yes, describe the rental terms and options.

Describe common elements and recreational facilities

Exterior-Only Inspection Residential Appraisal Report   File

This report form is designed to report an appraisal of a one-unit property or a one-unit property with an accessory unit; including a unit in a planned unit development (PUD). This report form is not designed to report an appraisal of a manufactured home or a unit in a condominium or cooperative project.

This appraisal report is subject to the following scope of work, intended use, intended user, definition of market value, statement of assumptions and limiting conditions, and certifications. Modifications, additions, or deletions to the intended use, intended user, definition of market value, or assumptions and limiting conditions are not permitted. The appraiser may expand the scope of work to include any additional research or analysis necessary based on the complexity of this appraisal assignment. Modifications or deletions to the certifications are also not permitted. However, additional certifications that do not constitute material alterations to this appraisal report, such as those required by law or those related to the appraiser's continuing education or membership in an appraisal organization, are permitted.

SCOPE OF WORK: The scope of work for this appraisal is defined by the complexity of this appraisal assignment and the reporting requirements of this appraisal report form, including the following definition of market value, statement of assumptions and limiting conditions, and certifications. The appraiser must, at a minimum: (1) perform a visual inspection of the exterior areas of the subject property from at least the street, (2) inspect the neighborhood, (3) inspect each of the comparable sales from at least the street, (4) research, verify, and analyze data from reliable public and/or private sources, and (5) report his or her analysis, opinions, and conclusions in this appraisal report.

The appraiser must be able to obtain adequate information about the physical characteristics (including, but not limited to, condition, room count, gross living area, etc.) of the subject property from the exterior-only inspection and reliable public and/or private sources to perform this appraisal. The appraiser should use the same type of data sources that he or she uses for comparable sales such as, but not limited to, multiple listing services, tax and assessment records, prior inspections, appraisal files, information provided by the property owner, etc.

INTENDED USE: The intended use of this appraisal report is for the lender/client to evaluate the property that is the subject of this appraisal for a mortgage finance transaction.

INTENDED USER: The intended user of this appraisal report is the lender/client.

DEFINITION MARKET VALUE: The most probable price which a property should bring in a competitive and open market under all conditions requisite to a fair sale, the buyer and seller, each acting prudently, knowledgeably and assuming the price is not affected by undue stimulus. Implicit in this definition is the consummation of a sale as of a specified date and the passing of title from seller to buyer under conditions whereby: (1) buyer and seller are typically motivated; (2) both parties are well informed or well advised, and each acting in what he or she considers his or her own best interest; (3) a reasonable time is allowed for exposure in the open market; (4) payment is made in terms of cash in U. S. dollars or in terms of financial arrangements comparable thereto; and (5) the price represents the normal consideration for the property sold unaffected by special or creative financing or sales concessions* granted by anyone associated with the sale.

*Adjustments to the comparables must be made for special or creative financing or sales concessions. No adjustments are necessary for those costs which are normally paid by sellers as a result of tradition or law in a market area; these costs are readily identifiable since the seller pays these costs in virtually all sales transactions. Special or creative financing adjustments can be made to the comparable property by comparisons to financing terms offered by a third party institutional lender that is not already involved in the property or transaction. Any adjustment should not be calculated on a mechanical dollar for dollar cost of the financing or concession but the dollar amount of any adjustment should approximate the market's reaction to the financing or concessions based on the appraiser's judgment.

STATEMENT OF ASSUMPTIONS AND LIMITING CONDITIONS: The appraiser's certification in this report is subject to the following assumptions and limiting conditions:

1. The appraiser will not be responsible for matters of a legal nature that affect either the property being appraised or the title to it, except for information that he or she became aware of during the research involved in performing this appraisal. The appraiser assumes that the title is good and marketable and will not render any opinions about the title.

2. The appraiser has examined the available flood maps that are provided by the Federal Emergency Management Agency (or other data sources) and has noted in this appraisal report whether any portion of the subject site is located in an identified Special Flood Hazard Area. Because the appraiser is not a surveyor, he or she makes no guarantees, express or implied, regarding this determination.

3. The appraiser will not give testimony or appear in court because he or she made an appraisal of the property in question, unless specific arrangements to do so have been made beforehand, or as otherwise required by law.

4. The appraiser has noted in this appraisal report any adverse conditions (such as needed repairs, deterioration, the presence of hazardous wastes, toxic substances, etc.) observed during the inspection of the subject property or that he or she became aware of during the research involved in performing this appraisal. Unless otherwise stated in this appraisal report, the appraiser has no knowledge of any hidden or unapparent physical deficiencies or adverse conditions of the property (such as, but not limited to, needed repairs, deterioration, the presence of hazardous wastes, toxic substances, adverse environmental conditions, etc.) that would make the property less valuable, and has assumed that there are no such conditions and makes no guarantees or warranties, express or implied. The appraiser will not be responsible for any such conditions that do exist or for any engineering or testing that might be required to discover whether such conditions exist. Because the appraiser is not an expert in the field of environmental hazards, this appraisal report must not be considered as an environmental assessment of the property.

5. The appraiser has based his or her appraisal report and valuation conclusion for an appraisal that is subject to satisfactory completion, repairs, or alterations on the assumption that the completion, repairs, or alterations of the subject property will be performed in a professional manner.

113

Exterior-Only Inspection Residential Appraisal Report   File

APPRAISER'S CERTIFICATION: The Appraiser certifies and agrees that:

1. I have, at a minimum, developed and reported this appraisal in accordance with the scope of work requirements stated in this appraisal report.

2. I performed a visual inspection of the exterior areas of the subject property from at least the street. I reported the condition of the improvements in factual, specific terms. I identified and reported the physical deficiencies that could affect the livability, soundness, or structural integrity of the property.

3. I performed this appraisal in accordance with the requirements of the Uniform Standards of Professional Appraisal Practice that were adopted and promulgated by the Appraisal Standards Board of The Appraisal Foundation and that were in place at the time this appraisal report was prepared.

4. I developed my opinion of the market value of the real property that is the subject of this report based on the sales comparison approach to value. I have adequate comparable market data to develop a reliable sales comparison approach for this appraisal assignment. I further certify that I considered the cost and income approaches to value but did not develop them, unless otherwise indicated in this report.

5. I researched, verified, analyzed, and reported on any current agreement for sale for the subject property, any offering for sale of the subject property in the twelve months prior to the effective date of this appraisal, and the prior sales of the subject property for a minimum of three years prior to the effective date of this appraisal, unless otherwise indicated in this report.

6. I researched, verified, analyzed, and reported on the prior sales of the comparable sales for a minimum of one year prior to the date of sale of the comparable sale, unless otherwise indicated in this report.

7. I selected and used comparable sales that are locationally, physically, and functionally the most similar to the subject property.

8. I have not used comparable sales that were the result of combining a land sale with the contract purchase price of a home that has been built or will be built on the land.

9. I have reported adjustments to the comparable sales that reflect the market's reaction to the differences between the subject property and the comparable sales.

10. I verified, from a disinterested source, all information in this report that was provided by parties who have a financial interest in the sale or financing of the subject property.

11. I have knowledge and experience in appraising this type of property in this market area.

12. I am aware of, and have access to, the necessary and appropriate public and private data sources, such as multiple listing services, tax assessment records, public land records and other such data sources for the area in which the property is located.

13. I obtained the information, estimates, and opinions furnished by other parties and expressed in this appraisal report from reliable sources that I believe to be true and correct.

14. I have taken into consideration the factors that have an impact on value with respect to the subject neighborhood, subject property, and the proximity of the subject property to adverse influences in the development of my opinion of market value. I have noted in this appraisal report any adverse conditions (such as, but not limited to, needed repairs, deterioration, the presence of hazardous wastes, toxic substances, adverse environmental conditions, etc.) observed during the inspection of the subject property or that I became aware of during the research involved in performing this appraisal. I have considered these adverse conditions in my analysis of the property value, and have reported on the effect of the conditions on the value and marketability of the subject property.

15. I have not knowingly withheld any significant information from this appraisal report and, to the best of my knowledge, all statements and information in this appraisal report are true and correct.

16. I stated in this appraisal report my own personal, unbiased, and professional analysis, opinions, and conclusions, which are subject only to the assumptions and limiting conditions in this appraisal report.

17. I have no present or prospective interest in the property that is the subject of this report, and I have no present or prospective personal interest or bias with respect to the participants in the transaction. I did not base, either partially or completely, my analysis and/or opinion of market value in this appraisal report on the race, color, religion, sex, age, marital status, handicap, familial status, or national origin of either the prospective owners or occupants of the subject property or of the present owners or occupants of the properties in the vicinity of the subject property or on any other basis prohibited by law.

18. My employment and/or compensation for performing this appraisal or any future or anticipated appraisals was not conditioned on any agreement or understanding, written or otherwise, that I would report (or present analysis supporting) a predetermined specific value, a predetermined minimum value, a range or direction in value, a value that favors the cause of any party, or the attainment of a specific result or occurrence of a specific subsequent event (such as approval of a pending mortgage loan application).

19. I personally prepared all conclusions and opinions about the real estate that were set forth in this appraisal report. If I relied on significant real property appraisal assistance from any individual or individuals in the performance of this appraisal or the preparation of this appraisal report, I have named such individual(s) and disclosed the specific tasks performed in this appraisal report. I certify that any individual so named is qualified to perform the tasks. I have not authorized anyone to make a change to any item in this appraisal report; therefore, any change made to this appraisal is unauthorized and I will take no responsibility for it.

Exterior-Only Inspection Residential Appraisal Report   File

20. I identified the lender/client in this appraisal report who is the individual, organization, or agent for the organization that ordered and will receive this appraisal report.

21. The lender/client may disclose or distribute this appraisal report to: the borrower; another lender at the request of the borrower; the mortgagee or its successors and assigns; mortgage insurers; government sponsored enterprises; other secondary market participants; data collection or reporting services; professional appraisal organizations; any department, agency, or instrumentality of the United States; and any state, the District of Columbia, or other jurisdictions; without having to obtain the appraiser's or supervisory appraiser's (if applicable) consent. Such consent must be obtained before this appraisal report may be disclosed or distributed to any other party (including, but not limited to, the public through advertising, public relations, news, sales, or other media).

22. I am aware that any disclosure or distribution of this appraisal report by me or the lender/client may be subject to certain laws and regulations. Further, I am also subject to the provisions of the Uniform Standards of Professional Appraisal Practice that pertain to disclosure or distribution by me.

23. The borrower, another lender at the request of the borrower, the mortgagee or its successors and assigns, mortgage insurers, government sponsored enterprises, and other secondary market participants may rely on this appraisal report as part of any mortgage finance transaction that involves any one or more of these parties.

24. If this appraisal report was transmitted as an "electronic record" containing my "electronic signature," as those terms are defined in applicable federal and/or state laws (excluding audio and video recordings), or a facsimile transmission of this appraisal report containing a copy or representation of my signature, the appraisal report shall be as effective, enforceable and valid as if a paper version of this appraisal report were delivered containing my original hand written signature.

25. Any intentional or negligent misrepresentation(s) contained in this appraisal report may result in civil liability and/or criminal penalties including, but not limited to, fine or imprisonment or both under the provisions of Title 18, United States Code, Section 1001, et seq., or similar state laws.

SUPERVISORY APPRAISER'S CERTIFICATION: The Supervisory Appraiser certifies and agrees that:

1. I directly supervised the appraiser for this appraisal assignment, have read the appraisal report, and agree with the appraiser's analysis, opinions, statements, conclusions, and the appraiser's certification.

2. I accept full responsibility for the contents of this appraisal report including, but not limited to, the appraiser's analysis, opinions, statements, conclusions, and the appraiser's certification.

3. The appraiser identified in this appraisal report is either a sub-contractor or an employee of the supervisory appraiser (or the appraisal firm), is qualified to perform this appraisal, and is acceptable to perform this appraisal under the applicable state law.

4. This appraisal report complies with the Uniform Standards of Professional Appraisal Practice that were adopted and promulgated by the Appraisal Standards Board of The Appraisal Foundation and that were in place at the time this appraisal report was prepared.

5. If this appraisal report was transmitted as an "electronic record" containing my "electronic signature," as those terms are defined in applicable federal and/or state laws (excluding audio and video recordings), or a facsimile transmission of this appraisal report containing a copy or representation of my signature, the appraisal report shall be as effective, enforceable and valid as if a paper version of this appraisal report were delivered containing my original hand written signature.

APPRAISER

Signature _____
Name _____
Company Name _____
Company Address _____

Telephone Number _____
Email Address _____
Date of Signature and Report _____
Effective Date of Appraisal _____
State Certification # _____
or State License # _____
or Other (describe) _____ State # _____
State _____
Expiration Date of Certification or License _____
ADDRESS OF PROPERTY APPRAISED

_____

_____

APPRAISED VALUE OF SUBJECT PROPERTY $ _____
LENDER/CLIENT
Name _____
Company Name _____
Company Address _____

_____

Email Address _____

SUPERVISORY APPRAISER (ONLY IF REQUIRED)

Signature _____
Name _____
Company Name _____
Company Address _____

_____

Telephone Number _____
Email Address _____
Date of Signature _____
State Certification # _____
or State License # _____
State _____
Expiration Date of Certification or License _____

SUBJECT PROPERTY
☐ Did not inspect exterior of subject property
☐ Did inspect exterior of subject property from street
   Date of Inspection _____

COMPARABLE SALES
☐ Did not inspect exterior of comparable sales from street
☐ Did inspect exterior of comparable sales from street
   Date of Inspection _____

115

Individual Condominium Unit Appraisal Report

File #

The purpose of this summary appraisal report is to provide the lender/client with an accurate, and adequately supported, opinion of the market value of the subject property.

Property Address	Unit # City State Zip Code

SUBJECT

Property Address   Unit #   City   State   Zip Code

Borrower   Owner of Public Record   County

Legal Description

Assessor's Parcel #   Tax Year   R.E. Taxes $

Project Name   Phase #   Map Reference   Census Tract

Occupant ☐ Owner ☐ Tenant ☐ Vacant   Special Assessments $ HOA $ ☐ per year ☐ per month

Property Rights Appraised ☐ Fee Simple ☐ Leasehold ☐ Other (describe)

Assignment Type ☐ Purchase Transaction ☐ Refinance Transaction ☐ Other (describe)

Lender/Client   Address

Is the subject property currently offered for sale or has it been offered for sale in the twelve months prior to the effective date of this appraisal? ☐ Yes ☐ No

Report data source(s) used, offering price(s), and date(s).

CONTRACT

I ☐ did ☐ did not analyze the contract for sale for the subject purchase transaction. Explain the results of the analysis of the contract for sale or why the analysis was not performed.

Contract Price $ Date of Contract   Is the property seller the owner of public record? ☐ Yes ☐ No   Data Source(s)

Is there any financial assistance (loan charges, sale concessions, gift or downpayment assistance, etc.) to be paid by any party on behalf of the borrower? ☐ Yes ☐ No
If Yes, report the total dollar amount and describe the items to be paid.

NEIGHBORHOOD

Note: Race and the racial composition of the neighborhood are not appraisal factors.

Neighborhood Characteristics	Condominium Unit Housing Trends	Condominium Housing		Present Land Use %	
Location ☐ Urban ☐ Suburban ☐ Rural	Property Values ☐ Increasing ☐ Stable ☐ Declining	PRICE	AGE	One-Unit	%
Built-Up ☐ Over 75% ☐ 25–75% ☐ Under 25%	Demand/Supply ☐ Shortage ☐ In Balance ☐ Over Supply	$ (000)	(yrs)	2-4 Unit	%
Growth ☐ Rapid ☐ Stable ☐ Slow	Marketing Time ☐ Under 3 mths ☐ 3–6 mths ☐ Over 6 mths	Low		Multi-Family	%
Neighborhood Boundaries		High		Commercial	%
		Pred.		Other	%

Neighborhood Description

Market Conditions (including support for the above conclusions)

PROJECT SITE

Topography   Size   Density   View

Specific Zoning Classification   Zoning Description

Zoning Compliance ☐ Legal ☐ Legal Nonconforming – Do the zoning regulations permit rebuilding to current density? ☐ Yes ☐ No
☐ No Zoning ☐ Illegal (describe)

Is the highest and best use of the subject property as improved (or as proposed per plans and specifications) the present use? ☐ Yes ☐ No If No, describe

Utilities	Public	Other (describe)		Public	Other (describe)	Off-site Improvements—Type	Public	Private
Electricity	☐	☐	Water	☐	☐	Street	☐	☐
Gas	☐	☐	Sanitary Sewer	☐	☐	Alley	☐	☐

FEMA Special Flood Hazard Area ☐ Yes ☐ No   FEMA Flood Zone   FEMA Map #   FEMA Map Date

Are the utilities and off-site improvements typical for the market area? ☐ Yes ☐ No If No, describe

Are there any adverse site conditions or external factors (easements, encroachments, environmental conditions, land uses, etc.)? ☐ Yes ☐ No If Yes, describe

PROJECT INFORMATION

Data source(s) for project information

Project Description ☐ Detached ☐ Row or Townhouse ☐ Garden ☐ Mid-Rise ☐ High-Rise ☐ Other (describe)

General Description	General Description	Subject Phase	If Project Completed	If Project Incomplete
# of Stories	Exterior Walls	# of Units	# of Phases	# of Planned Phases
# of Elevators	Roof Surface	# of Units Completed	# of Units	# o f Planned Units
☐ Existing ☐ Proposed	Total # Parking	# of Units For Sale	# of Units for Sale	# of Units for Sale
☐ Under Construction	Ratio (spaces/units)	# of Units Sold	# of Units Sold	# of Units Sold
Year Built	Type	# of Units Rented	# of Units Rented	# of Units Rented
Effective Age	Guest Parking	# of Owner Occupied Units	# of Owner Occupied Units	# of Owner Occupied Units

Project Primary Occupancy ☐ Principal Residence ☐ Second Home or Recreational ☐ Tenant

Is the developer/builder in control of the Homeowners' Association (HOA)? ☐ Yes ☐ No

Management Group – ☐ Homeowners' Association ☐ Developer ☐ Management Agent – Provide name of management company.

Does any single entity (the same individual, investor group, corporation, etc.) own more than 10% of the total units in the project? ☐ Yes ☐ No If Yes, describe

Was the project created by the conversion of an existing building(s) into a condominium? ☐ Yes ☐ No If Yes, describe the original use and the date of conversion.

Are the units, common elements, and recreation facilities complete (including any planned rehabilitation for a condominium conversion)? ☐ Yes ☐ No If No, describe

Is there any commercial space in the project? ☐ Yes ☐ No If Yes, describe and indicate the overall percentage of the commercial space.

Freddie Mac Form 465   March 2005   Page 1 of 6   Fannie Mae Form 1073   March 2005

Individual Condominium Unit Appraisal Report

File #

PROJECT INFORMATION

Describe the condition of the project and quality of construction.

Describe the common elements and recreational facilities.

Are any common elements leased to or by the Homeowners' Association? ☐ Yes ☐ No If Yes, describe the rental terms and options.

Is the project subject to ground rent? ☐ Yes ☐ No If Yes, $ _____ per year (describe terms and conditions)

Are the parking facilities adequate for the project size and type? ☐ Yes ☐ No If No, describe and comment on the effect on value and marketability.

PROJECT ANALYSIS

I ☐ did ☐ did not analyze the condominium project budget for the current year. Explain the results of the analysis of the budget (adequacy of fees, reserves, etc.), or why the analysis was not performed.

Are there any other fees (other than regular HOA charges) for the use of the project facilities? ☐ Yes ☐ No If Yes, report the charges and describe.

Compared to other competitive projects of similar quality and design, the subject unit charge appears ☐ High ☐ Average ☐ Low If High or Low, describe

Are there any special or unusual characteristics of the project (based on the condominium documents, HOA meetings, or other information) known to the appraiser? ☐ Yes ☐ No If Yes, describe and explain the effect on value and marketability.

Unit Charge $ _____ per month X 12 = $ _____ per year   Annual assessment charge per year per square feet of gross living area = $ _____

Utilities included in the unit monthly assessment ☐ None ☐ Heat ☐ Air Conditioning ☐ Electricity ☐ Gas ☐ Water ☐ Sewer ☐ Cable ☐ Other (describe)

UNIT DESCRIPTION

General Description	Interior materials/condition	Amenities	Appliances	Car Storage
Floor #	Floors	☐ Fireplace(s) #	☐ Refrigerator	☐ None
# of Levels	Walls	☐ Woodstove(s) #	☐ Range/Oven	☐ Garage ☐ Covered ☐ Open
Heating Type Fuel	Trim/Finish	☐ Deck/Patio	☐ Disp ☐ Microwave	# of Cars
☐ Central AC ☐ Individual AC	Bath Wainscot	☐ Porch/Balcony	☐ Dishwasher	☐ Assigned ☐ Owned
☐ Other (describe)	Doors	☐ Other	☐ Washer/Dryer	Parking Space #

Finished area **above** grade contains: _____ Rooms _____ Bedrooms _____ Bath(s) _____ Square Feet of Gross Living Area Above Grade

Are the heating and cooling for the individual units separately metered? ☐ Yes ☐ No If No, describe and comment on compatibility to other projects in the market area.

Additional features (special energy efficient items, etc.)

Describe the condition of the property (including needed repairs, deterioration, renovations, remodeling, etc.).

Are there any physical deficiencies or adverse conditions that affect the livability, soundness, or structural integrity of the property? ☐ Yes ☐ No If Yes, describe

Does the property generally conform to the neighborhood (functional utility, style, condition, use, construction, etc.)? ☐ Yes ☐ No If No, describe

---

PRIOR SALE HISTORY

I ☐ did ☐ did not research the sale or transfer history of the subject property and comparable sales. If not, explain

My research ☐ did ☐ did not reveal any prior sales or transfers of the subject property for the three years prior to the effective date of this appraisal.

Data source(s)

My research ☐ did ☐ did not reveal any prior sales or transfers of the comparable sales for the year prior to the date of sale of the comparable sale.

Data source(s)

Report the results of the research and analysis of the prior sale or transfer history of the subject property and comparable sales (report additional prior sales on page 3).

ITEM	SUBJECT	COMPARABLE SALE # 1	COMPARABLE SALE # 2	COMPARABLE SALE # 3
Date of Prior Sale/Transfer				
Price of Prior Sale/Transfer				
Data Source(s)				
Effective Date of Data Source(s)				

Analysis of prior sale or transfer history of the subject property and comparable sales.

Freddie Mac Form 465   March 2005   Page 2 of 6   Fannie Mae Form 1073   March 2005

117

Individual Condominium Unit Appraisal Report

File #

| There are | comparable properties currently offered for sale in the subject neighborhood ranging in price from $ | | | to $ | | |

| There are | comparable sales in the subject neighborhood within the past twelve months ranging in sale price from $ | | | to $ | | |

FEATURE	SUBJECT	COMPARABLE SALE # 1		COMPARABLE SALE # 2		COMPARABLE SALE # 3	
Address and Unit #							
Project Name and Phase							
Proximity to Subject							
Sale Price	$		$		$		$
Sale Price/Gross Liv. Area	$ sq. ft.	$ sq. ft.		$ sq. ft.		$ sq. ft.	
Data Source(s)							
Verification Source(s)							
VALUE ADJUSTMENTS	DESCRIPTION	DESCRIPTION	+(-) $ Adjustment	DESCRIPTION	+(-) $ Adjustment	DESCRIPTION	+(-) $ Adjustment
Sale or Financing Concessions							
Date of Sale/Time							
Location							
Leasehold/Fee Simple							
HOA Mo. Assessment							
Common Elements and Rec. Facilities							
Floor Location							
View							
Design (Style)							
Quality of Construction							
Actual Age							
Condition							
Above Grade Room Count	Total	Bdrms.	Baths	Total	Bdrms.	Baths	Total	Bdrms.	Baths	Total	Bdrms.	Baths
Gross Living Area	sq. ft.	sq. ft.		sq. ft.		sq. ft.	
Basement & Finished Rooms Below Grade							
Functional Utility							
Heating/Cooling							
Energy Efficient Items							
Garage/Carport							
Porch/Patio/Deck							
Net Adjustment (Total)		☐ + ☐ -	$	☐ + ☐ -	$	☐ + ☐ -	$
Adjusted Sale Price of Comparables		Net Adj. % Gross Adj. %	$	Net Adj. % Gross Adj. %	$	Net Adj. % Gross Adj. %	$

(left margin vertical label: SALES COMPARISON APPROACH)

Summary of Sales Comparison Approach

Indicated Value by Sales Comparison Approach $

INCOME APPROACH TO VALUE (not required by Fannie Mae)

(left margin vertical label: INCOME)

Estimated Monthly Market Rent $ X Gross Rent Multiplier   = $ Indicated Value by Income Approach

Summary of Income Approach (including support for market rent and GRM)

Indicated Value by: Sales Comparison Approach $ Income Approach (if developed) $

(left margin vertical label: RECONCILIATION)

This appraisal is made ☐ "as is", ☐ subject to completion per plans and specifications on the basis of a hypothetical condition that the improvements have been completed, ☐ subject to the following repairs or alterations on the basis of a hypothetical condition that the repairs or alterations have been completed, or ☐ subject to the following required inspection based on the extraordinary assumption that the condition or deficiency does not require alteration or repair:

Based on a complete visual inspection of the interior and exterior areas of the subject property, defined scope of work, statement of assumptions and limiting conditions, and appraiser's certification, my (our) opinion of the market value, as defined, of the real property that is the subject of this report is
$, as of   , which is the date of inspection and the effective date of this appraisal.

Freddie Mac Form 465   March 2005   Page 3 of 6   Fannie Mae Form 1073   March 2005

Individual Condominium Unit Appraisal Report

File #

This report form is designed to report an appraisal of a unit in a condominium project or a condominium unit in a planned unit development (PUD). This report form is not designed to report an appraisal of a manufactured home or a unit in a cooperative project.

This appraisal report is subject to the following scope of work, intended use, intended user, definition of market value, statement of assumptions and limiting conditions, and certifications. Modifications, additions, or deletions to the intended use, intended user, definition of market value, or assumptions and limiting conditions are not permitted. The appraiser may expand the scope of work to include any additional research or analysis necessary based on the complexity of this appraisal assignment. Modifications or deletions to the certifications are also not permitted. However, additional certifications that do not constitute material alterations to this appraisal report, such as those required by law or those related to the appraiser's continuing education or membership in an appraisal organization, are permitted.

SCOPE OF WORK: The scope of work for this appraisal is defined by the complexity of this appraisal assignment and the reporting requirements of this appraisal report form, including the following definition of market value, statement of assumptions and limiting conditions, and certifications. The appraiser must, at a minimum: (1) perform a complete visual inspection of the interior and exterior areas of the subject unit, (2) inspect and analyze the condominium project, (3) inspect the neighborhood, (4) inspect each of the comparable sales from at least the street, (5) research, verify, and analyze data from reliable public and/or private sources, and (6) report his or her analysis, opinions, and conclusions in this appraisal report.

INTENDED USE: The intended use of this appraisal report is for the lender/client to evaluate the property that is the subject of this appraisal for a mortgage finance transaction.

INTENDED USER: The intended user of this appraisal report is the lender/client.

MARKET VALUE: The most probable price which a property should bring in a competitive and open market under all conditions requisite to a fair sale, the buyer and seller, each acting prudently, knowledgeably and assuming the price is not affected by undue stimulus. Implicit in this definition is the consummation of a sale as of a specified date and the passing of title from seller to buyer under conditions whereby: (1) buyer and seller are typically motivated; (2) both parties are well informed or well advised, and each acting in what he or she considers his or her own best interest; (3) a reasonable time is allowed for exposure in the open market; (4) payment is made in terms of cash in U. S. dollars or in terms of financial arrangements comparable thereto; and (5) the price represents the normal consideration for the property sold unaffected by special or creative financing or sales concessions* granted by anyone associated with the sale.

*Adjustments to the comparables must be made for special or creative financing or sales concessions. No adjustments are necessary for those costs which are normally paid by sellers as a result of tradition or law in a market area; these costs are readily identifiable since the seller pays these costs in virtually all sales transactions. Special or creative financing adjustments can be made to the comparable property by comparisons to financing terms offered by a third party institutional lender that is not already involved in the property or transaction. Any adjustment should not be calculated on a mechanical dollar for dollar cost of the financing or concession but the dollar amount of any adjustment should approximate the market's reaction to the financing or concessions based on the appraiser's judgment.

STATEMENT OF ASSUMPTIONS AND LIMITING CONDITIONS: The appraiser's certification in this report is subject to the following assumptions and limiting conditions:

1. The appraiser will not be responsible for matters of a legal nature that affect either the property being appraised or the title to it, except for information that he or she became aware of during the research involved in performing this appraisal. The appraiser assumes that the title is good and marketable and will not render any opinions about the title.

2. The appraiser has provided a sketch in this appraisal report to show the approximate dimensions of the improvements. The sketch is included only to assist the reader in visualizing the property and understanding the appraiser's determination of its size.

3. The appraiser has examined the available flood maps that are provided by the Federal Emergency Management Agency (or other data sources) and has noted in this appraisal report whether any portion of the subject site is located in an identified Special Flood Hazard Area. Because the appraiser is not a surveyor, he or she makes no guarantees, express or implied, regarding this determination.

4. The appraiser will not give testimony or appear in court because he or she made an appraisal of the property in question, unless specific arrangements to do so have been made beforehand, or as otherwise required by law.

5. The appraiser has noted in this appraisal report any adverse conditions (such as needed repairs, deterioration, the presence of hazardous wastes, toxic substances, etc.) observed during the inspection of the subject property or that he or she became aware of during the research involved in performing this appraisal. Unless otherwise stated in this appraisal report, the appraiser has no knowledge of any hidden or unapparent physical deficiencies or adverse conditions of the property (such as, but not limited to, needed repairs, deterioration, the presence of hazardous wastes, toxic substances, adverse environmental conditions, etc.) that would make the property less valuable, and has assumed that there are no such conditions and makes no guarantees or warranties, express or implied. The appraiser will not be responsible for any such conditions that do exist or for any engineering or testing that might be required to discover whether such conditions exist. Because the appraiser is not an expert in the field of environmental hazards, this appraisal report must not be considered as an environmental assessment of the property.

6. The appraiser has based his or her appraisal report and valuation conclusion for an appraisal that is subject to satisfactory completion, repairs, or alterations on the assumption that the completion, repairs, or alterations of the subject property will be performed in a professional manner.

119

Individual Condominium Unit Appraisal Report

APPRAISER'S CERTIFICATION: The Appraiser certifies and agrees that:

1. I have, at a minimum, developed and reported this appraisal in accordance with the scope of work requirements stated in this appraisal report.

2. I performed a complete visual inspection of the interior and exterior areas of the subject property. I reported the condition of the improvements in factual, specific terms. I identified and reported the physical deficiencies that could affect the livability, soundness, or structural integrity of the property.

3. I performed this appraisal in accordance with the requirements of the Uniform Standards of Professional Appraisal Practice that were adopted and promulgated by the Appraisal Standards Board of The Appraisal Foundation and that were in place at the time this appraisal report was prepared.

4. I developed my opinion of the market value of the real property that is the subject of this report based on the sales comparison approach to value. I have adequate comparable market data to develop a reliable sales comparison approach for this appraisal assignment. I further certify that I considered the cost and income approaches to value but did not develop them, unless otherwise indicated in this report.

5. I researched, verified, analyzed, and reported on any current agreement for sale for the subject property, any offering for sale of the subject property in the twelve months prior to the effective date of this appraisal, and the prior sales of the subject property for a minimum of three years prior to the effective date of this appraisal, unless otherwise indicated in this report.

6. I researched, verified, analyzed, and reported on the prior sales of the comparable sales for a minimum of one year prior to the date of sale of the comparable sale, unless otherwise indicated in this report.

7. I selected and used comparable sales that are locationally, physically, and functionally the most similar to the subject property.

8. I have not used comparable sales that were the result of combining a land sale with the contract purchase price of a home that has been built or will be built on the land.

9. I have reported adjustments to the comparable sales that reflect the market's reaction to the differences between the subject property and the comparable sales.

10. I verified, from a disinterested source, all information in this report that was provided by parties who have a financial interest in the sale or financing of the subject property.

11. I have knowledge and experience in appraising this type of property in this market area.

12. I am aware of, and have access to, the necessary and appropriate public and private data sources, such as multiple listing services, tax assessment records, public land records and other such data sources for the area in which the property is located.

13. I obtained the information, estimates, and opinions furnished by other parties and expressed in this appraisal report from reliable sources that I believe to be true and correct.

14. I have taken into consideration the factors that have an impact on value with respect to the subject neighborhood, subject property, and the proximity of the subject property to adverse influences in the development of my opinion of market value. I have noted in this appraisal report any adverse conditions (such as, but not limited to, needed repairs, deterioration, the presence of hazardous wastes, toxic substances, adverse environmental conditions, etc.) observed during the inspection of the subject property or that I became aware of during the research involved in performing this appraisal. I have considered these adverse conditions in my analysis of the property value, and have reported on the effect of the conditions on the value and marketability of the subject property.

15. I have not knowingly withheld any significant information from this appraisal report and, to the best of my knowledge, all statements and information in this appraisal report are true and correct.

16. I stated in this appraisal report my own personal, unbiased, and professional analysis, opinions, and conclusions, which are subject only to the assumptions and limiting conditions in this appraisal report.

17. I have no present or prospective interest in the property that is the subject of this report, and I have no present or prospective personal interest or bias with respect to the participants in the transaction. I did not base, either partially or completely, my analysis and/or opinion of market value in this appraisal report on the race, color, religion, sex, age, marital status, handicap, familial status, or national origin of either the prospective owners or occupants of the subject property or of the present owners or occupants of the properties in the vicinity of the subject property or on any other basis prohibited by law.

18. My employment and/or compensation for performing this appraisal or any future or anticipated appraisals was not conditioned on any agreement or understanding, written or otherwise, that I would report (or present analysis supporting) a predetermined specific value, a predetermined minimum value, a range or direction in value, a value that favors the cause of any party, or the attainment of a specific result or occurrence of a specific subsequent event (such as approval of a pending mortgage loan application).

19. I personally prepared all conclusions and opinions about the real estate that were set forth in this appraisal report. If I relied on significant real property appraisal assistance from any individual or individuals in the performance of this appraisal or the preparation of this appraisal report, I have named such individual(s) and disclosed the specific tasks performed in this appraisal report. I certify that any individual so named is qualified to perform the tasks. I have not authorized anyone to make a change to any item in this appraisal report; therefore, any change made to this appraisal is unauthorized and I will take no responsibility for it.

20. I identified the lender/client in this appraisal report who is the individual, organization, or agent for the organization that ordered and will receive this appraisal report.

Individual Condominium Unit Appraisal Report

21. The lender/client may disclose or distribute this appraisal report to: the borrower; another lender at the request of the borrower; the mortgagee or its successors and assigns; mortgage insurers; government sponsored enterprises; other secondary market participants; data collection or reporting services; professional appraisal organizations; any department, agency, or instrumentality of the United States; and any state, the District of Columbia, or other jurisdictions; without having to obtain the appraiser's or supervisory appraiser's (if applicable) consent. Such consent must be obtained before this appraisal report may be disclosed or distributed to any other party (including, but not limited to, the public through advertising, public relations, news, sales, or other media).

22. I am aware that any disclosure or distribution of this appraisal report by me or the lender/client may be subject to certain laws and regulations. Further, I am also subject to the provisions of the Uniform Standards of Professional Appraisal Practice that pertain to disclosure or distribution by me.

23. The borrower, another lender at the request of the borrower, the mortgagee or its successors and assigns, mortgage insurers, government sponsored enterprises, and other secondary market participants may rely on this appraisal report as part of any mortgage finance transaction that involves any one or more of these parties.

24. If this appraisal report was transmitted as an "electronic record" containing my "electronic signature," as those terms are defined in applicable federal and/or state laws (excluding audio and video recordings), or a facsimile transmission of this appraisal report containing a copy or representation of my signature, the appraisal report shall be as effective, enforceable and valid as if a paper version of this appraisal report were delivered containing my original hand written signature.

25. Any intentional or negligent misrepresentation(s) contained in this appraisal report may result in civil liability and/or criminal penalties including, but not limited to, fine or imprisonment or both under the provisions of Title 18, United States Code, Section 1001, et seq., or similar state laws.

SUPERVISORY APPRAISER'S CERTIFICATION: The Supervisory Appraiser certifies and agrees that:

1. I directly supervised the appraiser for this appraisal assignment, have read the appraisal report, and agree with the appraiser's analysis, opinions, statements, conclusions, and the appraiser's certification.

2. I accept full responsibility for the contents of this appraisal report including, but not limited to, the appraiser's analysis, opinions, statements, conclusions, and the appraiser's certification.

3. The appraiser identified in this appraisal report is either a sub-contractor or an employee of the supervisory appraiser (or the appraisal firm), is qualified to perform this appraisal, and is acceptable to perform this appraisal under the applicable state law.

4. This appraisal report complies with the Uniform Standards of Professional Appraisal Practice that were adopted and promulgated by the Appraisal Standards Board of The Appraisal Foundation and that were in place at the time this appraisal report was prepared.

5. If this appraisal report was transmitted as an "electronic record" containing my "electronic signature," as those terms are defined in applicable federal and/or state laws (excluding audio and video recordings), or a facsimile transmission of this appraisal report containing a copy or representation of my signature, the appraisal report shall be as effective, enforceable and valid as if a paper version of this appraisal report were delivered containing my original hand written signature.

APPRAISER

Signature _____
Name _____
Company Name _____
Company Address _____
_____
Telephone Number _____
Email Address _____
Date of Signature and Report _____
Effective Date of Appraisal _____
State Certification # _____
or State License # _____
or Other _____ State # _____
State _____
Expiration Date of Certification or License _____

ADDRESS OF PROPERTY APPRAISED

_____
_____
APPRAISED VALUE OF SUBJECT PROPERTY $_____
LENDER/CLIENT
Name _____
Company Name _____
Company Address _____
Email Address _____

SUPERVISORY APPRAISER (ONLY IF REQUIRED)

Signature _____
Name _____
Company Name _____
Company Address _____
_____
Telephone Number _____
Email Address _____
Date of Signature _____
State Certification # _____
or State License # _____
State _____
Expiration Date of Certification or License _____

SUBJECT PROPERTY
☐ Did not inspect subject property
☐ Did inspect exterior of subject property from street
　 Date of Inspection _____
☐ Did inspect interior and exterior of subject property
　 Date of Inspection _____

COMPARABLE SALES
☐ Did not inspect exterior of comparable sales from street
☐ Did inspect exterior of comparable sales from street
　 Date of Inspection _____

121

Small Residential Income Property Appraisal Report   File

The purpose of this summary appraisal report is to provide the lender/client with an accurate, and adequately supported, opinion of the market value of the subject property.

Property Address	City State Zip Code
Borrower Owner of Public Record	County
Legal Description	

SUBJECT

Assessor's Parcel #	Tax Year	R.E. Taxes $
Neighborhood Name	Map Reference	Census Tract

Occupant ☐ Owner ☐ Tenant ☐ Vacant   Special Assessments $ ☐ PUD   HOA $ ☐ per year ☐ per month

Property Rights Appraised ☐ Fee Simple ☐ Leasehold ☐ Other (describe)

Assignment Type ☐ Purchase Transaction ☐ Refinance Transaction ☐ Other (describe)

Lender/Client   Address

Is the subject property currently offered for sale or has it been offered for sale in the twelve months prior to the effective date of this appraisal? ☐ Yes ☐ No

Report data source(s) used, offering price(s), and date(s).

CONTRACT

I ☐ did ☐ did not analyze the contract for sale for the subject purchase transaction. Explain the results of the analysis of the contract for sale or why the analysis was not performed.

Contract Price $ Date of Contract   Is the property seller the owner of public record? ☐ Yes ☐ No Data Source(s)

Is there any financial assistance (loan charges, sale concessions, gift or downpayment assistance, etc.) to be paid by any party on behalf of the borrower? ☐ Yes ☐ No
If Yes, report the total dollar amount and describe the items to be paid.

NEIGHBORHOOD

Note: Race and the racial composition of the neighborhood are not appraisal factors.

Neighborhood Characteristics			2-4 Unit Housing Trends			2-4 Unit Housing		Present Land Use %	
Location ☐ Urban ☐ Suburban ☐ Rural			Property Values ☐ Increasing ☐ Stable ☐ Declining			PRICE	AGE	One-Unit	%
Built-Up ☐ Over 75% ☐ 25–75% ☐ Under 25%			Demand/Supply ☐ Shortage ☐ In Balance ☐ Over Supply			$ (000)	(yrs)	2-4 Unit	%
Growth ☐ Rapid ☐ Stable ☐ Slow			Marketing Time ☐ Under 3 mths ☐ 3–6 mths ☐ Over 6 mths			Low		Multi-Family	%
Neighborhood Boundaries						High		Commercial	%
						Pred.		Other	%

Neighborhood Description

Market Conditions (including support for the above conclusions)

SITE

Dimensions   Area   Shape   View

Specific Zoning Classification   Zoning Description

Zoning Compliance ☐ Legal ☐ Legal Nonconforming (Grandfathered Use) ☐ No Zoning ☐ Illegal (describe)

Is the highest and best use of the subject property as improved (or as proposed per plans and specifications) the present use? ☐ Yes ☐ No If No, describe

Utilities	Public	Other (describe)		Public	Other (describe)	Off-site Improvements—Type	Public	Private
Electricity	☐	☐	Water	☐	☐	Street	☐	☐
Gas	☐	☐	Sanitary Sewer	☐	☐	Alley	☐	☐

FEMA Special Flood Hazard Area ☐ Yes ☐ No FEMA Flood Zone   FEMA Map #   FEMA Map Date

Are the utilities and off-site improvements typical for the market area? ☐ Yes ☐ No If No, describe

Are there any adverse site conditions or external factors (easements, encroachments, environmental conditions, land uses, etc.)? ☐ Yes ☐ No If Yes, describe

IMPROVEMENTS

General Description	Foundation	Exterior Description materials/condition	Interior materials/condition
Units ☐ Two ☐ Three ☐ Four	☐ Concrete Slab ☐ Crawl Space	Foundation Walls	Floors
☐ Accessory Unit (describe below)	☐ Full Basement ☐ Partial Basement	Exterior Walls	Walls
# of Stories # of bldgs.	Basement Area sq. ft.	Roof Surface	Trim/Finish
Type ☐ Det. ☐ Att. ☐ S-Det./End Unit	Basement Finish %	Gutters & Downspouts	Bath Floor
☐ Existing ☐ Proposed ☐ Under Const.	☐ Outside Entry/Exit ☐ Sump Pump	Window Type	Bath Wainscot
Design (Style)	Evidence of ☐ Infestation	Storm Sash/Insulated	**Car Storage**
Year Built	☐ Dampness ☐ Settlement	Screens	☐ None
Effective Age (Yrs)	**Heating/Cooling**	**Amenities**	☐ Driveway # of Cars
Attic ☐ None	☐ FWA ☐ HWBB ☐ Radiant	☐ Fireplace(s) # ☐ Woodstove(s) #	Driveway Surface
☐ Drop Stair ☐ Stairs	☐ Other Fuel	☐ Patio/Deck ☐ Fence	☐ Garage # of Cars
☐ Floor ☐ Scuttle	☐ Central Air Conditioning	☐ Pool ☐ Porch	☐ Carport # of Cars
☐ Finished ☐ Heated	☐ Individual ☐ Other	☐ Other	☐ Att. ☐ Det. ☐ Built-in

# of Appliances Refrigerator   Range/Oven   Dishwasher   Disposal   Microwave   Washer/Dryer   Other (describe)

Unit # 1 contains:	Rooms	Bedroom(s)	Bath(s)	Square feet of Gross Living Area
Unit # 2 contains:	Rooms	Bedroom(s)	Bath(s)	Square feet of Gross Living Area
Unit # 3 contains:	Rooms	Bedroom(s)	Bath(s)	Square feet of Gross Living Area
Unit # 4 contains:	Rooms	Bedroom(s)	Bath(s)	Square feet of Gross Living Area

Additional features (special energy efficient items, etc.)

Describe the condition of the property (including needed repairs, deterioration, renovations, remodeling, etc.).

122

Small Residential Income Property Appraisal Report   File

IMPROVEMENTS

Are there any physical deficiencies or adverse conditions that affect the livability, soundness, or structural integrity of the property? ☐ Yes ☐ No   If Yes, describe

Does the property generally conform to the neighborhood (functional utility, style, condition, use, construction, etc.)? ☐ Yes ☐ No   If No, describe

Is the property subject to rent control? ☐ Yes ☐ No   If Yes, describe

COMPARABLE RENTAL DATA

The following properties represent the most current, similar, and proximate comparable rental properties to the subject property. This analysis is intended to support the opinion of the market rent for the subject property.

FEATURE	SUBJECT	COMPARABLE RENTAL # 1	COMPARABLE RENTAL # 2	COMPARABLE RENTAL # 3
Address				
Proximity to Subject				
Current Monthly Rent	$	$	$	$
Rent/Gross Bldg. Area	$ sq. ft.	$ sq. ft.	$ sq. ft.	$ sq. ft.
Rent Control	☐ Yes ☐ No	☐ Yes ☐ No	☐ Yes ☐ No	☐ Yes ☐ No
Data Source(s)				
Date of Lease(s)				
Location				
Actual Age				
Condition				
Gross Building Area				

Unit Breakdown	Rm Count	Size Sq. Ft.		Rm Count	Size Sq. Ft.	Monthly Rent	Rm Count	Size Sq. Ft.	Monthly Rent	Rm Count	Size Sq. Ft.	Monthly Rent
	Tot	Br	Ba	Tot	Br	Ba		Tot	Br	Ba		Tot	Br	Ba
Unit # 1						$			$			$
Unit # 2						$			$			$
Unit # 3						$			$			$
Unit # 4						$			$			$
Utilities Included				

Analysis of rental data and support for estimated market rents for the individual subject units reported below (including the adequacy of the comparables, rental concessions, etc.)

SUBJECT RENT SCHEDULE

Rent Schedule: The appraiser must reconcile the applicable indicated monthly market rents to provide an opinion of the market rent for each unit in the subject property.

	Leases		Actual Rent			Opinion Of Market Rent		
	Lease Date		Per Unit		Total	Per Unit		Total
Unit #	Begin Date	End Date	Unfurnished	Furnished	Rent	Unfurnished	Furnished	Rent
1			$	$	$	$	$	$
2								
3								
4								

Comment on lease data	Total Actual Monthly Rent	$	Total Gross Monthly Rent	$
	Other Monthly Income (itemize)	$	Other Monthly Income (itemize)	$
	Total Actual Monthly Income	$	Total Estimated Monthly Income	$

Utilities included in estimated rents ☐ Electric ☐ Water ☐ Sewer ☐ Gas ☐ Oil ☐ Cable ☐ Trash collection ☐ Other (describe)

Comments on actual or estimated rents and other monthly income (including personal property)

PRIOR SALE HISTORY

I ☐ did ☐ did not research the sale or transfer history of the subject property and comparable sales. If not, explain

My research ☐ did ☐ did not reveal any prior sales or transfers of the subject property for the three years prior to the effective date of this appraisal.

Data source(s)

My research ☐ did ☐ did not reveal any prior sales or transfers of the comparable sales for the year prior to the date of sale of the comparable sale.

Data source(s)

Report the results of the research and analysis of the prior sale history of the subject property and comparable sales (report additional prior sales on page 4).

ITEM	SUBJECT	COMPARABLE SALE # 1	COMPARABLE SALE # 2	COMPARABLE SALE # 3
Date of Prior Sale/Transfer				
Price of Prior Sale/Transfer				
Data Source(s)				
Effective Date of Data Source(s)				

Analysis of prior sale history for the subject property and comparable sales

123

Small Residential Income Property Appraisal Report   File

| There are _____ comparable properties currently offered for sale in the subject neighborhood ranging in price from $ _____ to $ _____ . |
| There are _____ comparable sales in the subject neighborhood within the past twelve months ranging in sale price from $ _____ to $ _____ . |

FEATURE	SUBJECT	COMPARABLE SALE # 1	COMPARABLE SALE # 2	COMPARABLE SALE # 3
Address				
Proximity to Subject				
Sale Price	$	$	$	$
Sale Price/Gross Bldg. Area	$ sq. ft.	$ sq. ft.	$ sq. ft.	$ sq. ft.
Gross Monthly Rent	$	$	$	$
Gross Rent Multiplier				
Price Per Unit	$	$	$	$
Price Per Room	$	$	$	$
Price Per Bedroom	$	$	$	$
Rent Control	☐ Yes ☐ No	☐ Yes ☐ No	☐ Yes ☐ No	☐ Yes ☐ No
Data Source(s)				
Verification Source(s)				

VALUE ADJUSTMENTS	DESCRIPTION	DESCRIPTION	+ (-) Adjustment	DESCRIPTION	+ (-) Adjustment	DESCRIPTION	+ (-) Adjustment
Sale or Financing Concessions							
Date of Sale/Time							
Location							
Leasehold/Fee Simple							
Site							
View							
Design (Style)							
Quality of Construction							
Actual Age							
Condition							
Gross Building Area							
Unit Breakdown	Total Bedrooms Baths	Total Bdrms Baths		Total Bdrms Baths		Total Bdrms Baths	
Unit # 1							
Unit # 2							
Unit # 3							
Unit # 4							
Basement Description							
Basement Finished Rooms							
Functional Utility							
Heating/Cooling							
Energy Efficient Items							
Parking On/Off Site							
Porch/Patio/Deck							
Net Adjustment (Total)		☐ + ☐ -	$	☐ + ☐ -	$	☐ + ☐ -	$
Adjusted Sale Price of Comparables		Net Adj. % Gross Adj. %	$	Net Adj. % Gross Adj. %	$	Net Adj. % Gross Adj. %	$
Adj. Price Per Unit (Adj. SP Comp / # of Comp Units)	$	$		$		$	
Adj. Price Per Room (Adj. SP Comp / # of Comp Rooms)	$	$		$		$	
Adj. Price Per Bedrm (Adj. SP Comp / # of Comp Bedrooms)	$	$		$		$	

The letters S A L E S   C O M P A R I S O N   A P P R O A C H appear vertically along the left margin of the sales comparison grid.

| Value Per Unit | $ _____ X _____ Units = $ _____ | Value Per GBA $ _____ X _____ GBA = $ _____ |
| Value Per Rm. | $ _____ X _____ Rooms = $ _____ | Value Per Bdrms. $ _____ X _____ Bdrms. = $ _____ |

Summary of Sales Comparison Approach including reconciliation of the above indicators of value.

Indicated Value by Sales Comparison Approach $ _____

INCOME

Total gross monthly rent $ _____ X gross rent multiplier (GRM) _____ = $ _____   Indicated value by the Income Approach _____

Comments on income approach including reconciliation of the GRM _____

RECONCILIATION

Indicated Value by: Sales Comparison Approach $ _____   Income Approach $ _____   Cost Approach (if developed) $ _____

This appraisal is made ☐ "as is", ☐ subject to completion per plans and specifications on the basis of a hypothetical condition that the improvements have been completed, ☐ subject to the following repairs or alterations on the basis of a hypothetical condition that the repairs or alterations have been completed, or ☐ subject to the following required inspection based on the extraordinary assumption that the condition or deficiency does not require alteration or repair:

Based on a complete visual inspection of the interior and exterior areas of the subject property, defined scope of work, statement of assumptions and limiting conditions, and appraiser's certification, my (our) opinion of the market value, as defined, of the real property that is the subject of this report is $ _____ , as of _____ , which is the date of inspection and the effective date of this appraisal.

124

Small Residential Income Property Appraisal Report   File

ADDITIONAL COMMENTS

COST APPROACH TO VALUE (not required by Fannie Mae)

Provide adequate information for the lender/client to replicate the below cost figures and calculations.

Support for the opinion of site value (summary of comparable land sales or other methods for estimating site value)

ESTIMATED ☐ REPRODUCTION OR ☐ REPLACEMENT COST NEW

Source of cost data	OPINION OF SITE VALUE	= $
Quality rating from cost service Effective date of cost data	Dwelling Sq. Ft. @ $	=$
Comments on Cost Approach (gross building area calculations, depreciation, etc.)	Sq. Ft. @ $	=$
	Garage/Carport Sq. Ft. @ $	=$
	Total Estimate of Cost-New	= $
	Less Physical	Functional	External
	Depreciation	=$( )
	Depreciated Cost of Improvements	=$
	"As-is" Value of Site Improvements	=$

Estimated Remaining Economic Life (HUD and VA only)   Years | Indicated Value By Cost Approach   =$

PROJECT INFORMATION FOR PUDs (if applicable)

Is the developer/builder in control of the Homeowners' Association (HOA)? ☐ Yes ☐ No   Unit type(s) ☐ Detached ☐ Attached

Provide the following information for PUDs ONLY if the developer/builder is in control of the HOA and the subject property is an attached dwelling unit.

Legal name of project

Total number of phases   Total number of units   Total number of units sold

Total number of units rented   Total number of units for sale   Data source(s)

Was the project created by the conversion of an existing building(s) into a PUD? ☐ Yes ☐ No If Yes, date of conversion

Does the project contain any multi-dwelling units? ☐ Yes ☐ No Data source(s)

Are the units, common elements, and recreation facilities complete? ☐ Yes ☐ No If No, describe the status of completion.

Are the common elements leased to or by the Homeowners' Association? ☐ Yes ☐ No If Yes, describe the rental terms and options.

Describe common elements and recreational facilities.

125

Freddie Mac Form 72 March 2005   Page 4 of 7   Fannie Mae Form 1025 March 2005

Small Residential Income Property Appraisal Report File

This report form is designed to report an appraisal of a two- to four-unit property, including a two- to four-unit property in a planned unit development (PUD). A two- to four-unit property located in either a condominium or cooperative project requires the appraiser to inspect the project and complete the project information section of the Individual Condominium Unit Appraisal Report or the Individual Cooperative Interest Appraisal Report and attach it as an addendum to this report.

This appraisal report is subject to the following scope of work, intended use, intended user, definition of market value, statement of assumptions and limiting conditions, and certifications. Modifications, additions, or deletions to the intended use, intended user, definition of market value, or assumptions and limiting conditions are not permitted. The appraiser may expand the scope of work to include any additional research or analysis necessary based on the complexity of this appraisal assignment. Modifications or deletions to the certifications are also not permitted. However, additional certifications that do not constitute material alterations to this appraisal report, such as those required by law or those related to the appraiser's continuing education or membership in an appraisal organization, are permitted.

SCOPE OF WORK: The scope of work for this appraisal is defined by the complexity of this appraisal assignment and the reporting requirements of this appraisal report form, including the following definition of market value, statement of assumptions and limiting conditions, and certifications. The appraiser must, at a minimum: (1) perform a complete visual inspection of the interior and exterior areas of the subject property, (2) inspect the neighborhood, (3) inspect each of the comparable sales from at least the street, (4) research, verify, and analyze data from reliable public and/or private sources, and (5) report his or her analysis, opinions, and conclusions in this appraisal report.

INTENDED USE: The intended use of this appraisal report is for the lender/client to evaluate the property that is the subject of this appraisal for a mortgage finance transaction.

INTENDED USER: The intended user of this appraisal report is the lender/client.

DEFINITION OF MARKET VALUE: The most probable price which a property should bring in a competitive and open market under all conditions requisite to a fair sale, the buyer and seller, each acting prudently, knowledgeably and assuming the price is not affected by undue stimulus. Implicit in this definition is the consummation of a sale as of a specified date and the passing of title from seller to buyer under conditions whereby: (1) buyer and seller are typically motivated; (2) both parties are well informed or well advised, and each acting in what he or she considers his or her own best interest; (3) a reasonable time is allowed for exposure in the open market; (4) payment is made in terms of cash in U. S. dollars or in terms of financial arrangements comparable thereto; and (5) the price represents the normal consideration for the property sold unaffected by special or creative financing or sales concessions* granted by anyone associated with the sale.

*Adjustments to the comparables must be made for special or creative financing or sales concessions. No adjustments are necessary for those costs which are normally paid by sellers as a result of tradition or law in a market area; these costs are readily identifiable since the seller pays these costs in virtually all sales transactions. Special or creative financing adjustments can be made to the comparable property by comparisons to financing terms offered by a third party institutional lender that is not already involved in the property or transaction. Any adjustment should not be calculated on a mechanical dollar for dollar cost of the financing or concession but the dollar amount of any adjustment should approximate the market's reaction to the financing or concessions based on the appraiser's judgment.

STATEMENT OF ASSUMPTIONS AND LIMITING CONDITIONS: The appraiser's certification in this report is subject to the following assumptions and limiting conditions:

1. The appraiser will not be responsible for matters of a legal nature that affect either the property being appraised or the title to it, except for information that he or she became aware of during the research involved in performing this appraisal. The appraiser assumes that the title is good and marketable and will not render any opinions about the title.

2. The appraiser has provided a sketch in this appraisal report to show the approximate dimensions of the improvements, including each of the units. The sketch is included only to assist the reader in visualizing the property and understanding the appraiser's determination of its size.

3. The appraiser has examined the available flood maps that are provided by the Federal Emergency Management Agency (or other data sources) and has noted in this appraisal report whether any portion of the subject site is located in an identified Special Flood Hazard Area. Because the appraiser is not a surveyor, he or she makes no guarantees, express or implied, regarding this determination.

4. The appraiser will not give testimony or appear in court because he or she made an appraisal of the property in question, unless specific arrangements to do so have been made beforehand, or as otherwise required by law.

5. The appraiser has noted in this appraisal report any adverse conditions (such as needed repairs, deterioration, the presence of hazardous wastes, toxic substances, etc.) observed during the inspection of the subject property or that he or she became aware of during the research involved in performing this appraisal. Unless otherwise stated in this appraisal report, the appraiser has no knowledge of any hidden or unapparent physical deficiencies or adverse conditions of the property (such as, but not limited to, needed repairs, deterioration, the presence of hazardous wastes, toxic substances, adverse environmental conditions, etc.) that would make the property less valuable, and has assumed that there are no such conditions and makes no guarantees or warranties, express or implied. The appraiser will not be responsible for any such conditions that do exist or for any engineering or testing that might be required to discover whether such conditions exist. Because the appraiser is not an expert in the field of environmental hazards, this appraisal report must not be considered as an environmental assessment of the property.

6. The appraiser has based his or her appraisal report and valuation conclusion for an appraisal that is subject to satisfactory completion, repairs, or alterations on the assumption that the completion, repairs, or alterations of the subject property will be performed in a professional manner.

126

Small Residential Income Property Appraisal Report   File

APPRAISER'S CERTIFICATION: The Appraiser certifies and agrees that:

1. I have, at a minimum, developed and reported this appraisal in accordance with the scope of work requirements stated in this appraisal report.

2. I performed a complete visual inspection of the interior and exterior areas of the subject property, including all units. I reported the condition of the improvements in factual, specific terms. I identified and reported the physical deficiencies that could affect the livability, soundness, or structural integrity of the property.

3. I performed this appraisal in accordance with the requirements of the Uniform Standards of Professional Appraisal Practice that were adopted and promulgated by the Appraisal Standards Board of The Appraisal Foundation and that were in place at the time this appraisal report was prepared.

4. I developed my opinion of the market value of the real property that is the subject of this report based on the sales comparison and income approaches to value. I have adequate market data to develop reliable sales comparison and income approaches to value for this appraisal assignment. I further certify that I considered the cost approach to value but did not develop it, unless otherwise indicated in this report.

5. I researched, verified, analyzed, and reported on any current agreement for sale for the subject property, any offering for sale of the subject property in the twelve months prior to the effective date of this appraisal, and the prior sales of the subject property for a minimum of three years prior to the effective date of this appraisal, unless otherwise indicated in this report.

6. I researched, verified, analyzed, and reported on the prior sales of the comparable sales for a minimum of one year prior to the date of sale of the comparable sale, unless otherwise indicated in this report.

7. I selected and used comparable sales that are locationally, physically, and functionally the most similar to the subject property.

8. I have not used comparable sales that were the result of combining a land sale with the contract purchase price of a home that has been built or will be built on the land.

9. I have reported adjustments to the comparable sales that reflect the market's reaction to the differences between the subject property and the comparable sales.

10. I verified, from a disinterested source, all information in this report that was provided by parties who have a financial interest in the sale or financing of the subject property.

11. I have knowledge and experience in appraising this type of property in this market area.

12. I am aware of, and have access to, the necessary and appropriate public and private data sources, such as multiple listing services, tax assessment records, public land records and other such data sources for the area in which the property is located.

13. I obtained the information, estimates, and opinions furnished by other parties and expressed in this appraisal report from reliable sources that I believe to be true and correct.

14. I have taken into consideration the factors that have an impact on value with respect to the subject neighborhood, subject property, and the proximity of the subject property to adverse influences in the development of my opinion of market value. I have noted in this appraisal report any adverse conditions (such as, but not limited to, needed repairs, deterioration, the presence of hazardous wastes, toxic substances, adverse environmental conditions, etc.) observed during the inspection of the subject property or that I became aware of during the research involved in performing this appraisal. I have considered these adverse conditions in my analysis of the property value, and have reported on the effect of the conditions on the value and marketability of the subject property.

15. I have not knowingly withheld any significant information from this appraisal report and, to the best of my knowledge, all statements and information in this appraisal report are true and correct.

16. I stated in this appraisal report my own personal, unbiased, and professional analysis, opinions, and conclusions, which are subject only to the assumptions and limiting conditions in this appraisal report.

17. I have no present or prospective interest in the property that is the subject of this report, and I have no present or prospective personal interest or bias with respect to the participants in the transaction. I did not base, either partially or completely, my analysis and/or opinion of market value in this appraisal report on the race, color, religion, sex, age, marital status, handicap, familial status, or national origin of either the prospective owners or occupants of the subject property or of the present owners or occupants of the properties in the vicinity of the subject property or on any other basis prohibited by law.

18. My employment and/or compensation for performing this appraisal or any future or anticipated appraisals was not conditioned on any agreement or understanding, written or otherwise, that I would report (or present analysis supporting) a predetermined specific value, a predetermined minimum value, a range or direction in value, a value that favors the cause of any party, or the attainment of a specific result or occurrence of a specific subsequent event (such as approval of a pending mortgage loan application).

19. I personally prepared all conclusions and opinions about the real estate that were set forth in this appraisal report. If I relied on significant real property appraisal assistance from any individual or individuals in the performance of this appraisal or the preparation of this appraisal report, I have named such individual(s) and disclosed the specific tasks performed in this appraisal report. I certify that any individual so named is qualified to perform the tasks. I have not authorized anyone to make a change to any item in this appraisal report; therefore, any change made to this appraisal is unauthorized and I will take no responsibility for it.

20. I identified the lender/client in this appraisal report who is the individual, organization, or agent for the organization that ordered and will receive this appraisal report.

127

Small Residential Income Property Appraisal Report   File

21. The lender/client may disclose or distribute this appraisal report to: the borrower; another lender at the request of the borrower; the mortgagee or its successors and assigns; mortgage insurers; government sponsored enterprises; other secondary market participants; data collection or reporting services; professional appraisal organizations; any department, agency, or instrumentality of the United States; and any state, the District of Columbia, or other jurisdictions; without having to obtain the appraiser's or supervisory appraiser's (if applicable) consent. Such consent must be obtained before this appraisal report may be disclosed or distributed to any other party (including, but not limited to, the public through advertising, public relations, news, sales, or other media).

22. I am aware that any disclosure or distribution of this appraisal report by me or the lender/client may be subject to certain laws and regulations. Further, I am also subject to the provisions of the Uniform Standards of Professional Appraisal Practice that pertain to disclosure or distribution by me.

23. The borrower, another lender at the request of the borrower, the mortgagee or its successors and assigns, mortgage insurers, government sponsored enterprises, and other secondary market participants may rely on this appraisal report as part of any mortgage finance transaction that involves any one or more of these parties.

24. If this appraisal report was transmitted as an "electronic record" containing my "electronic signature," as those terms are defined in applicable federal and/or state laws (excluding audio and video recordings), or a facsimile transmission of this appraisal report containing a copy or representation of my signature, the appraisal report shall be as effective, enforceable and valid as if a paper version of this appraisal report were delivered containing my original hand written signature.

25. Any intentional or negligent misrepresentation(s) contained in this appraisal report may result in civil liability and/or criminal penalties including, but not limited to, fine or imprisonment or both under the provisions of Title 18, United States Code, Section 1001, et seq., or similar state laws.

SUPERVISORY APPRAISER'S CERTIFICATION: The Supervisory Appraiser certifies and agrees that:

1. I directly supervised the appraiser for this appraisal assignment, have read the appraisal report, and agree with the appraiser's analysis, opinions, statements, conclusions, and the appraiser's certification.

2. I accept full responsibility for the contents of this appraisal report including, but not limited to, the appraiser's analysis, opinions, statements, conclusions, and the appraiser's certification.

3. The appraiser identified in this appraisal report is either a sub-contractor or an employee of the supervisory appraiser (or the appraisal firm), is qualified to perform this appraisal, and is acceptable to perform this appraisal under the applicable state law.

4. This appraisal report complies with the Uniform Standards of Professional Appraisal Practice that were adopted and promulgated by the Appraisal Standards Board of The Appraisal Foundation and that were in place at the time this appraisal report was prepared.

5. If this appraisal report was transmitted as an "electronic record" containing my "electronic signature," as those terms are defined in applicable federal and/or state laws (excluding audio and video recordings), or a facsimile transmission of this appraisal report containing a copy or representation of my signature, the appraisal report shall be as effective, enforceable and valid as if a paper version of this appraisal report were delivered containing my original hand written signature.

APPRAISER

Signature _____
Name _____
Company Name _____
Company Address _____
_____
Telephone Number _____
Email Address _____
Date of Signature and Report _____
Effective Date of Appraisal_____
State Certification # _____
or State License # _____
or Other (describe)_____ State # _____
State_____
Expiration Date of Certification or License _____

ADDRESS OF PROPERTY APPRAISED

_____
_____

APPRAISED VALUE OF SUBJECT PROPERTY $ _____

LENDER/CLIENT

Name _____
Company Name _____
Company Address _____
_____
Email Address _____

SUPERVISORY APPRAISER (ONLY IF REQUIRED)

Signature _____
Name _____
Company Name _____
Company Address _____
_____
Telephone Number_____
Email Address _____
Date of Signature _____
State Certification # _____
or State License # _____
State _____
Expiration Date of Certification or License_____

SUBJECT PROPERTY

☐ Did not inspect subject property
☐ Did inspect exterior of subject property from street
   Date of Inspection _____
☐ Did inspect interior and exterior of subject property
   Date of Inspection_____

COMPARABLE SALES

☐ Did not inspect exterior of comparable sales from street
☐ Did inspect exterior of comparable sales from street
   Date of Inspection_____

Glossary

A

Amortization Elimination of a debt with a series of equal payments (principle and interest) at regular time intervals.

Anticipation An economic theory that says value is created by the expectation of future benefits, such as profit, pleasure, tax shelter, production, income, etc. Anticipation is the foundation for the income approach.

Appraiser's Peers Other appraisers with expertise and competency in a similar type of assignment.

Appurtenant Rights Rights that go with ownership of real property. They are usually transferred with the property, but may be sold separately. This is a legal term referring to both physical and non-physical appurtenances.

B

Balance A condition that exists in the real estate market when there are slightly more homes available than buyers.

Band of Investment A technique for determining an overall capitalization rate by weighting and combining the various components of an investment.

Bias A preference or inclination that precludes an appraiser's impartiality, independence, or objectivity in an assignment.

Bracketing A process in which an appraiser identifies a probable value range, most often by identifying values of properties that are inferior and those that are superior. The appraiser then determines where an opinion of value for the subject should fall within that range.

Buyer's Market A situation in the real estate market in which buyers have a large selection of properties from which to choose.

C

Change A principle affecting value in real estate that says all factors that influence real estate—physical, economic, governmental, and social—are constantly changing, and, thus, property value itself is subject to constant change.

Characteristics of Value Also known as D-U-S-T. The characteristics of value are Demand, Utility, Scarcity, and Transferability.

Client The party (or parties) who engage an appraiser (by employment or contract) in a specific assignment.

Comparable Property Possesses many of the same appeal factors, but the buyer for one property may not necessarily be interested in the comparable property.

Competition Two or more parties, properties, etc., trying to obtain the same thing.

Competitive Property Those that compete head to head. A potential buyer for one property would also be interested in the competitive property.

Compound Interest Interest paid on previously earned interest based on the original principal amount. The more frequent the compounding period and the higher the effective interest rate, the greater the impact on the calculation.

Conditions of Sale Atypical motivations of the parties of a transaction (usually make the sale non-arm's length).

Confidential information Information that is either identified by the client as confidential when providing it to an appraiser and that is not available from any other source; or classified as confidential or private by applicable law or regulation.

Conformity The theory that says a particular property achieves its maximum value when it is surrounded by properties that are similar in style, function, and utility. Also called **Homogeneity**.

Contract Rent What tenants are actually paying in rent, as stated in the terms of the lease.

Contributory Value The theory that a particular item or feature of a property is worth only what it actually contributes in value to that parcel of real estate.

Credible Worthy of belief.

Curable Item Repairable or able to be fixed; something that can be repaired or replaced at a reasonable cost with the value added to the property being more than the cost.

D

Date of Report An indication of the perspective from which the appraiser is examining the market.

Debt Service The amount of funds required to make periodic payments of principal and interest to the lender.

Decline The third stage a neighborhood goes through in its life cycle, when property values begin to fall as demand falls.

Deed An instrument that conveys the grantor's interest in real property.

Deferred Maintenance A physical deterioration that has occurred because of a failure to perform regular maintenance and upkeep.

Deficit Rent The resulting difference when the market rent exceeds the contract rent.

Direct Capitalization An income method that converts a property's single-year net operating income (NOI) into a value indication by applying an overall capitalization rate: NOI ÷ Overall Capitalization Rate = Value.

Discount Points An amount paid to a lender (1% of loan amount) when a loan is made to make up the difference between the current market interest rate and the rate a lender gives a borrower on a note. Discount points increase a lender's yield on a note, allowing the lender to give a borrower a lower interest rate.

Discounting The process, by some investors, that uses the principles of TVM to convert future income or cash flows into present value, at a specified interest rate.

District An area consisting of one particular land use. There could be several districts within a neighborhood and several neighborhoods comprising a market area.

Dominant Tenement A property that benefits from an easement.

E

Easement A right to use some part of another person's real property for a particular purpose. An easement is irrevocable and creates an interest in the property.

Easement Appurtenant An easement that burdens one piece of land for the benefit of another.

Easement in Gross An easement that benefits a person instead of a particular property; there is a dominant tenant, but no dominant tenement.

Economic Life The period of time when a structure contributes positively to a property's value - considers physical deterioration, functional obsolescence, and external obsolescence.

Effective Age Estimated by an appraiser and based on all forces of physical deterioration and functional and external obsolescence.

Effective Date Establishes the context for the value opinion.

Effective Gross Income (EGI) Potential gross income, less vacancy and collection losses.

EGIM A factor derived and applied using EGI—the amount after estimated vacancy has been deducted from PGI.

Elements of Comparison Characteristics of a property or a transaction that can be used to explain differences in the price paid in a transaction.

Equity Capitalization Rate The capitalization rate applied to the expectation of return on equity (symbolized by R_E).

Excess Rent The resulting difference when the contract rent exceeds the market rent.

Excess Site A site that is not needed to support the existing improvements or highest and best use. Could have sell-off

potential or be needed for future expansion of the existing or anticipated improvements.

External Obsolescence When something outside the boundaries of a property and the control of the property owner makes it less desirable. The factors causing the obsolescence may be economic or location factors.

Extraordinary Assumption An assignment specific assumption as of the effective date regarding uncertain information used in an analysis which, if found to be false, could alter the appraiser's opinions or conclusions.

F

Fee Simple The greatest estate (ownership) one can have in real property; it is freely transferable and inheritable, and of indefinite duration, with no conditions on the title. Often called **fee simple absolute** or **fee title**.

Fixed Expenses Ongoing operating expenses that do not vary based on occupancy levels of the property (e.g., taxes and insurance).

External Obsolescence When something outside the boundaries of a property and the control of the property owner makes it less desirable. The factors causing the obsolescence may be economic or location factors.

Functional Utility When a building has the adequate design and features to be used as intended.

Future Value Amount of money that an investment (either a single payment or an annuity) at a fixed interest rate, for a specified period of time, will grow to in the future.

G

General Data Information that covers the forces that affect property values, but are not directly related to a particular piece of property. General data covers **p**hysical, **e**conomic, **g**overnmental, and **s**ocial factors (**P E G S**) and can be local or national.

Gentrification The process of rapid revitalization of properties in a neighborhood, which causes current residents to be displaced.

Government Sponsored Enterprises (GSEs) A financial services corporation created by the United States Congress. Their function is to enhance the flow of credit to targeted sectors of the economy and to make those segments of the capital market more efficient and transparent.

Gross Adjustments The overall total of all adjustments applied regardless of whether the adjustment is applied as a positive or a negative. (For example, a +$1,000 and a -$1,000 adjustment would result in $2,000 gross adjustments.)

Gross Income Multiplier (GIM) A factor that takes into account income derived from all sources of a property (e.g., vending, storage units).

Gross Lease A property lease for which the landlord pays all expenses related to the operation of the property.

Gross Rent Multiplier (GRM) A factor derived from comparable rental data, which is then used to develop an opinion of value of the subject property.

Growth The first stage a neighborhood goes through in its life cycle, when property values rise as development activity begins and continues.

H

Highest and Best Use The most profitable, legally permitted, economically feasible, and physically possible use of a piece of property.

Hypothetical Condition That which is contrary to what exists, but is supposed for the purpose of analysis.

I

Incurable Item Something that cannot be repaired or replaced at a reasonable cost with the cost of the repair being more than the value added to a property.

Intended Use The use(s) of an appraiser's reported appraisal or appraisal review assignment results, as identified by the appraiser based on communication with the client at the time of the assignment.

Intended User The client and any other party as identified, by name or type, as users of the appraisal or appraisal review report by the appraiser on the basis of communication with the client at the time of the assignment.

IVR A formula or technique that derives an overall capitalization rate: Income (NOI) ÷ Value (Sale Price) = Rate.

J

Jurisdictional Exception An assignment condition that voids the force of a part or parts of USPAP, when compliance with part or parts of USPAP is contrary to law or public policy applicable to the assignment.

L

Lease Conveyance of a leasehold estate from the fee owner to a tenant; a contract for which one party pays the other rent in exchange for possession of real estate.

Leased Fee Estate The landlord's ownership interest in property.

Leased Fee Interest Defined by the amount of contract rent over and above market rent.

Leasehold Estate An estate that gives the holder (tenant) a temporary right to possession, without title. Also called **Less-than-Freehold Estate**.

Leasehold Interest Defined by the amount of rent that is less than market rent (amount of difference between contract and market rent).

Lessee A person who leases property; a tenant.

Lessor A person who leases property to another; a landlord.

Life Estate A freehold estate that lasts only as long as a specified person lives.

Life Tenant Someone who owns a life estate; the person entitled to possession of the property during the measuring life.

Limiting Conditions Statement by the appraiser explaining the framework used to reach the appraisal value.

Linkages The proximity of property to common destinations and conveniences, and the time required to reach those places.

Long-lived Item A component of a structure that is not expected to be replaced during the life of a property.

M

Market Area 1. The broadest of all terms identifying the boundaries of a particular area. Market area takes into account the land uses and characteristics of typical market participants within the defined area. 2. An area where properties would be located which would be considered competition for the subject property.

Market Rent What the property could rent for in the open market if currently vacant and available.

Mortgage Capitalization Rate A return on the money lent in an investment (symbolized by R_M).

Mortgage Constant The ratio between annual debt service and loan principal.

Multiplier A factor that is derived from market data and applied to the subject's market rent or income to produce a value indication in an income approach.

N

Negative Leasehold When contract rent is more than market rent (an advantage to the lessor).

Neighborhood Any constant, contiguous area that may be identified by similar characteristics of physical boundaries. A compilation or group of complimentary land uses.

Net Adjustments The sum of the adjustments taking into account whether the adjustment was a positive or a negative. (For example, a +$1,000 and a -$1,000 adjustment would result in $0 net adjustments.)

Net Lease A property lease for which the tenant pays all utilities and certain expenses, in addition to rent payments.

Net Operating Income Income after expenses.

O

Operating Expenses Day-to-day costs of running a building, like repairs and maintenance, but not including debt service or depreciation.

Overage Rent A percentage of business sales a tenant's business has generated paid in addition to rent payments.

Overall Capitalization Rate Used to interpret a property's single year net operating income to the property's value using direct capitalization (symbolized by R_O).

Overall Yield Rate Considers a series of annual figures over the entire investment period as well as reversion.

P

Paired Data Analysis The process of determining the value of specific property characteristics or features by comparing pairs of similar properties. Also called **Matched Pair Analysis**.

Partial Interest Any interest in real estate that one may have, other than the full bundle of rights.

PGIM A factor derived from, and applied to, the total gross income generated by the property without vacancy being considered.

Physical Deterioration The diminishment of condition of a structure or other improvement; or a component of the structure or improvement due to age, the elements, or other forces.

Positive Leasehold When contract rent is less than market rent (an advantage to the lessee).

Potential Gross Income (PGI) The income that could be produced by a property in an ideal situation, with no vacancy or collection losses.

Present Value An amount today that is equivalent to a future payment, or series of payments (annuity), based on a specified interest rate, for a specific period of time.

Primary Data Data that is obtained directly by the appraiser.

Principle of Consistent Use Holds that land cannot be valued for one use, while the improvements are valued at another use.

Progression A principle that says the value of a home is positively affected by the other homes in an area. Usually said about the "worst" home in the "best" area.

Q

Qualitative Analysis A method used after any quantitative adjustments have been applied that employs the appraiser's judgment in forming opinions relying on such methods as relative comparison analysis (bracketing), ranking analysis, and/or personal interviews. The method requires good judgment and reasoning skills of the appraiser.

Quantitative Adjustments A method that requires the recognition of the differences between the comparable data and the subject property and assigning either a market derived dollar or percentage amount as an adjustment.

R

Reconciliation Analyzing the values derived from the different appraisal approaches to arrive at a final opinion of value.

Regression A principle that says the value of a home is negatively affected by the other homes in an area. Usually said about the "best" home in the "worst" area.

Regression Analysis A statistical measure that attempts to ascertain the source of change in variables.

Remainderman The party in a life estate who is entitled to the remainder of the property interest after the life estate is terminated.

Rent Roll Briefly details the unit information, such as lease terms, contract rent, as well as the effective date of the leases that are in place for the property.

Rent Survey A compilation of the rents being generated (and often rent history) in a particular market for a particular property type.

Report Any communication, written or oral, of an appraisal or appraisal review that is transmitted to the client or a party authorized by the client upon completion of an assignment.

Reserves for Replacement An amount of money set aside for future replacement of major items, such as the roof or heating system. Also called **Reserves**.

Reverse Polish Notation (RPN) A formal logic system used in the HP-12C calculator that allows mathematical equations to be expressed by pressing the arithmetic operations key (+, -, x, ÷) after the numbers or variables have been keyed.

Reversionary Benefit Typically a sum, often stated in a dollar amount, that a property owner will receive when or if he sells the property at the end of the investment term.

Revitalization The final stage a neighborhood goes through in its life cycle, when property values rise again as demand increases, resulting in increased renovation and rehabilitation. *See:* **Gentrification.**

S

Scatter Diagram Graphs used to study the relationship between two variables.

Scope of Work The type and extent of research and analyses in an appraisal or appraisal review assignment.

Secondary Data Data that is compiled by other parties and used by the appraiser.

Seller's Market A situation in the real estate market where sellers can choose from a large number of buyers looking for property in an area.

Servient Tenement A property that is burdened by an easement.

Short-lived Item A component of a structure that is expected to be replaced during the life of a property.

Signature Personalized evidence indicating authentication of the work performed by the appraiser and the acceptance of the responsibility for content, analyses, and the conclusions in the report.

Sinking Fund Factor Amount set aside on a periodic basis so that, when compounded at a given interest rate for a defined term, it will accumulate to a specified future sum.

Specific Data Information that is relevant to the subject property. There are two types of specific data.

Stability The second stage a neighborhood goes through in its life cycle, when the area is built up to the point where there is little, if any, vacant property. Also called **equilibrium**.

Substitution Theory that an informed buyer will not pay more for a home than a comparable substitute.

Surplus Site A site that is not needed for the highest and best use of the subject and does not have potential for sell-off or an autonomous highest and best use.

T

Timeshares Grant the right to use (or possess) a property for a specified period of time (the right may or may not be accompanied with an ownership interest in the property).

Time Value of Money (TVM) The concept that a dollar today is usually worth more than receiving a dollar at some point in the future.

Transition A complete change of land use.

U

Uniform Appraisal Dataset (UAD) Defines all fields required for an appraisal submission for specific appraisal forms and standardizes definitions and responses for a key subset of fields to enhance data quality and promote consistency.

Uniform Standards of Professional Appraisal Practice (USPAP) Professional appraisal standards promulgated by The Appraisal Foundation, and widely recognized throughout the United States as accepted standards of appraisal practice.

Unit of Comparison A component with which a property can be divided for the purpose of comparison such as square foot, living unit, etc.

URAR (Uniform Residential Appraisal Report) Developed collaboratively by Fannie Mae and Freddie Mac for use with a mortgage finance transaction of single-family residential property. Also adopted by other entities such as FHA, VA, and some primary lenders for residential appraisal reporting.

Useful Life Relates to the period of time a structure or a component of the structure can be expected to function for the purpose it was designed for and applies only to physical deterioration.

V

Variable Expenses Operating expenses necessary to the property, but usually dependent on the property's occupancy level.

VIM A formula used to derive the appropriate multiplier from the transaction data: V (sale price) ÷ I (gross monthly rent) = M (multiplier).

W

Workfile The documentation necessary to support the appraiser's analyses, opinions, and conclusions.